TARGETED

Guns may be as American as apple pie, but what does it mean to own a gun north of the 49th parallel? While policy battles over gun control are often associated with American politics, debates about gun control are raging in Canada, prompting Canadian gun owners to transition from hobbyists to advocates. In *Targeted*, Noah S. Schwartz provides an insider's perspective on gun culture in Canada, unpacking the differences between Canadian and American gun activism. He explores how Canadians interpret the rising pro-gun movement in the country, its self-perception, its goals, and the strategies and funding sources that sustain it.

Arguing that a distinct pro-gun culture is emerging in Canada, *Targeted* highlights how the demands of the movement are closely linked to significant divisions in Canadian politics, such as the rural-urban divide and western alienation. Rather than viewing gun ownership as an unassailable constitutional right, the book reveals how Canadian gun owners frame their demands as a call for fair treatment from their leaders.

NOAH S. SCHWARTZ is an assistant professor of political science at the University of the Fraser Valley.

Targeted

Citizenship, Advocacy, and Gun Control in Canada

NOAH S. SCHWARTZ

UNIVERSITY OF TORONTO PRESS
Toronto Buffalo London

© University of Toronto Press 2025
Toronto Buffalo London
utppublishing.com
Printed in Canada

ISBN 978-1-4875-6229-8 (cloth)   ISBN 978-1-4875-6233-5 (EPUB)
ISBN 978-1-4875-6231-1 (paper)   ISBN 978-1-4875-6232-8 (UPDF)

Publication cataloguing information is available from Library and Archives Canada.

Cover design: Val Cooke
Cover image: iStock.com/StockSeller_ukr

This book has been published with the help of a grant from the Federation for
the Humanities and Social Sciences, through the Awards to Scholarly
Publications Program, using funds provided by the Social Sciences and
Humanities Research Council of Canada.

University of Toronto Press acknowledges the financial assistance to its
publishing program of the Canada Council for the Arts and the Ontario
Arts Council, an agency of the Government of Ontario.

Canada Council   Conseil des Arts
for the Arts   du Canada

ONTARIO ARTS COUNCIL
CONSEIL DES ARTS DE L'ONTARIO
an Ontario government agency
un organisme du gouvernement de l'Ontario

Funded by the   Financé par le
Government   gouvernement
of Canada   du Canada

Canadä

Contents

Acronyms & Key Terms

Assault Weapon – There is no universally accepted definition for an "assault weapon." The military definition of an assault weapon refers to a firearm chambered in an intermediate cartridge capable of firing in both fully automatic and semi-automatic fashion. These firearms were adopted after the Second World War, when armies noticed that the high-powered rifles issued to troops were unnecessary and wasteful at the short engagement distances soldiers now faced. The term was adopted by gun advertisers to sell modified civilian versions of military firearms that are not capable of fully automatic fire. Gun control advocates then adopted the term to capitalize on public confusion surrounding their capabilities.[1]

"Assault-Style" Weapon – Term adopted by the Federal Liberal government after consulting on a proposed assault weapons ban in 2018.[2]

ATT – Authorization to Transport. Given to owners of restricted or prohibited firearms by the RCMP Canadian Firearm Centre to allow them to take a restricted or prohibited firearm from one place to another, such as from their house to the range, a tournament, or a gunsmith.

Automatic Firearms – Sometimes called "fully automatic firearms" or "full autos." These firearms will continue to fire as long as the user depresses the trigger, or until the magazine runs out of ammunition. Not to be confused with semi-automatic firearms, which only fire a single bullet with each pull of the trigger.

Cartridge – Often erroneously referred to as a bullet. A cartridge consists of a casing which holds the bullet in place during storage, a bullet, powder, and a primer. The hammer of a firearm hits the primer once the trigger is pulled. The primer ignites the powder, which propels the bullet.

CCFR – Canadian Coalition for Firearm Rights. Newest major Canadian gun rights group, founded in 2015.

CFO – Chief Firearms Officer.

CFP – Canadian Firearms Program. Administered by the RCMP. Program that manages the licensing and regulation of firearms in Canada.

Concealed Carry – Laws that allow ordinary citizens to carry concealed firearms in public. These laws have become increasingly popular in the United States since the 1980s.

CSAAA – Canadian Sporting Arms and Ammunition Association. Lobby group representing the firearms and ammunition industry in Canada.

CSSA – Canadian Shooting Sports Association. Gun rights group in Canada.

FAC – Firearms Acquisition Certificate. An early form of firearm licensing in Canada. Brought in by Bill C-51 in 1977. The predecessor to the PAL/RPAL.

High-Capacity Magazines (Standard Capacity Magazines) – There is no universally accepted definition for what constitutes a high-capacity magazine. In the United States, bans on these accessories generally limit capacity to ten rounds, whereas Canadian law has limited detachable long-gun magazines to five rounds since 1991. These are sometimes called Standard Capacity Magazines by pro-gun advocates, since many long guns like the AR-15 would come from the factory with a thirty-round magazine.

Long-Gun Registry – Created in 1995 through the Canadian Firearms Act and dismantled in 2012 by the Harper Government. Required that all long guns (rifles and shotguns) be registered with the Canadian Firearms Program.

Magazine – A magazine is the portion of a firearm that holds the cartridges. They can be fixed or removable.

Military-Style Assault Weapon – See Assault Weapon.

NFA – National Firearms Association. Canadian gun rights group.

Non-restricted Firearms – Any firearm considered by the RCMP to be non-restricted. Mostly bolt, lever, and hinge-action rifles and shotguns.

PAL – Possession and Acquisition Licence, required to own non-restricted firearms in Canada.

Restricted Firearm – Any firearm determined by the RCMP to be restricted. Mostly handguns.

RCMP – Royal Canadian Mounted Police. Federal police force of Canada.

RCMP CFC – Royal Canadian Mounted Police Canadian Firearm Centre. In charge of administering the Canadian Firearms Program.

RPAL – Restricted Possession and Acquisition Licence, required to own restricted firearms in Canada.

Semi-Automatic Firearm – Sometimes called "autoloaders." These firearms fire a single round with each depression of the trigger. Different from automatic firearms, which continue to fire as long as the trigger is depressed.

Timeline of Contemporary Gun Control in Canada

1977 – Bill C-51 passed. Establishes firearms classification system (restricted – handguns, certain semi-automatics, non-restricted – most long-guns, prohibited – short-barreled pistols, fully automatic firearms, etc.). Creates Firearms Acquisition Certificate with background check to buy guns.[1]

6 December 1989 – Ecole Polytechnique shooting. Strong pro-control advocacy coalition emerges, led by survivors Heidi Rathjen and Wendy Cuckier.[2]

July–September 1990 – Kanesatake Resistance (Oka Crisis) pits armed Indigenous protestors against Canadian military. Debate over how much this influenced government decision on C-17.[3]

1991 – Bill C-17 – Created mandatory firearms safety course and twenty-eight-day waiting period.[4] Prohibited high-capacity magazines and created safe storage laws.[5]

1992–3 – Two more lower-level spree shootings. Liberals take power.

1995 – Bill C-68 – Centralizes Canada's gun control laws in the Firearms Act. Creates long-gun registry.

2012 – Bill C-19 – Repeals the unpopular and expensive[6] long-gun registry.[7]

2018 – Bill C-71 – Extends background checks from five years to lifetime. Requires firearms sellers to keep list of purchase records that can be accessed by police (some argue a de facto registry).

2020 – Using an order-in-council (OIC), the Liberal government bans over 1,500 models of firearms.

2022 – Liberal government freezes handgun sales. Handguns can still be used, but may no longer be transferred, purchased, inherited, or sold.

TARGETED

1
Introduction

The sale and consumption of alcohol in Canada comes with a large social cost. This cost can be measured in lives, in years, and in dollars. Every year, alcohol results in 15,000 preventable deaths in Canada, and 90,000 hospitalizations. The Canadian Centre for Substance Use & Addiction (CCSA) estimates that over 240,000 years of life are lost because of alcohol.[1] Alcohol use is also a major factor in violent crime. In a study of violent offenders in British Columbia, where I live and teach, researchers estimated that 28 per cent of violent crimes happened while the perpetrator was under the influence of alcohol.[2] The World Health Organization (WHO) also notes that "strong links" exist between alcohol use and intimate partner violence.[3] It is estimated that impacts on Canada's healthcare system, criminal justice system, and labour productivity equal about $14.6 billion.[4] The CCSA attracted considerable media attention when they released new guidelines on alcohol consumption that recommended that Canadian adults consume no more than two alcoholic beverages per week.[5]

Now, imagine that a government, galvanized by a resurgent prohibitionist movement, proposed banning the sale of alcohol in Canada. If you are one of the two-thirds of Canadians over fifteen years of age who enjoy consuming alcohol, you would likely be upset. You might think: why should I, as a person who enjoys alcohol responsibly, be denied my simple pleasure due to the actions of others who abuse it? Turning to your knowledge of historical experience, you might opine that if we prohibit alcohol, malcontents will find a way to manufacture it illegally or smuggle it into the country. Or they might turn to other drugs, like marijuana.

The prohibitionists in this imagined scenario might acknowledge that though prohibition is unlikely to be a complete success, it will certainly make it harder for people to acquire alcohol, even if the determined criminal element will find a way to manufacture or smuggle it. It will raise prices on the black market, making it unavailable to many. Further, turning to marijuana might be better for many people, as it is less addictive.

Responding to this backlash, the government proposes a compromise between the prohibitionists and drinkers. It introduces an alcohol licence. To purchase beer and wine, you must apply for a licence, submit to regular background checks, take a course on responsible drinking, report any past mental health issues, and solicit the approval of your intimate partner or any exes with whom you have been in a relationship within the past two years. You must agree to store your alcohol under lock and key so that minors or unlicensed individuals cannot have easy access. Those seeking to enjoy hard liquor must apply for an additional licence. Hard liquor can now only be consumed at licensed establishments, under the supervision of bartenders. There are strict zoning requirements around where these bars can be located, and you must drive an hour outside of town to find the nearest tavern. Still, you are a responsible drinker, and these limitations seem reasonable to you, given the social cost of alcohol use.

Years go by, and you grow accustomed to these restrictions. You happily apply for your licence, lock up your alcohol, and drive to the bar occasionally for a Scotch with your friends. The time you spend at the bar is your social time. You connect with friends, relax, unwind, and enjoy your beverage responsibly.

The social ills caused by alcohol are reduced but can never be entirely eliminated. Alcohol flows across the border from the United States, and the occasional bad actor applies for a licence and then sells alcohol on the black market. Some make homemade alcohol to sell or consume.

The precedent for regulation has been set. A more prohibitionist government comes to power and soon decides to crack down further. The sale of hard liquor is now frozen. You can drink what is in your cellar, but once it is gone you cannot buy more. Even worse, some types of alcohol that have been safely consumed for centuries are now considered too dangerous to own. The government proposes buying them back from their owners at a fraction of the price paid.

Your collection of scotch whisky includes antiques, spirits of historical significance that you have spent years collecting. Now they will end up in the gutter. With a limited supply of hard liquor, your friends go to the bar less and less frequently, saving their last drops for special occasions. Your social group melts away. Every sip of whisky reminds you that your stock is shrinking, and soon you will never taste it again.

Given the title and subject of this book, you have likely drawn the link that I sought between this hypothetical resurgence of a prohibition movement in Canada and the gun control debate. This thought experiment is not intended to argue against gun control. That is certainly not the purpose of this book. As we will see, many Canadian gun owners support the robust gun control laws that Canada has had in place for decades.

What this exercise is instead intended to do is to put you, the reader, in the shoes of a Canadian pro-gun advocate. If you, like the majority of Canadians, are not a gun owner, it may be difficult to understand why 2.2 million Canadians cling so tightly to their firearms, despite the social cost they incur. This social cost, after all, is the totality of your understanding of gun use, just as it has been the almost exclusive focus of news reports and academic studies of firearms.[6]

Understanding Canadian gun owners, and the political movements that represent them is central to the purpose and argument of this book. I do not ask you to agree with the people whose stories you will read in this book, but I do ask you to understand them.

Since the 1970s, heated debates around gun control have taken place in Canada, usually after major focusing events like the École Polytechnique shooting in 1989, the Kanesatake Resistance (Oka Crisis), or the 2020 mass shooting in Portapique, Nova Scotia. Firearms policy in Canada arguably still constitutes a wicked problem for policymakers, characterized by deep polarization and increasingly hostile rhetoric. The issue is often understood through the lens of the left-right partisan divide. Conservatives, we are told, support loosening restrictions on private firearm ownership, and Liberals or progressives support tightening it. As we will see, the reality is more complicated.

Though not as powerful or ubiquitous as the American National Rifle Association, Canada has a highly motivated grassroots movement of gun owners that have worked tirelessly to oppose recent changes to Canada's gun control laws. The movement is well-organized, drawing on a pre-existing network of ranges and clubs across the country, and well-funded through donations from passionate members of the community. They have a lot at stake in policy debates over gun control; not only their property, but leisure pursuits to which they have devoted considerable time, money, and energy. Though advocates acknowledge that no constitutional right to gun ownership exists in Canada, the movement has recently begun to refer to the term "firearm rights." For example, one of Canada's newest and most energetic pro-gun groups in recent years has been the Canadian Coalition for Firearm Rights (CCFR).

This book will explore several key questions related to gun politics in Canada. How can we understand the rise of such a movement in Canada and reconcile the grassroots strength of this movement with the significant expansion of gun control in Canada since the 1970s? How does this movement understand itself and frame its goals? How can we make sense of the gun debate in Canada, and especially the language around rights being used by pro-gun advocates?

As we will see, the pro-gun movement in Canada sees itself as a highly regulated group of Canadians that works hard to comply with our nation's strict gun laws. As a result of Canadian political culture and institutions, a unique vision of gun rights has emerged in Canada, distinct from the focus on self-defence and Jeffersonian Republicanism south of the border. Gun rights in Canada are tied to conceptualizations of citizenship and the expectation that citizens have of fair treatment by their government.

The link between citizenship and gun ownership is more explicit south of the border due to the doctrine of armed citizenship that, emerging from the American Revolution, has been preserved and repurposed by the American pro-gun movement,[7] leading to the expansion of policies like concealed carry laws.[8] The same connection has not emerged from Canadian history. Instead of a right of citizenship, firearm ownership has been conceived of as a privilege in Canadian legal doctrine and the wider Canadian society. At the same time debates over gun control still involve discussions of rights and what it means to be a Canadian citizen. Rather than being imagined as a right to gun ownership, from the perspective of gun owners, demands for gun rights are demands for the rights of citizens to be dealt with fairly by their leaders.

Three key concepts will be central to the book's exploration of Canadian gun politics. First, leisure culture, or communities that emerge around shared identities tied to sports or hobbies, will be used to explain the formation of the pro-gun movement in Canada. Second, citizenship regimes, or what it means to be a citizen at a particular time and place, will help us to understand institutional arrangements that shape gun politics in Canada, and the demands of the pro-gun movement. Third, looking at the concept of alienation will help us to unpack the grievances of gun owners; grievances that are both unique to the community and connected to rural and western alienation.

Firearms policy is chronically underexplored in Canadian political science and public policy. There are few books on gun control in Canada written by political scientists. In addition to exploring the contemporary iteration of the pro-gun movement, this book attempts to fill this gap. Unlike other texts on gun control, it offers a first-person view of the Canadian pro-gun movement. Throughout the book, you will be introduced to a variety of advocates, lobbyists, and ordinary Canadians. You will meet people like Rick, a Métis Canadian hunter, for whom firearms are a tool to practise his culture and exercise his treaty rights, as well as connect with family and nature. People like Tracey Wilson, a self-described suburban grandma who would become one of Canada's foremost gun lobbyists after a run-in with police left her feeling like a second-class citizen because she chooses to hunt and shoot. You will meet people like Kevin, a Chinese Canadian businessman for whom the Glock handgun and AR-15 rifle are not weapons of mass destruction, but tools to unwind after a long day at the office. These stories are as essential as any quantitative data point for understanding the Canadian gun debate, and the people who advocate so passionately within it.

Methods and Outline

This project began in the spring of 2020, in the middle of a global pandemic. With Canadians locked down at home, researchers also needed to pivot to find new ways of conducting our craft. Given the salience of gun politics in the wake of the Nova Scotia shooting that spring, and the subsequent order-In-council banning what the government later labelled "assault-style weapons," I saw an opportunity to survey Canadian gun owners.

How to do this was another matter. While survey data on gun ownership is plentiful in the United States, it is virtually unheard of in Canada. As a result, to study the opinions of Canadian gun owners, I needed to build my own dataset. I created a survey of Canadian gun owners, which was disseminated through the email list of two major firearms advocacy groups and several provincial hunting groups. From a methodological perspective this was a less-than-ideal method of data collection, but given the glaring absence of such data on gun owners in Canada, there were few other options.

Survey data was collected using Qualtrics and included digital safeguards to prevent answers by bots. The survey was open to respondents between April and June of 2020 and received 16,880 responses. Given that at the time there were 2,183,827 licensed gun owners in Canada, this represented approximately 0.77 per cent of the target population. The dataset was compared with basic demographic information made public by the RCMP related to gun licences in Canada, and the data was regionally representative with the exception of Quebec, which was underrepresented, and Alberta, which was overrepresented.

The data clearly come with some important limitations. It cannot be used to make comparisons between gun owners and the broader population given that it is not a random sample. Further, using the mailing list of groups of leisure communities means that the survey may not have reached populations with more utilitarian reasons for owning firearms, such as ranchers or farmers, for whom firearms are tools of necessity rather than tools of leisure. That said, it does give us a good opportunity to examine the opinions of gun owners in Canada.

For the second phase of the project, in the fall of 2021 and winter of 2022, I conducted semi-structured Zoom interviews with fourteen advocates and lobbyists, and eighty-four Canadian gun owners. Interview participants were recruited using the mailing list of one of the major firearms advocacy groups in Canada. I met with participants over Zoom for short, semi-structured interviews that lasted from twenty minutes to several hours, depending on the time that the participant had to spare.

Once again, this data collection method comes with obvious limitations. Given the volunteer bias introduced by data collection, these interviews are intended to showcase the views and opinions of gun owners who are involved, at some level, in firearms advocacy in Canada. This compromise was necessary given the lack of data on gun ownership in Canada, and the challenges of collecting that data. Given that gun owners make up a small percentage of the Canadian public, less than 6 per cent, it would be prohibitively expensive and logistically challenging to reach them using established random sampling techniques.

Further, by using the mailing list of a pro-gun group, I was able to mitigate issues of participant trust that might have arisen given the perceived anti-gun bias in academia.

With the exception of the professional advocates I spoke to, who agreed to share their real names, all participant names used in this project are pseudonyms assigned using a random name generator. To avoid applying a veneer of whiteness, I tried to ensure that the pseudonyms used were appropriate to the person's cultural group and gender, using the heritage-related filters that the name generator provided me with.

The advocates I spoke to were predominantly from pro-gun groups, with a few notable exceptions. This was not intentional. While recruiting participants for my research, I reached out to invite pro-control groups to participate in interviews, but these requests were either rejected or ignored. I suspect this is related to several opinion pieces that I have written in defence of evidence-based firearm policy in Canada.[9]

The semi-structured interviews were audio-recorded with the consent of participants. Interview data was then analysed thematically using NVIVO 13, a qualitative research analysis tool. When conducting thematic analysis, researchers search for and interpret "patterns of meaning ('themes') within qualitative data."[10] Conducting thematic analysis in this way is an inductive rather than deductive approach, and coding is "treated as an organic and flexible process" based on deep engagement with the data. Rather than approaching the data with a codebook in mind, themes are identified throughout the course of the research.[11]

Some of the common themes became clear after only a few interviews, as they were repeated often by participants. For example, after dozens of participants noted similar feelings of being targeted by politicians, media, and Canadian law, it became clear that these were important themes to touch on in the book. Other themes emerged by looking for common phrases or groupings in NVIVO. These themes would later become headings for various sections of the book. For example, the themes of family, friendship, community, competition, heritage, relaxation, and fun were the most commonly cited reasons for gun ownership by participants, and thus became sub-headings within chapter 3's discussion of why anyone in Canada "needs" a gun.

The next chapter introduces the book's approach to understanding pro-gun advocacy in Canada. It gives a short history of gun control legislation, including a first-person account of gun licensing in Canada, before explaining the relationship between the three key themes of the book: citizenship, leisure culture, and alienation.

Chapter 3 explores gun culture in Canada and provides evidence for my claim that there is a unique Canadian leisure culture surrounding gun ownership. I will demonstrate that while US gun culture has changed dramatically since the 1980s, largely as a result of the liberalization of concealed-carry laws, Canadian gun culture has remained frozen in time.

Chapter 4 will outline the Canadian gun debate and describe the political opportunity structure that pro-gun groups advocate within. There, I show how key Canadian institutions shape the environment in which the Canadian pro-gun movement operates: the Canadian Charter of Rights and Freedoms, the courts, Parliament, the party and interest group systems, federalism, and Indigenous treaties. I also emphasize the influence of public opinion, the media and Canadian political culture, as well as rural and western alienation.

In Chapter 5, I outline the Canadian model of gun rights, showing how Canadian gun owners have moved from leisure to politics when mobilized to defend their avocation. In chapter 6, I present data from my surveys of pro-gun advocates in Canada and seek to take stock of the movement. This includes examining the people who make up the movement, and the key tactics that it uses to advocate for Canadian gun owners, such as lobbying, public relations, or coalition-building.

Finally, in chapter 7, I discuss the most recent legislative changes to Canada's gun control laws – Bill C-21 – and outline the major conclusions of the project, and the lessons it holds, as well as avenues for further research.

Some readers may be disappointed that this book avoids a lengthy discussion of the effectiveness of gun control policies. I felt, however, that this discussion was beyond the scope of this book. There is a large literature on this topic, and interested readers are encouraged to look at some of my past work on this subject.

2

Leisure Culture, Citizenship, and Alienation

Canadians have tended to define themselves, not in terms of their own national history and tradition, but rather by reference to what they are not: American.[1]

Seymour Martin Lipset

Guns are as American as apple pie – but what does it mean to own a gun north of the 49th parallel? What do I mean when I say that Canada has a gun culture, and how has that culture organized itself politically? How do gun politics connect to questions of what it means to be a citizen of Canada, a rural Canadian, or a Western Canadian?

This chapter explores these questions. It begins with a brief history of contemporary Canadian gun control policy, as well as a first-person look into the licensing system under which Canadian gun owners are regulated. This is intended to give readers important context to understand the gun debate in Canada. Though most Canadians vaguely understand that Canada has laws governing the possession and use of firearms, these laws are poorly understood by the general public.[2] This public ignorance has a profound impact on the gun debate. It is thus important to clarify this at the outset of our discussion.

The chapter then moves on to flesh out the key concepts that will be essential to understanding the book's argument: leisure culture, citizenship, rural politics, and western alienation.

A Brief History of Contemporary Firearms Policy in Canada

This book focuses on gun advocacy in the second Trudeau era. To understand this particular period, however, it is worth exploring some of the history of firearm regulation in Canada. While most Canadians are vaguely aware that Canada has "gun control" and that the United

States allegedly does not, they are often surprised to learn that many of
these laws are of a more recent vintage.

While Canada has a long-established tradition of regulating handguns dating back to the late nineteenth century,[3] the regulation of
long guns in Canada is relatively recent, even of those capable of fully
automatic fire. After a series of spree shootings in the early 1970s, the
government passed Bill C-51, which laid the groundwork for Canada's
contemporary gun laws. The bill prohibited fully automatic firearms,[4]
which until then had been legal to own. It created the Firearm Acquisition Certificate and introduced a background check requirement to
purchase guns. It also created a firearms classification system, separating firearms into the categories of non-restricted, restricted, and prohibited. The non-restricted category is generally made up of long guns,
like rifles and shotguns. The restricted category included handguns
and rifles that the government considered to be particularly threaten-
ing, like the AR-15 rifle.[5] Finally, prohibited firearms are, as the name
suggests, illegal to possess except to those who owned the guns before
the ban, and were "grandfathered" into the policy.[6]

Some of my older participants looked back with fondness and nostal-
gia on earlier periods of firearms regulation in Canada, before Bill C-51.
Jackson, a Black man from the prairies now in his sixties, remembers
getting his first gun:

> When I was 13 years old, I asked my dad for a pellet gun. He said no. He
> said, if you're going to have a firearm, you're going to have a real firearm,
> and he bought me a .22. So, he said, I want you to be responsible. Because
> this can hurt somebody. Pellet guns, people play around with all the time.

Jackson laughed at my look of shock during our interview, acknowledging that by contemporary standards, it would be quite odd to allow
a 13-year-old to have their own rifle. He continued:

> So he bought me a .22 and he would take me out shooting with that. I
> had a lot of friends [that I would shoot with]. Back in those days ... when
> I was, you know, 14, 15 years old, you could go into a gun store yourself
> and buy your own firearm. You didn't have to be 18 or anything else like
> that. Right? It was completely different, like you could walk down the
> street carrying a .22 heading out to a field to go shoot gophers, and nobody
> would bat an eye at it. Today, try to do that. Good luck.[7]

Others took a different view of the more relaxed gun laws of the past.
Karl grew up in rural Alberta in the 1960s and 1970s. He remembered

having relatively free access to firearms from a young age. "I was using firearms quite early, and to be honest with you, that was really stupid of parents to let us [do that] as preteens, you know, with the prefrontal cortex development thing. We just didn't understand what kind of danger we were carrying around."[8] Since then, of course, Canada has introduced much stricter laws surrounding the use of firearms by young people. Situations like the one described later by Karl now seem unimaginable:

> When we were teenagers, we took our guns to school, if you can believe it. And we'd walk into our school with our rifles, unloaded, you know. Our mom and dad said you can't have a bullet in there [the chamber]. Okay, so we'd have the clips [sic] in our pocket, and we'd go in, and we would put the guns in our locker and the principal or the teacher in charge would say:
> "Is that gun loaded?"
> "Yes, it is."
> "Take the bolt out."
> Okay, we take the bolt out. We didn't have locks on our lockers. In the '60s, if someone had come up to us and said that in the future, young students are going to take rifles, they're going to go into schools, they're going to murder their fellow students, we would have laughed him out of the room. It just would be inconceivable to us that that would happen.[9]

The single most important date in the development of contemporary gun control in Canada is 6 December 1989. On that day, a misogynist terrorist[10] stormed the École Polytechnique in Montreal on an explicit mission to kill as many women as possible. Blaming feminists for his various personal problems, he ended the lives of fourteen women before taking his own.[11] While American pro-control advocates had long struggled to mobilize a powerful movement,[12] the political opportunity structure in Canada was more favourable, and an effective pro-control advocacy coalition emerged, led by survivors of the massacre, Heidi Rathjen and Wendy Cuckier.[13]

As this coalition reignited the gun debate in Canada, another gun-related incident caught the attention of the government. In the summer of 1990, a group of armed Mohawk protestors erected a barricade to protect their ancestral lands from being bulldozed to build a golf course and residential development. When the provincial police, Sûreté du Québec, launched a late-night raid in July at the request of the town's mayor, they were repulsed by gunfire from the protesters. The government soon deployed the Canadian Armed Forces, stationing 4,000 troops in the area. After seventy-eight days, the death of a police officer, and hundreds of injuries among the protestors, an end to the Kanesatake Resistance, or Oka Crisis, was negotiated.[14]

In 1991, Brian Mulroney's Progressive Conservative government passed Bill C-17, which was spearheaded by then Justice Minister and future Prime Minister Kim Campbell. This law created the mandatory firearms safety course and twenty-eight-day waiting period for firearms licences.[15] It prohibited removable magazines accepted by semi-automatic rifles that could hold more than five rounds of ammunition and introduced stringent laws regarding how gun owners could store their firearms. The law also changed the minimum barrel-length requirement for legal handguns, prohibiting guns that the government feared were too concealable.[16] While the attack on the École Polytechnique is often cited as precipitating the law, Bouchard questions whether the Kanesatake Resistance also influenced the government's decision.[17] Given that the fear of insurrection by armed minority groups has often been a motivation for the creation of gun-control laws in Canada[18] and the United States,[19] there could be some merit to this argument.

The contemporary pro-gun movement saw this legislation as a massive betrayal by a fellow conservative. Sheldon Clare, former president of the National Firearms Association (NFA), noted that he held Campbell in particular contempt. "I have more of a problem with Kim Campbell and what she did to firearms ownership than anybody else, frankly." Meanwhile, the Liberals argued that Campbell had not gone far enough and promised a universal firearms registry in an attempt to make Campbell look soft on guns.[20] Despite the Liberal threats to tighten gun laws even further, the pro-gun movement's feelings of betrayal drove them to work hard to stymie Campbell's re-election, and along with major blunders by the Progressive Conservative Campaign, this may have helped lead to the defeat of the PCs to Jean Chrétien's Liberals in 1993.[21]

In 1995, Liberal Prime Minister Jean Chrétien passed Bill C-68, which centralized Canada's gun laws in the Firearms Act, and created the infamous long-gun registry.[22] Though handguns had been registered in Canada since the 1930s, no such requirement existed for long guns before 1995.[23] The long-gun registry would prove controversial, eliciting strong opposition from hunters, sports shooters, and farmers. It would soon become deeply unpopular, as costs soared and proponents struggled to point to gains in public safety related to the registry.[24]

Stephen Harper's newly united Conservative Party was able to use the registry as a wedge issue during his election campaign to become prime minister in 2006. Six years later, the Harper government repealed the long-gun registry and ordered the data destroyed, a measure that would result in a court battle between Jean Charest's Liberal government in Quebec and the Federal Government.[25]

Toughening gun laws was a priority of the incoming Trudeau government following its election in 2015. In 2018, the government passed Bill C-71, which extended background checks on gun-licence applicants from five years to a lifetime and required firearms sellers to keep purchase records that could be accessed by police, something opponents have labelled a "back-door registry" in reference to the dismantled long-gun registry.[26] The bill also paved the way for the government to introduce further firearm bans.

In March of 2019, after a gunman killed fifty-one people in a mosque in Christchurch, New Zealand, the government in Wellington quickly moved to tighten the country's already strict gun laws, including a ban of what they labelled assault weapons, despite New Zealand's low rate of gun violence[27] and the fact that administrative errors in the licensing system had allowed the gunman to wrongfully receive a firearms licence.[28] Given the global attention paid to the struggles of the gun-control movement in the United States, the ban was lauded by the news media as a courageous and common-sense solution.

In this context, the Liberal government announced its intention to introduce a similar ban during the run-up to the 2019 election campaign.[29] On 1 May 2020, weeks after a gunman went on an overnight rampage in Portapique, Nova Scotia, claiming the lives of twenty-two people, the government announced a similar ban in Canada. Though it came to light that the killer was not a licensed firearms owner and had smuggled all but one of his firearms from the United States, the government took advantage of the agenda window provided by the tragedy to issue an order-in-council (OIC) prohibiting over 1,500 models of firearms. This included the infamous AR-15, as well as the Ruger Mini-14, which had been used at the École Polytechnique massacre in Montreal in 1989, though other firearms were caught up in the ban, including some large-calibre bolt-action hunting rifles.

Though the government went to great pains to frame the ban as something that would not impact hunters, an analysis by the Ontario Federation of Anglers and Hunters found that the majority of the newly prohibited firearms had been used regularly for hunting and pest control in Canada for decades.[30] Owners of newly prohibited firearms could not fire, sell, transfer, or return their firearms, but were required to keep them securely stored and await a government buyback program, which at time of writing has yet to materialize.

Critics of the policy pointed out that the ban did not prohibit all semi-automatic rifles, and the government refused to publicly divulge information related to how they selected firearms to include in the ban.[31] Many rifles, like the Soviet SKS or Israeli Tavor, which were functionally similar to an AR-15 or Ruger Mini-14, were still available. The inconsistencies in the policy, and the silence of the government about their selection criteria, opened room for speculation that the banned guns were chosen based on their reputation rather than their design.

After two years and mounting criticism regarding the struggles of the government to organize the buyback program,[32] as well as a tragic mass shooting at Uvalde, Texas, the government introduced Bill C-21, which would formalize and later expand the firearm prohibition, and introduce measures like red-flag laws and a freeze on the sale, transfer, or importation of handguns.

Criticism of the new law focused on two main arguments – redundancy and optics. First, handguns in Canada were already tightly controlled to the point where the new laws seemed unnecessary to critics. Further, though the government does not produce publicly available national data on the origin of crime guns, sporadic reports from the cities most impacted by gun violence demonstrate that the lion's share of handguns used in crimes in Canada are smuggled from the United States.[33] Several other measures within the bill, like red-flag laws, were actually minor tweaks to Canada's existing framework, which fulfil the same function. Second, the government received criticism for the timing of the announcement after a tragedy in the United States.[34] This was compounded when, weeks later, the public inquiry into the Nova Scotia shooting unearthed evidence that the RCMP police commissioner had allegedly, under the direction of the government, pressured the local police to release the details of the firearms used by the shooter, as they were "tied to pending legislation."[35]

Surveying the contemporary history of gun control legislation in Canada, a shift can be observed following the creation of the long-gun registry. Though gun control efforts before this period were not uncontroversial, they tended to include bipartisan input. For example, the most significant changes to Canada's gun laws happened under a Progressive Conservative government. Since the long-gun registry, gun politics seems to have succumbed to a wider trend of hyper-partisanship and wedge politics. This has been pursued by both Conservative and Liberal governments. Since the Harper government successfully leveraged the long-gun registry to shore up the support of his rural and western Canadian base, the Trudeau government continued the tradition, energizing voters in downtown Toronto, Montreal, and Vancouver with highly visible changes to Canada's gun laws.

A First-Person Look at Firearms' Licensing in Canada

This history may seem unimportant to those outside of the gun community, but my participants often referenced the process of firearms licensing in Canada during our discussions, given the impact this process has had on their lives. The process of getting a gun licence in Canada is not well understood by those outside the gun community or its regulators, so I felt some clarification was needed at the beginning of this book. As part of a past research project on gun policy which I conducted between 2017 and 2021, I felt that it would be useful to go through the licensing process to obtain a Restricted Possession and Acquisition Licence (RPAL), and an Ontario Outdoors Card, which would allow me to purchase hunting permits. I feel that sharing my experience with this process will help readers better understand how it works from the point of view of the regulated.

I took the Canadian Firearms Safety Course (CFSC) and Canadian Restricted Firearms Safety Course (CRFSC) in 2018. The first qualified me to possess non-restricted firearms in Canada, mostly long guns and shotguns. The second allowed me to own restricted firearms, which at that time included handguns and certain other firearms designated by the government as restricted. Using the internet, I located a community sports facility near my home, which at that time was in Ottawa, that offered both the CFSC and the CRFSC in the same weekend. I registered. Given the high demand for the course and low supply of instructors, there was a lengthy wait before I could take the class. At the time of writing, the class costs $300, including the textbook.

The class took place over the course of a weekend. This included Friday evening, and a full day both Saturday and Sunday. The course consisted of both theoretical and "practical" elements. I put "practical" in quotes because the Canadian Firearms Safety Class does not allow for the use of live firearms. Rather, students practise handling deactivated firearms and dummy ammunition. You never have to fire a shot.

Course material covered safe firearm handling, the rules of gun safety, and Canada's numerous regulations covering the safe storage and transportation of guns. But the course taught values as well. Students are drilled about the responsibility that comes with gun ownership, and the consequences of failing to follow the proper safety rules.

Given that I was applying for both a Possession and Acquisition Licence (PAL) and a Restricted Possession and Acquisition Licence

(RPAL), the course involved two written tests and two practical tests. Written tests needed to be passed with a score over 80 per cent. Practical tests involved showing the instructor that we could handle firearms safely. Major safety errors would result in an automatic failure, and instructors have the authority to fail anyone that they feel would not be a safe firearm owner.

After passing the test, the student is qualified to apply for their licence, which will cost an additional $63. This involves downloading and printing a form from the website of the Royal Canadian Mounted Police. It means acquiring passport photos and character references from two people who are eighteen years of age or older, are not your conjugal partner, and have known you for at least three years. It involves disclosing your mental health history to the RCMP, including past episodes of depression, substance abuse, or "emotional problems." It involves disclosing whether, in the past two years, you have had a breakup, job loss, or bankruptcy. In my case, I had experienced a breakup of a significant relationship a few months prior to taking the class. As a result, I had to contact my ex-partner and discuss with her why I was applying for the licence so that I could acquire her written consent for me to apply. Lying on the form is an offence under the Firearms Act.

Once all of this was done, I sent my application and waited. When the firearms centre received my application, it sat in a pile for twenty-eight days during the mandatory waiting period. After that, the overworked and underfunded employees of the Canadian Firearms Program did their best to get to it when they could.

The process of taking the Ontario Hunters Education Course was similar. Hunting is regulated by the provinces in Canada, rather than the RCMP. As a result, each province offers its own licensing system. While hunters can hunt outside of their provinces, they need to purchase special licences or tags to do this, which are often quite expensive.

This time, the course was offered in a rural area outside of Ottawa. The course involved 1.5 days of coursework, as well as a written and practical exam. The course covered additional firearms safety instruction, but mostly focused on matters related to hunting, including provincial, federal, and municipal hunting regulations, wilderness safety, species identification, and processing wild game. Like the CFSC/CRFSC, this course also focuses on stressing the importance of safe hunting practices but also touches on conservation ethics. After completing the course, the applicant can apply to the provincial government for a licence (in Ontario this is called an Outdoors Card), which allows one to buy species-specific licences and tags.

Provincial conservation officers are responsible for enforcing many laws and regulations related to hunting in Canada. They patrol popular hunting and fishing spots to ensure that everyone involved is properly licenced and following the laws and regulations. Hunting without the proper permit, called poaching, carries serious penalties.

Not all hunters in Canada use firearms. Some use bows or cross-bows in addition to, or in lieu of, a firearm. Governments incentivize archery hunting by providing longer seasons and more opportunities for archery hunters, given the increased level of difficulty involved.

This licensing process for firearms and hunting is important, as it helps to keep Canadians safe. It is a regulatory system shaped by Canada's history of gun violence, and by policymakers' decisions at key times and places. The requirement for spousal consent, or the consent of an ex-partner, for example, is quite logical and useful to help prevent domestic abusers from acquiring firearms.

At the same time, for the applicant, the process can feel invasive. Exposing the intimate details of your life to your country's national police force, a force with a rather complicated history with regard to human rights, makes one feel vulnerable. Contacting an ex-partner to talk about gun licensing is stressful and humiliating. The licensing process is also costly, both in terms of time and financial commitment.

The process is designed to inculcate both knowledge and values into the minds of participants, whether that be a respect for the danger firearms pose and a desire to use them responsibly, or the ethics of wildlife conservation, which will be discussed in detail in later chapters. At the same time, the process also creates a sense of collective identity in participants as licence holders. Having sacrificed time, privacy, and money for the privilege of their licence, gun owners feel that they have entered into a covenant with their government, entitling them to use the tools for which they are licenced. It is unsurprising, then, that gun owners would view changes to this regime as a betrayal.

Making Sense of Gun Culture: Leisure Culture and Social Movements in Canadian Politics

The battle over gun control in Canada is a battle between competing movements with different visions of the country. Participating in movements allows ordinary citizens to take part in the democratic process beyond casting ballots every four years. In the 1960s, a new type of collective actor emerged. Labelled "new social movements," these initiatives coalesced around identities and values rather than material goals and were increasingly transnational in scope.[36] These movements have profoundly transformed western society and remain an important vehicle for democratic participation.

Like any group involved in the creation of public policy, social movements occupy an environment filled with both opportunities and challenges. Some are unique to a given movement, while others are generalizable. The most significant common challenge groups and movements face is known as the free-rider problem. First identified by Olson,[37] this explains how it is rational for citizens to sit on the sidelines while a small number of motivated actors engage in advocacy. In the Canadian context, movements face institutional barriers as well. For example, financial support for advocacy from the government has declined in recent years.[38]

To better understand how movements overcome these barriers, a robust literature has emerged examining collective action in a variety of contexts such as the rights revolution,[39] the feminist movement,[40] the environment,[41] 2SLGBTQ+ rights,[42] and disability rights.[43] While most of the literature has focused on left-wing movements, a few scholars have tackled right-wing social movements in Canada, such as the wider conservative movement,[44] the evangelical movement,[45] and the anti-abortion/pro-life movement.[46]

Authors have applied several theories to explain the success or failure of certain social movements, including pluralism,[47] resource mobilization theory,[48] Marxist and neo-Marxist theory,[49] feminist theory,[50] and others. This literature has shed light on how identity impacts politics, and how identities like race, class, sexuality, and gender create linkages around which social movements can mobilize.

But what about leisure culture? The literature has not yet examined how leisure-based cultural identities inspire advocacy and shape the way that actors in the system navigate the political world.

In June of 1971, John Meisel, Canadian Political Science Association (CPSA) president and founding editor of the *Canadian Journal of Political Science* (*CJPS*), gave a presidential address in which he asked scholars of Canadian politics to take leisure culture seriously.[51] Meisel noted that leisure culture was increasingly important in post-industrial societies, where the free time provided to the growing middle class by technological innovations allowed more Canadians to enjoy leisure pursuits. He argued that leisure culture both shaped and was shaped by formal politics. That is, leisure culture helps to shape political culture, in that it influences "both the demands people make on the political system and the support they bring it." At the same time, by regulating and funding culture, sport, and leisure, the government in turn influences leisure.[52]

Despite the passing of several decades, leisure remains an understudied concept in political science. Sociologists have developed a robust literature on serious leisure, thanks to the work of pioneers like Stebbins,[53] but little work has been done in the field of political science to capture the influence of leisure on politics and political behaviour.

While leisure had traditionally been conceptualized by scholars as the "happy, carefree refuge from our earnest pursuit of money and social standing," Stebbins argued that for many people, serious leisure activities were not merely distractions from life's problems, but much more serious pursuits.[54] Serious leisure pursuits include things like volunteer work, amateurism, and hobbyist endeavours. Serious leisure is distinguished from what Stebbins calls casual leisure by six core characteristics: (1) durable benefits, (2) effort, (3) perseverance, (4) careerism, (5) ethos, and (6) identity.

Casual leisure, like watching television, having sex, or going to a party, provides immediate gratification,[55] while serious leisure pursuits provide long-term benefits like: "self-actualization, self-enrichment, recreation or renewal of self, feelings of accomplishment, enhancement of self-image, self-expression, social interaction and belongingness, and lasting physical products of the activity."[56] Because of these benefits, participants expend tremendous effort and resources to gain skills, knowledge, and training in their given activity. This might involve taking classes, reading books, or scouring the internet and social media for information on their hobby or sport. Those involved in serious leisure will engage in their pursuit for decades, often persevering through difficult conditions like injuries or embarrassments. Participants in serious leisure often have secondary careers alongside their leisure activities, facilitated by the rise of social media and e-commerce websites like YouTube and Etsy. Finally, serious leisure activities often develop a unique ethos, or shared "beliefs, values, moral principles, norms and performance standards." Thus, serious leisure activities become a component of participants' identities.[57]

Since Stebbins first coined the term, a substantial literature has emerged on serious leisure in the fields of sociology and the subfield of leisure studies.[58] Serious leisure has been linked to many positive outcomes for participants, such as personal growth and happiness,[59] life satisfaction,[60] and reduced stress.[61] A major benefit of serious leisure is its ability to foster community-building and social interaction at a time where meeting people and forming communities seems to be becoming more challenging.[62] Further, several studies have demonstrated that serious leisure is linked to successful aging among senior citizens in the United States,[63] Canada,[64] Iran,[65] and South Korea.[66]

Various authors have proposed that gun ownership, participation in the shooting sports, gun collecting, and hunting, form the basis for serious leisure identities.[67] Research on target shooters in the United States has demonstrated that participants are deeply engaged in their sport, with almost 80 per cent of participants having participated in target shooting for more than fifteen years. Further, over 57 per cent were involved in reloading their own ammunition, a labourious and time-consuming process that takes a significant amount of up-front investment and training.[68] Ethnographic research on American hunters has demonstrated that "Hunting is deeply intertwined with rural family traditions."[69] Participants' identities were closely linked to the practice of hunting. The authors found that "our informants constructed their hunting identity as central and foundational."[70] Further, Hubbs's[71] ethnography of tactical shooters in Saskatchewan notes that these shooters exist as part of a serious leisure community that bonds members and creates strong social ties, fellowship, and an intense feeling of belonging.

Participants in serious leisure activities are often tied together by a shared leisure culture. In the case of firearm enthusiasts, this is referred to in the literature as "gun culture."[72] Gun culture is often thought of as a uniquely American phenomenon, especially since Hofstadter's[73] famous lament that America was the only industrialized nation that retained such a culture. Detractors like Hofstadter usually use the term pejoratively to describe American culture as a whole. In other words, they say that America *is* a gun culture. This of course is a generalization that ignores the vast number of Americans for whom guns are objects of fear and derision. As I have argued in the past, it is more accurate to say that within the vast and diverse American society resides a significant gun culture, a community that shares cultural practices, jargon, and understandings of the world.[74]

Gun culture, conceptualized in this way, can be recognized in countries around the world that still allow some level of civilian gun ownership, and Canada is no exception. Canadian gun culture is markedly different from its American counterpart, largely due to its collision with government institutions and regulations, but also due to Canada's unique political culture.

Culture is important to political scientists because of how it informs political beliefs, creates social identities, and motivates political behaviour. The concept of culture can help us to reconcile institutional and rational choice approaches to political science with a social movements approach. While individuals often act rationally, based on interests, culture can help to unpack how individuals understand their interest. By informing the way that people understand the world, culture can function similarly to ideology in forming the basis of political beliefs. American commentators have noted the emergence of a gun-centric political ideology south of the border.[75] Further, there is evidence that at least a sizeable corps of gun owners in Canada have been activated politically by changes to Canada's gun regulations under the former Trudeau government.[76]

This book will add quantitative and qualitative data to the discussion of gun ownership as serious leisure in Canada, demonstrating that this community fits Stebbins's definition of serious leisure. This is important for scholars of political science to unpack, because it allows us to make sense of pro-gun advocacy – a social movement formed not around class, race, gender, or indigeneity, but rather shared belonging in a different type of community. The concept of leisure helps us understand how pastimes can become politics.

Serious leisure pursuits involve significant material and temporal commitments, and inspire a collective ethos, identity, and culture. It is unsurprising, then, that serious leisure can have political implications, especially at a time when culture-war politics are increasingly salient. Thus far, a few authors writing in sociology have used ethnographic research to study how serious leisure can serve as a motivation for political participation. For example, looking at off-road driving enthusiasts in the United States, Rosenbaum notes: "As individuals ground a sense of self and community in their leisure activities, they are likely to take action to protect the foundation of their identity narratives when opposing forces threaten these foundations."[77] Rosenbaum demonstrated that the "Jeepers" that he studied were highly motivated towards political action when their access to off-road driving trails was threatened by government regulation. His participants used similar strategies and techniques to those of other new social movements.[78]

Other scholars have examined how a motorcycle-rights movement emerged from a collection of motorcycle clubs in Indiana in response to mandatory helmet laws,[79] and how outdoor recreation enthusiasts were mobilized to advocate for environmental politics.[80]

Sociologists of serious leisure often study the behaviour of individuals within the community or focus on the role of larger structural factors, such as consumer culture and gender, in shaping how people participate in their leisure activities. For example, Anderson and Taylor[81] compare how skydivers and gun collectors create identity narratives to mediate their relationship with outsider communities that misunderstand their hobbies. They do not look, however, at how the formal political realm shapes the context in which this identity construction takes place. What is missing is an account of what happens to serious leisure communities when their pursuit becomes a site of societal contestation.

How does leisure culture impact politics in Canada? I propose that the answer lies in an examination of group politics, given that social movements and advocacy groups are an important way in which Canadians can make demands on their government. As we will see, serious leisure pursuits, when contested, can serve as a powerful driver motivating supporters towards collective action, even in the face of hostile political opportunity structures.

Using the leisure culture approach contributes to our understanding of political mobilization. Rational choice theorists since Olson[82] have maintained that the interest-group system favours small groups and concentrated, selective interests. Given that it is natural for individuals to try to "free ride" on the advocacy work of others, as they can attain the same benefits without having to incur any personal or financial sacrifices, movements representing collective interests struggle to maintain participation and mobilize resources.[83] Given that firearm rights, as conceptualized by pro-gun advocates, are a collective good, with the potential to be enjoyed by a wide swathe of Canadians, it would be expected that most everyday Canadian gun owners would not be involved in advocacy.

Neopluralists, on the other hand, while abandoning some of the early assumptions of pluralist theory, have shifted the focus to examine how advocacy groups have proliferated in the face of barriers to collective action.[84] Various pathways to group formation have been proposed: from policy entrepreneurs who take it upon themselves to launch and lead groups[85] to patrons who supply interest groups with much-needed resources, to social movements, issue networks, and selective benefits that groups can offer.[86] I contend that leisure culture can serve as another pathway to group formation. Members of leisure communities, like the Canadian community of gun owners or "gun culture," represent cohesive latent groups[87] that, when challenged by restrictive legislation, can be more easily mobilized towards advocacy.

As we will see, the firearms policy subsystem in Canada looks remarkably neopluralist, with advocacy coalitions competing in a system of countervailing power. This does not mean that all coalitions are equal. While leisure culture and the rural-urban divide can help to explain the relatively successful mobilization of the pro-gun movement in Canada, the pro-control coalition has been dominant in influencing Canada's gun policy since the 1990s, despite having few material resources and a shallow membership base. This is largely due to the political opportunity structure in Canada, especially for institutions and public opinion, which heavily favours the pro-control coalition.

Rights Claims and Citizenship

How does the Canadian gun culture articulate its demands? How does the movement engage in what political scientists and scholars of human rights call "rights claiming"[88]; that is, using the discourse of rights to make claims of their government and of society? The key to unpacking this is understanding the concept of citizenship, and debates over what citizenship means in the Canadian political context. As we will see, Canadian gun owners see themselves as highly regulated citizens who have made considerable personal sacrifices – of privacy, of time, and of money – to participate in their chosen avocation. Recent changes to Canada's gun laws are seen by those within the culture as a betrayal of that compromise and a breach of the relationship of trust they expect governments to have with their citizens. Understanding what citizenship means to people is thus key to understanding the movement.

Further, unpacking how powerful Canadian institutions have shaped what it means to be Canadian also helps us to understand why the pro-gun movement has faced an uphill battle in the court of public opinion. While arms bearing is central to many narratives of American identity, constructions of Canadianness in the later twentieth and early twenty-first centuries do not include an armed citizenry. While this may seem obvious, a brief overview of the history of guns in Canada will show it was not inevitable.

Over the past three decades, discussions of citizenship in Canadian political science have tended to centre on three themes: multiculturalism, Quebecois Nationalism, and Indigenous politics.[89] Given the context of Canadian political culture, little attention has been paid in Canada to questions of armed citizenship so prevalent south of the border.

Citizenship is a complex concept distinct from nationality, designed to separate inhabitants of a given territorial unit into categories. These categories of citizen and non-citizen lay out the boundaries regarding "to whom the state owes protection and the persons who owe the state loyalty."[90] Citizenship involves incorporating a particular set of practices into state institutions. These practices relate to how states wield power to regulate markets, communities, and individuals. Citizenship rights limit state actions, shape how power is distributed in society, and serve to demarcate full membership in the political community. The way that citizenship is conceptualized, however, is not static, but changes over time and place.[91] A citizen of the Roman Empire in the year 250 CE would conceive of citizenship quite differently than a citizen of Italy today, just as what it means to be a citizen of Canada has shifted over time. Thus, the term "citizenship regime" refers to what it means to be a citizen at a particular place and time.[92] Citizenship regimes do not emerge from nowhere: they are shaped by politicians and political and cultural institutions.

Citizenship regimes serve four functions: the "responsibility mix," setting out rights and obligations, limiting access to politics, and delineating the borders of belonging. The first involves defining the boundaries of responsibility among the major components of any society: the state, civil society, families, and the individual. The second ascribes a set of rights and responsibilities to those who belong in society: citizens.[93] This in turn leads to the creation of distinct citizenship norms: ideas about what it means to be a good citizen.[94] The third, laying out governance practices that govern how people in society participate in political decision-making, and which claims and voices are considered legitimate. And, finally, establishing the boundaries of the nation – who belongs and who does not.[95]

The post-war period in Canada led to the creation of a new citizenship regime that found its ultimate form in the Canadian Charter of Rights and Freedoms. This political project involved many institutions, from the Citizenship Act of 1947 onward. Heavily influenced by Liberal party policies, it "assigned an active role to the state, in order to promote social justice; accepted a guiding role for the state in economic development; [and] recognized a single Canadian community, albeit one composed of francophones and anglophones, as well as individuals of diverse ethnic origins."[96] This citizenship regime created policies that most Canadians now take for granted, such as Canada's official bilingualism policy or policy of multiculturalism.

This was part of an attempt to create a Canadian identity that began among central Canadian intellectuals after the First World War. It was a way to try to unite Canadians from all provinces and territories under a common banner, and to distance Canada from both British political influence and American cultural influence, especially the United States' "excessive liberalism." As a result, cultural institutions were an important part of this citizenship regime. Cultural institutions like the Canadian Broadcasting Corporation (CBC), National Film Board, Canada Council, Radio-Canada, and others all played a central role in the creation of a new Canadian identity. But "the core of the citizenship regime was a strong and active federal government, providing and protecting the social rights of individuals and the culture of Canada." Making these institutions bilingual was an important way of reconciling French and English Canada under a single citizenship regime.[97]

This idea of Canadian citizenship was not without its critics. Some rural and Western Canadians felt citizenship in Canada had been constructed along central and urban Canadian norms and values. Central aspects of "Canadianness," such as anti-Americanism[98] or bilingualism, generally reflect the experiences of urban and central Canada,[99] leading to a sense of western and rural alienation that saturates Canadian politics and the gun debate.

Citizenship regimes are also inherently tied to questions of risk, as the idea of citizenship in Canada emerged as a way of mitigating risk. In the past, it was the responsibility of the individual, family, and civil society to manage risk. In the post-war period, state institutions like the welfare state were created to mitigate the risks inherent in capitalist societies that had historically been shouldered by families or charitable organizations, mostly religious charities.[100]

Gun control is an extension of this idea that the government, not the individual and family, bear a responsibility for managing collective risks. While the government regulated guns before this period, gun control historically in Canada was tied more overtly to questions of race, class, and power. That is, most gun laws were used to disarm populations that the government deemed untrustworthy, a category that over time included Indigenous peoples, Acadians, Irish immigrant labourers, and other groups. It was only in the 1970s that Canada's contemporary gun control regime began to take shape, applying gun control laws equally to all populations.[101]

Given the association between firearms and Americanness,[102] the civilian possession of guns was not incorporated into this citizenship regime. It might seem obvious that it would not be – however, this was not an inevitability. We often forget that Canada and the United States share a political lineage. Past iterations of citizenship regimes, descending from the British tradition, placed a greater emphasis on arms bearing to what it meant to be a loyal subject of the crown. This tradition dates back at least as far as the English Revolution (1642–51) and Glorious Revolution (1688), after which the English Bill of Rights declared "That Subjects which are Protestants, may have Arms for their Defence suitable to their Condition, and as are allowed by Law."[103] This British right to arms-bearing was intimately connected with participation in the militia, and the citizenship norm that good British subjects should take responsibility for the defence of realm.[104]

The legal commentaries of William Blackstone, a British law professor at Oxford, published between 1765 and 1770, further cemented this tradition and were a significant inspiration for the American Second Amendment. Blackstone identified three natural rights that people possess: "personal security, personal liberty, and private property."[105] These are further buttressed by five "auxiliary rights." The first three specified British political institutions to which the people could appeal: parliament, the sovereign, and the courts. Should these fail, the subjects' fourth right was to petition parliament or the sovereign. Finally, the fifth right was armed resistance.[106] Blackstone's work was so influential in British North America that it was even cited by Canadian Prime Minister Sir John A. Macdonald in Parliament during debates over the regulation of revolvers in early post-confederation Canada.[107]

Throughout early Canadian history, the government encouraged the practice of rifle shooting among Canadian men as part of its defence policy, motivated first by fear of American invasion and then by the need to produce soldiers for the great wars of the twentieth century. The government funded the Dominion of Canada Rifle Association to encourage Canadian men to take up rifle shooting, which would become "the first sports organization in Canada to receive federal funding in the form of annual grants."[108]

At the same time as the government was paying middle-class white men to shoot, gun control laws denied access to firearms to those whom the colonial and then Canadian governments considered unworthy, dangerous, or other.[109] Throughout British North America, gun control laws were used to disarm Indigenous peoples and forbid the trade of firearms with them. In the eighteenth century, gun-control laws were used to disarm French Canadians and pave the way for the expulsion of the Acadians. They were also used to disarm unruly Irish canal workers in the 1840s, Indigenous and Métis participants in the Northwest resistance, German and Austro-Hungarian Canadians during the First World War, non-citizens during the inter-war period following the Winnipeg General strike, and later alleged Bolsheviks.[110] This history makes it clear that questions of citizenship and belonging are central to the gun debate. Being a fully recognized British subject or Canadian citizen came with both the right and duty to arm oneself.

I do not cite this, as some have, to establish a historical right to bear arms in Canada.[111] I instead raise this point to demonstrate, first, that the decision to exclude armed citizenship from what it meant to be Canadian was not an inevitability. Gun control laws are part of a citizenship regime because they contribute to determining who is and who is not a full citizen in the eyes of the state by denoting who can and who cannot be trusted with dangerous technology. Second, changes in citizenship regimes are reflected in not just firearms policies, but the public debate on guns in society and the way that political actors assert citizenship rights.

The contemporary Canadian gun debate is heavily influenced by the post-war citizenship regime, which tacitly accepts that the federal government should have expansive powers to regulate the risk posed by firearms in the public interest (unlike in the United States), with an ideological focus on Canadian distinctiveness and anti-Americanism shaped by Central Canadian values. As we will see, Canadian gun owners see themselves as responsible, law-abiding Canadian citizens. Much of their anger, and political mobilization, comes from the feeling that their rights as citizens are being infringed upon by changes to Canada's gun control laws. The right they assert is not to bear arms for personal defence or the defence of the state, but the expectation that citizens be treated fairly by their government.

Rural Politics and Western Alienation

It is impossible to talk about the gun debate in Canada without discussing the politics of rural and western Canada. Gun culture in Canada is strongest in rural areas, with easy access to land for hunting and sports shooting, and in western Canada, defined here as the area between Manitoba and the interior of British Columbia. Rural and western Canada fit uncomfortably into the image of Canadian identity that forms the heart of the contemporary citizenship regime.

Guns have played and continue to play an important role in rural life. For many, though not all, rural Canadians, guns are useful tools on the farm and in the woods. Firearms are also an important tool for Canada's Indigenous peoples, many of whom live in rural and remote regions. According to Alison De Groot, spokesperson for the gun industry in Canada, 85–90 per cent of active firearms businesses in Canada are located in non-urban, rural, and remote areas.[112]

Rural Canada has become more than just a place; it is an important marker of identity. Human beings form emotional attachments to places that influence how they navigate the social world.[113] As a result, a distinct rural social identity has emerged in the United States[114] and Canada[115] that influences how citizens see politics, and their relationship with the urban realm in a way that transcends class and age gaps. It has led rural residents to feel that there are foundational differences in lifestyles and values between rural and urban citizens.[116] Economic and political shifts in rural Canada brought on by globalization and neoliberal policies, like the demise of family farms in favour of large agro-businesses, urbanization,[117] and the centralization of government in urban centres,[118] have left many rural Canadians feeling left behind by economic progress and excluded from political decision-making.

This has created a new politics of rural resentment[119] to which gun politics is intimately connected.

Policy differences between urban and rural areas are nothing new. The needs and values of urban and rural areas are often in competition. Policies that work well in urban areas may impose extra costs on rural areas. Some policies that favour rural folk, like liberalized gun laws, may offend the sensibilities of urban Canadians. At the same time, there are also spheres where urban and rural citizens need one another. Rural natural resources provide the raw materials for city life, and – to paraphrase a famous bumper sticker – farmers feed cities. At the same time, urban technology and cultural production make life in rural areas easier and more enjoyable. Rural Canadians often travel to cities for recreation, such as shopping or dining, while urban Canadians enjoy access to the outdoors at cottages, campgrounds, or national parks near rural towns.[120]

The politics of rural resentment shifts the conversation away from economic exchange towards cultural differences. Three overarching themes emerge from the politics of rural consciousness: first, the belief that decision-makers in urban centres regularly ignore the needs of rural areas; second, the feeling that rural folks receive fewer resources from the state than those in urban areas; and third, that decision-makers in cities ignore the distinct values of rural Canadians.[121] These values include community, resourcefulness, self-sufficiency, and the expectation of fair treatment by others.[122]

Canada is currently experiencing the "most profound urban-rural divide in support for major political parties in the country's history." While Canada has experienced urban-rural division in the past, it has never been as dramatic as in the period following the consolidation of the modern Conservative Party in 2003. This divide has partisan implications, with Liberals dominating in urban Canada and the Conservatives in rural Canada.[123]

Feelings of rural resentment are deeply connected to gun politics. It is no coincidence that the Liberal Party, so dominant in urban areas, has become the party of increased gun control. The impetus for gun control initiatives often arises from violent crime in urban areas, whether mass shootings in large Canadian cities like Montreal, or gang violence during Toronto's "Summer of the Gun." At the same time, levels of gun ownership are higher in rural areas, and rural gun owners feel unfairly targeted by these measures. To many rural folks I spoke with, this was yet another example of big city decision-makers privileging the values of anti-gun urbanites over the needs of rural Canadians, contributing to the latter feeling like second-class citizens.

The politics of western alienation are also important to discussions of gun politics in Canada. Rural resentment in Canada is deeply connected to feelings of alienation felt by western Canada, and to the agrarian populist tradition extending back to Henry Wise Wood's United Farmers of Alberta.[124] Rural and western alienation, while distinct phenomena, become linked or "layered" together into the way that people understand or make sense of politics.[125] Because these grievances are longstanding and deeply held, they go beyond any single policy issue, emerging and remerging at different times and places in Canada's political history, and in response to diverse political and social issues.[126]

Unlike other forms of political alienation, western alienation does not stem from economic roots, as the prairie provinces tend to be fairly prosperous and western alienation is not concentrated among economically marginalized westerners.[127] Rather, western alienation can better be seen as a political ideology,[128] interpretive framework, or counter-narrative[129] through which westerners view politics in Canada. Western alienation has less to do with economic structures in Canada and more to do with political institutions like party politics, federalism, and Parliament that create the rules of the game for decision-making in Canada – rules the west sees as slanted against its interests.[130]

When Canada was born, the vast majority of the population, eight in ten Canadians, lived in Ontario and Quebec.[131] As a result, the values of central Canada at this time came to be treated as core Canadian values – bilingualism, anti-Americanism, and "pragmatic elitism." As Canada expanded westward and new population booms happened, these central values made less sense in the west. French-Canadian populations in the west were significantly smaller than not just English-Canadians, but many of the new linguistic minorities moving to Canada. Without deep-rooted historical memory of the War of 1812, anti-Americanism was not as prevalent in the west. "The experiences and challenges of the west were different from those in central Canada."[132] Westerners felt that the central Canadian narrative, the idea of what it meant to be Canadian, had been defined in the east and did not fit neatly into western life.

Western alienation plays a significant role in the gun debate in Canada. The contemporary Canadian citizenship regime, shaped as it was by eastern Canadian institutions and their anti-American sensibilities, has created a public image of what it means to be Canadian that is anathema to firearms ownership. As gun ownership is concentrated in the west of Canada, the federal government's perceived attack on gun ownership fits neatly into the perception that eastern Canadian decision-makers routinely ignore western Canadian concerns.

3
Canadian Gun Culture

Hunting represents an enduring connection with our honourable past. By hunting and eating what I kill, I reaffirm my connection to the natural world and my place in it. To put it another way, you can't understand the world without eating some of it.[1]

Robert Sopuck.

The above quote illustrates the fact that serious leisure pursuits, like hunting, often have deep meanings to those who take part in them. Over 2.2 million Canadians hold licences that allow them to acquire and own firearms and participate in leisure activities related to gun ownership: sports shooting, hunting, and collecting. Though Canadian gun culture looks very different from its American counterpart, and by virtue of Canada's strict regulation of gun ownership is a much more exclusive club, there is a significant gun-owning community here.

Despite a large literature on serious leisure in sociology, few political scientists have explored how leisure-based groups make political claims and influence policy. The pro-gun movement in Canada is an important case study, as it is the largest and most successful leisure-based movement in Canada.

To understand firearms advocacy, we need to understand the people these advocates represent. The pro-gun movement in Canada is a grassroots movement, composed of members of a community. In this chapter, I will sketch a picture of Canadian gun culture. I will tackle the questions: Who are Canadian gun owners? Why does anyone in Canada need a gun? What is Canadian gun culture like, and how is it different from the American version? What is serious leisure, and why is it important for our understanding of advocacy and social movements? Answering these questions is key to understanding pro-gun advocacy in Canada.

Gun Culture 1.0 Redux

The term "gun culture" is contentious, often associated with critiques of widespread firearms ownership in the United States. The term was coined by an American historian, Richard Hofstadter, and was intended to carry a pejorative connotation. Hofstadter made the claim that America was unique among developed nations in maintaining a sizable gun culture.[2] In recent years, the community has reappropriated the term and has begun to use it internally. Due to the central importance of multiculturalism in Canadian culture and law, claims to the existence of a gun culture have even become the foundations of legal challenges to gun control policies.

I contend that a unique gun culture exists in Canada, different from its American counterpart in important ways. This culture, a set of ideas, traditions, symbols, and practices, is shared by a community of Canadian gun owners. It is practised on the skeet field and in the deer stand, in conversations among friends over beers or coffee, or in online chatrooms. The gun culture has also led to the emergence of a unique and politicized gun-owner social identity.[3]

Communities of gun owners are highly regulated citizens. As a result, regulations and laws shape gun culture, just as the advocacy of those within the culture seeks to further shape laws and regulations. Until the 1970s, Canadian and American gun culture were very similar, with the notable exception of handgun ownership. This was much more widespread in the United States than in Canada, given the absence of handgun regulation in many states and the more stringent regulation in Canada. During this period, there was also a significant exchange between American and Canadian gun communities, a tradition that persists to this day in the form of cross-border shooting competitions and the exchange, mostly south to north, of online content on platforms like YouTube.

This culture has changed over time. It's first iteration, Gun Culture 1.0 developed in the United States and Canada during the late nineteenth and early twentieth centuries, as guns became industrially mass-produced and available to a growing middle class as a source of recreation and a way of reconnecting with nature.[4] While guns were "tools of necessity" in colonial America and pre-confederation Canada, increasing urbanization and the closing of the frontier transformed them into tools of leisure.[5] During this period, rifle shooting grew in popularity across the English-speaking world with the support of governments, who saw the value in training their populations in marksmanship. In Canada, the *Militia Act* of 1868 allowed for the creation of the Dominion of Canada Rifle Association (DCRA). The DCRA built gun ranges, organized competitions across the country, and was the first sports organization in Canada to be federally funded.[6] In the United States, the government looked north following the Civil War. With the help of consultants from Canada, it created the National Rifle Association (NRA), whose original mission was to foster marksmanship amongst the US population by organizing competitions and classes.[7] Similar organizations emerged at the state and then national level in Australia[8] and also in New Zealand.[9]

Gun Culture 1.0 was centred around recreational target shooting and hunting. It was generally male-dominated, given the prevalent gender norms of the time, and was limited for the most part to white settler populations.

Scholars studying American gun culture have noted a shift, which began in the 1970s, between Gun Culture 1.0 and Gun Culture 2.0. First coined by Yamane,[10] the term Gun Culture 2.0 captures the shift in focus of American gun culture from hunting and sports shooting to self-defence. It was linked to increasing concern about crime and violence during this period[11] and was catalysed by the liberalization of concealed-carry laws[12] in the 1980s.[13] These laws, which made it easier for Americans to carry concealed firearms in public spaces, either by acquiring a licence or through what is called permitless carry, have allowed more people to carry handguns than at any time in America's history.[14] This shift can be captured not only in carry permits, but in survey data and through content analysis. For example, while in 1978, 71 per cent of Americans surveyed owned firearms for leisure purposes, by 2015, 63 per cent named personal protection as their primary reason for gun ownership.[15] Further, tracing advertisements in the NRA's *American Rifleman Magazine*, Yamane et al. catalogue a change over the years, from advertisements primarily focused on hunting and sports shooting to those promoting self-defence-related products.[16]

Scholars have explained this shift by looking at the reinvigorated gun rights movement in the United States during the period between the late 1960s and the turn of the century. In the 1960s, crime rates began to rise, and in 1968 the United States passed the *Gun Control Act*, the first federal firearms legislation since before the Second World War.[17] This galvanized the gun-rights movement, shifting the NRA from an occasional advocate to a political juggernaut.[18] With a grassroots army of supporters, the NRA was able to advocate effectively at the state level, where most American gun policy contests are settled. Between 1961 and 2013, the number of states with permissive "shall-issue" concealed carry laws jumped to forty.[19] In addition to the state-level advocacy efforts of the NRA and other groups, this change was also catalysed by the rise in crime associated with the crack cocaine epidemic in the 1980s, and ironically, by the 1994 Assault Weapons Ban, which pushed the firearms industry to focus more on handgun sales.[20]

While recreational shooting and hunting were primarily concentrated among rural Americans and white middle-class men, self-defence is a more universal concern. As a result, Gun Culture 2.0 in the United States has become increasingly diverse, as more women, people of colour, 2SLBTQ+ folks, political moderates, and even liberals join. This new generation of gun owners is more likely to own handguns than long guns and to own guns solely for the purposes of self-defence.[21]

The association between firearms and self-protection has transcended the boundaries of race, gender, sexual orientation, and class. For example, 2020 saw a massive surge in gun purchases, driven by the fear and uncertainty of the COVID-19 pandemic, the Trump presidency, and the racial tensions caused by the horrific murder of George Floyd by Minneapolis police and the ensuing protests. During this period, 18 per cent of American households purchased a gun.[22] Seventy per cent of those buying a gun during this period cited self-protection as their reason for doing so. Though the majority of new gun buyers were white, African Americans were overrepresented as a percentage of the population of first-time gun buyers.[23] Gun purchases by African Americans in the United States increased by 58.2 per cent in 2020,[24] and the National African American Gun Owners Association (NAAGA) grew by 25 per cent.[25] While the association between Americans and guns is often imagined as timeless, it is clear that the relationship has changed since the 1960s, along with the laws that regulate gun use.

American politicians and courts loosened gun laws after the 1980s, but Canadian legislators took a different approach and continued the construction of Canada's extensive gun control infrastructure. Unlike the United States, where firearms policy is primarily concentrated at the state level, national governments in Canada managed to successfully centralize gun laws at the federal level, starting in 1977 with the passage of Bill C-51.

As a result, the same cultural shift towards handguns and a focus on self-defence has not occurred in Canada. Canadian gun culture is very much rooted in the practices of Gun Culture 1.0: hunting and sports shooting. Handgun shooting, while widespread in Canada, is much less common than in the United States. Those who own handguns must demonstrate that they are active sports shooters by maintaining a membership at a club or range. Self-defence is not a legal reason to own a handgun in Canada, and the strict safe-storage laws make using a

Table 3.1. Type of Guns Owned by Survey Respondents

Firearm Type	Percentage of Participants Owned
Rifles	
Non-restricted single-action rifles	76%
Non-restricted semi-automatic rifles	65%
Restricted rifles	40%
Shotguns (non-restricted)	78%
Handguns (restricted)	63%
Muzzle-Loading Firearms (non-restricted)	18%

handgun for self-defence in the home challenging, and in public spaces virtually impossible.

These nuances are not often presented in the public discussion on firearms policy in Canada, which the media often frame in the same language as the American gun debate. Exacerbating this problem, little research in Canada attempts to better understand gun use and the political opinions of Canadian gun owners, despite a recent surge in US research on this topic. As a result, my survey sought to understand how Canadian gun owners use their firearms, and what their opinions are on government firearms policy. The findings are consistent with the limited research that has probed the differences between Canadian and American gun owners. Canadian gun owners tend to see firearms less as symbols of broader political values, as Americans do, and more as tools to participate in sports and activities.[26] This does not mean that firearms lack meaning for their owners, but that these meanings are personal and instrumental, and less tied to political culture or fear of crime.

Participants in my online survey mostly owned long guns. The most common firearms my participants reported owning were shotguns, at 78 per cent, and non-restricted[27] rifles, at 76 per cent. A further 65 per cent owned non-restricted semi-automatic rifles, while 40 per cent owned restricted semi-automatic rifles, and 63 per cent owned handguns (see Table 3.1). Handgun ownership was overrepresented in the survey, given that only a quarter of licensed gun owners in Canada possess an RPAL that would allow them to purchase handguns, and only half of those with the licence actually own one.[28] The overrepresentation of handgun ownership indicates that individuals who own restricted firearms like handguns or semi-automatic carbines may be more likely to be politically engaged. This is logical, given that most proposed gun control legislation targets these firearms.

Even with the inflated number of handgun owners in the sample, Canadian gun owners differ from their American counterparts in the types of guns they own and the reasons they own them. In America, handguns are the most popular type of firearm (72 per cent) compared to rifles (62 per cent) and shotguns (54 per cent). Americans who only own a single firearm consistently choose a handgun (62 per cent) rather than a rifle (22 per cent) or shotgun (16 per cent).[29]

Further, Americans overwhelmingly own firearms out of concern for personal protection, with 67 per cent of American gun owners claiming that self-defence is their main reason for owning a gun.[30] Most of my participants owned firearms for sports shooting and hunting. When asked if they had ever acquired a firearm for personal, home, or farm protection, only 35 per cent answered in the affirmative. Of this minority group, about a quarter (24 per cent) cited protection from wild animals as the reason for this purchase. Only 21 per cent of those who answered yes acquired a firearm due to concerns regarding crime, and 17 per cent due to concerns regarding social unrest.

Canadian gun enthusiasts tend to own and use their firearms for sporting and hunting purposes. Target shooters made up the largest demographic in the sample. Ninety per cent of those in my sample reported participating in target shooting, with 67 per cent reporting taking part in hunting. Fifty-five per cent reported taking part in shotgun sports, like skeet, trap, and sporting clays, with 24 per cent participating in dynamic shooting competitions like IPSIC, 3-Gun, or IDPA, and 7 per cent being cowboy action shooters. About 46 per cent noted that they collected firearms, and 47 per cent reported engaging in casual backyard shooting, referred to as plinking.

Why Does Anyone "Need" A Gun?

"Why does anyone in this city need to have a gun at all?"[31] This 2018 quote by then-Toronto mayor John Tory speaks to a lack of awareness on the part of mainstream Canadian society of the leisure community that exists within their midst. Many Canadians, especially those from urban areas, may genuinely have never met a hunter or sports shooter. It is therefore useful to explore the motivations that gun owners have for wanting to possess potentially deadly weapons, before moving into a deeper discussion of Canadian gun regulation and culture. These explanations highlight that firearms are both *useful* and *meaningful* objects for the people who own and use them. For gun enthusiasts, firearms are tools for recreation or subsistence; objects to collect; witnesses to history; and useful for protection from four-legged threats. On a social level, firearms have deep meanings to their owners that extend beyond mere utility. Firearms as objects serve to connect communities and families in ways rarely acknowledged in the popular debates on gun control. One cannot adequately understand the policy debate on gun control without grasping this.

Unlike the United States, which recognizes gun ownership as a constitutional right, the Canadian government and courts consider firearm ownership in Canada to be a privilege. There are several justifications accepted by the RCMP to apply for a firearm licence: for hunting, sports shooting, collecting, or if your job requires it. Those needing to carry a firearm for professional purposes must apply for an Authorization to Carry (ATC), which is tightly restricted. Few professions qualify for these licences. For example, while armoured car drivers are often granted ATCs, security guards in Canada are rarely armed. In rural areas, the most common reason to require an ATC is heightened risk of contact with dangerous animals. These licences are often held by professionals such as fur trappers or prospectors.

Gun ownership in Canada is most often associated with hunting, and 1.3 million Canadians[32] regularly take to the woods in search of game. Because of the relative abundance of public land, called Crown Land, Canadian hunters have the opportunity to harvest a variety of animals, from small game species like hare or game birds, to large game like deer, elk, and moose. Hunters also engage in pest and predator control, hunting species like coyotes who can threaten children and small animals, or gophers who destroy farmers' fields. For many rural Canadians, hunting is a way of life.

But hunting is not the only reason that Canadians own firearms. Shooting sports are also popular in Canada. As of 2019, 1.4 million Canadians regularly took part in these sports.[33] This includes Olympic sports like static target shooting with rifles and handguns, and the Olympic shotgun sports: skeet and trap shooting. It also includes more recent dynamic competitions like IPSIC handgun competitions, long-range shooting, three-gun, cowboy action shooting, and positional rifle shooting competitions. While traditional target-shooting competitions require firing from fixed positions, like a bench rest, these new sports often involve moving to different positions and shooting larger steel targets. The dynamic nature of these contests has boosted their popularity among gun owners.

The domestic firearms and ammunition industry is quite small in Canada, and most firearms-related products are imported from the United States. Despite this, sports shooting and hunting still represent a significant sector of the Canadian economy, contributing around 8.5 billion dollars annually, and employing 48,000 Canadians.[34] As of 2019, there are 4,437 businesses in Canada authorized to sell, possess, handle, or display firearms, as well as 1,400 licensed shooting ranges across the country. These businesses must register with the Canadian Firearms Program and are regularly inspected for safety and regulatory compliance.[35] Firearms retailers in Canada tend to be small businesses, many of them family-owned, with about 85–90 per cent servicing non-urban, rural, and remote communities.[36]

The participants that I interviewed provided a variety of motivations for gun ownership. The first was of course the legal justification used to apply for their firearms licence. The RCMP and Canadian Firearms Act lay out lawful purposes for which ordinary people can acquire a firearm, generally limited to hunting, sports shooting, and collecting for non-restricted firearms, and sports shooting and collecting for restricted firearms.[37] Of the gun owners that I interviewed, 66.7 per cent reported taking part in shooting sports, 51.2 per cent hunting, 61.9 per cent casual plinking, and 35.7 per cent collecting. Beyond the legal justification for gun ownership, participants listed a variety of reasons for wanting to own guns.

Scholar David Yamane has built a brand from the adage "guns are normal, and normal people use guns." It derived from his observation that while gun ownership was normative for millions of Americans, scholars studying guns focused almost solely on their criminal misuse.[38] For many Canadians, like their American neighbours, guns were a normal part of growing up. This was certainly the case among participants who grew up in rural areas. Others were drawn to gun ownership later in life, especially those in suburban and urban areas who were less likely to have grown up around guns but have woven firearms into the fabric of their social lives, families, and leisure time. When speaking to gun owners about why firearms are important to them, several themes emerged: family, friendship, community, a connection to the past, competition, relaxation, and sometimes simply "fun."

Family

For many rural Canadians, guns are an important part of family life, deeply connected to rural economies, subsistence, leisure, and heritage. Regardless of which part of the country they came from, rural gun owners asserted that firearms were woven into the fabric of their heritage, relationships, and family activities.

For Aaron, who grew up in a rural prairie town, guns were a normal part of a rural upbringing:

> Firearms have always been a part of my family's background and life, I guess you could say. I'm from southwest Saskatchewan, and our folks have been there since like 1886, and they've always had them. My dad always had firearms and so he introduced me to that at a very young age.[39]

Paul is now retired, but grew up in a small community in Ontario. He also felt that hunting and shooting were a significant part of his heritage. He proudly recounted the story of his father, who was born in the wilderness of northern Ontario, the son of a one-legged fur trapper and a schoolteacher.

> He was a trapper up there. I mean, people trapped in the wintertime. He lost his leg because he also worked in the mill in the lumber industry ... He just trapped in the wintertime with only one leg, and my dad told me he lost it very high up close to the hip. I can't even imagine, you know, how hard that life must have been.

When Paul was fifteen, his father accompanied him to get his hunting licence and began to take him on hunting trips. Only then was he allowed to inherit his grandfather's legacy: several firearms that Paul treasures to this day.[40] The hardships his father endured in the wilderness, and the firearms connected to those experiences, clearly formed an important part of Paul's personal story.

Rick is a Métis Canadian, born and raised in rural Manitoba to a family of hunters. Hunting and firearms were a way of putting food on the table, but also an integral part of his family's leisure time:

> We grew up in a farm in Manitoba, and my dad was a hunter, and my grandfather was a hunter. It's been something that's been taught through the family. It was always accessible. We had, you know, not only pastureland, but we had bush[41] very close to our house that we hunted in. Even growing up, so five, six, seven years old, I was out in the bush with my dad. I didn't carry a rifle or anything at the time, but I was spending time with him, and I was learning the trade just because it was normal. That's what we did as a family.

For Rick, firearms were another tool of farm and rural life. "It was never a hidden thing in the family, it was always an open thing. Just like a car, or a knife, or the tractor, it was a tool to do a job, as long as you respected it that way. If you didn't, you got held to account. Absolutely."

Rick has enjoyed passing on this tradition to his children. When asked what values he associated with firearms ownership, he answered:

> It's bonding time, family time. It's an opportunity to get out to share something with my kids. I think that responsible gun ownership comes with a lot of, it's redundant to say, but it comes with a lot of responsibilities. Understanding those and being able to teach those to my kids, I think that creates a bond.[42]

Rural gun cultures not only exist among Indigenous Canadians and those of Western European origin, but among more recent immigrant groups as well, as rural gun cultures have been transplanted globally. Growing up in rural Ontario, hunting and sports shooting were a part of Flora's upbringing, and her Greek ancestry:

> My grandparents and my dad, they all immigrated here from Greece. Trapshooting and upland hunting are pretty popular over there. So that's kind of how we got into it. There's a lot of the Greek-Italian kind of Mediterranean hunting community that we hang out with. All my family back in Greece, they all have bird dogs.

Now a graduate student in her early twenties, Flora grew up going to the gun club with her dad and got her licence as soon as she was able to. Her father, a successful competitive trap shooter, taught her to shoot, and instilled in her a deep respect for firearms and gun safety. Like many devoted competitors, Flora visits the gun range at least three times a week during competition season, going through at least 200 shells in a single session. She started shooting competitively in 2016, and since then has competed in national and international tournaments. When asked about memories of competitions that were especially meaningful to her, she mentioned the time she was able to compete with her father, grandfather, brother, and uncle.

> That's pretty special, I think, to just have like, you know, the whole family on the [shooting] line. My very first Canadian [championship], I was not very good. My first year was definitely a learning curve. But I shot a 94 in the Canadian handicap and ended up shooting off against my dad. My dad's, like, a twenty-seven-year veteran, like Hall of Famer, and I beat him. I mean, it was low yardage, but everyone was freaking out over that.[43]

Participants often noted the links that guns had helped them forge bonds with family members. This was especially common among the women that I interviewed, who often cited the important role firearms played in their relationship with their fathers. When asked about the personal meaning of guns to her, Debbie, who was taught how to shoot and hunt by her late father, replied: "Just going hunting with my dad ... him showing me how to do it. Just, really good memories of him. And I'll always have those. He's passed on. So, every time I go, I think of him and I smile. It's happy memories of time I got to spend with him."[44]

For Colleen, firearms were also an important part of her relationship with her father, who passed on the tradition of hunting to her in her late teens. Though she now works in the entertainment industry in a large Canadian city, guns and hunting are still a significant element of the bond with her father and family.

> My dad's oldest daughter, my half-sister, passed away in 2009. She left behind four kids; the youngest is a six-year-old that has little memories of her mom. She came to visit us and wanted to go to the gun range, because she heard stories about how her mom was a great shot with a .22. Firearms allowed her to participate in something that her mom really enjoyed.[45]

Lindsay grew up in a small town in Prince Edward Island. Hunting was a part of her earliest memories with her father. Too young then to wield a gun herself, Lindsay learned the important hard work that goes into hunting before the guns even come out of their cases. "I would help with our decoys[46] if we were in a field. I helped carry everything. I mean, it was also like pretty good exercise, and I learned good survival skills. We would build fires and stuff."

When she was old enough, Lindsay finally learned how to shoot under her father's watchful eye. "I like to say I was the firstborn son. I would go to the range of my dad on most weekends. We always went through all the rules, like all the safety regulations, everything like that. I loved being on the range and just the range culture in general."[47]

Beyond the firing range, the hunting camp is an important rural family tradition for many. Because large-game hunting seasons can be quite short, many rural hunters time their vacations around these brief periods. While not all family members participate in the hunt, families often gather at the hunt camp and share in the meat that the hunters harvest.

Every year in November, for example, Debbie's family gathers at their deer camp. While some family members come and go throughout the week, Debbie noted that at any given time, there are usually ten to fifteen family members and friends in the camp.[48]

Roderick also grew up in a rural area, though he now lives in suburban Alberta. He spoke of the family hunt camp as an important part of the tradition of firearms in his family. Especially important to him was the practice of sharing food in the camp. As any hunter can tell you, behind every successful hunt is a handful of unsuccessful ones. But any meat that was harvested by Roderick's family was shared with everyone at the family hunt camp. This created a sense of togetherness for the family and made sure everyone had something to eat during the evening's family fun time. While some family members might go off hunting during the day, the evenings were spent together as a family.[49]

Family was also important for urban and suburban Canadians who own guns, though they may not have come from the same heritage of firearm ownership as their rural counterparts. Sometimes, this family connection to firearms was transplanted, as they or their parents moved from a rural to urban area or watched their once rural town be absorbed by increasingly sprawling cities. For others, the family connection to firearms was new, unique to their nuclear family unit.

Kane is a young East Asian man who grew up in British Columbia. His connection to firearms came through his grandfather, who was a guide and outfitter across the province. Kane described to me the pride he felt when he got to travel with his grandfather, now in his mid-seventies, to one of the old mountain ranges where his grandfather used to guide fly-in hunting trips. "We flew to the old range of mountains where he used to spend years in the middle of nowhere hunting. We got to revisit these spots with him. And that's just an amazing thing to be able to do."[50]

For others, firearms allowed them to find a common activity with family members that they had fallen out with. Mireille lives and grew up in a large city in the province of Quebec, where gun ownership is not common. After her parents split and her father, who served in the Air Force, was posted to Nova Scotia, she was mostly raised by her mother, who did not own guns. She got into the hobby later in life alongside her partner. When she re-connected with her father, who moved back to Quebec after retiring, shooting was a way to find common ground after such a long time apart, and bond over their family history. Given that she was the only child in the family to have a firearm licence, her father left her an antique shotgun that had belonged to her grandfather. "So, you know, I got to connect with my dad in a way that I wouldn't have without that." Mireille feels that this side of firearm ownership is rarely represented in public portrayals of the hobby. "I think there are so many positives that aren't portrayed (in the media). You can have that whole side of connecting with people, going out together, shooting together, and developing relationships that people never think about because, 'oh my god, scary guns.'"[51]

The shooters I spoke to often had deep emotional connections to memories attached to specific firearms. Bruce, a competitive amateur sports shooter and hunter, learned how to use guns from his uncle. When talking about memories attached to certain firearms, Bruce mentioned a rifle that was particularly meaningful to him due to its connection to those memories.

> I was talking about the rifle that ... [*participant pauses and begins to cry*]. I'm sorry if I get all teary-eyed on this one, but the original rifle that my uncle had taken me hunting with. He passed a couple of years ago, and I managed to recoup that (the rifle) from my aunt [*pause*] ... Sorry ... I mean, this rifle represents probably ten years of memories of me hunting with my uncle. It's not something you go to Cabela's[52] and replace, you know?[53]

Overcome with emotion, Bruce broke down crying when talking about the rifle and the connection that he had shared between himself and his uncle. The intimacy of this moment drove home to me the deep meanings that these objects take on to their owners. Beyond simple constructions of wood, polymer, and steel, they are imbued with memories, affect, and deep meanings. For Bruce, the .22 rifle that his uncle taught him to shoot with was a meaningful object, not just another gun that you can buy at a sporting-goods store.

New Canadians or Canadians descended from more recent immigrant groups, and those from countries with no tradition of civilian gun ownership, face significant barriers to firearm ownership in Canada. Despite this, some families have built new traditions around gun ownership.

Zhi is a father and professional worker in urban Ontario. While he noted that he did not have the same ancestral connection to gun ownership as many rural gun owners, and his parents were anti-gun, going to the range has become an important ritual for his new family unit. With the nearest range two hours away, Zhi enjoys the drive, and time spent at the range, as it allows him to bond with his son: "It's the father-son time. It's really nice. When you get to see the sense of accomplishment. You see how happy it makes him."[54]

Similarly, Mani, a South Asian Canadian engineer and father, has raised two daughters in suburban Ontario. He took pride in sharing that his wife and two daughters are all licensed to own guns and that his daughters were getting started in the sport of target shooting. He shared memories of family range days when the girls were younger. With his oldest daughter off at university, and the youngest soon to follow, Mani finds it difficult to find ways to spend time with his kids, especially during the busy school year. But the family still reserves time during the summer to go out to the range together.

Mani was devastated when one of the guns he had purchased for his daughter to use was banned by the 2020 Order in Council, especially since the gun was a low-powered .22LR. Mani believes that model was targeted because of its tactical features, the very features that made it easier for his daughters to customize it to their frame. Unlike a traditional wooden-stock rifle, which is often standardized based on the average firearm consumer, who tends to be male, a "tactical"-looking rifle can be quickly adapted to the consumer's personal ergonomics. These features include things like an adjustable gun stock, which allows the user to shorten or lengthen various parts of the rifle, in the same way that an office worker might adjust the height of their chair to fit their own body.[55]

As a busy working professional and single mother of two children, Nicole was always trying to find ways to keep her boys active and busy. The boys became involved in Cadets, where they learned to shoot in biathlon competitions. When they were old enough, Nicole took them to do their PAL course so that they could "learn the safety and responsibility." Once they were properly licensed and the family could go out shooting, the practice became "family bonding time."

Nicole and her sons now enjoy not only shooting together but collecting historical firearms. Nicole's grandfather served in the Second World War, and collecting guns from the period has been a way for Nicole to connect with this heritage while also teaching her sons about history.

Nicole noted that she was proud of the sense of responsibility and environmental stewardship that she has instilled in her children through participation in shooting sports. Given the high price and long waiting list for range memberships in Alberta, she and her boys mostly shoot on Crown land. She always makes sure to bring a garbage bag with her when she goes to pick up trash others have left behind, and has instilled in her sons the importance of leaving the place cleaner than when you found it. She is proud of how responsible her sons have become:

I adopted my niece and nephew when they were quite young. So, I raised four kids. My nephew just got his PAL. So, for his birthday, he wanted to go out in the wilderness where we go. We had like a, I call it a tailgate party, but we have a barbecue, and if we can, and there's no fire ban, we'll have a fire.

My two sons were coaching their nephew on (firearm) safety. And I just stood back with a tremendous amount of pride. It actually made me quite emotional, because it was just a really fun day. But it was so controlled and professional, and not at all what people would think young people are out doing with guns.[56]

Friendship and Community

While participants reported the strong feeling of family bonding that comes with participating in gun culture, it is also central to many friendships and communities across Canada. The gun owners I spoke to often cited friendship and community as important parts of their participation in shooting sports, hunting, and collecting.

Pierre worried that as a Métis Canadian, he might not feel at home after moving to a predominantly white community. But since getting more involved, he has found acceptance and friendship. When asked what gun ownership means to him, he responded: "I think just being able to go down [to] the range with friends and have an afternoon of relaxing and plinking or running drills. It can be a really wonderful sense of community. Because once you're in the community, I find that you're *in* the community."[57]

Many urban gun owners, like Enzo, were introduced into the world of guns later in life through long-time friends. Enzo had always enjoyed martial arts and works as a Shaolin Kung Fu instructor in Ontario. He was never interested in becoming a gun owner, until a friend took him to the range. "A very good friend of mine ... her name is Jess. She got married to a very nice guy, Dan, and we became good friends. I mean, you know, between Jess and I, it's like a father-daughter kind of thing. I walked her down the aisle when she got married." For years, Enzo dodged Dan's invitations to go out and try shooting with him, but one day at the gym, when Dan insisted again, Enzo finally gave in and agreed. Enzo found the experience humbling, but also highly addictive. He enjoyed shooting, but also found the community and sense of camaraderie at the gun range an important part of why he became so involved in the hobby. Going down the rabbit hole has also deepened his relationship with Dan. Despite the fact that Dan was twenty years younger than Enzo, he became his shooting mentor. The two would go to the range, clean their guns together, and Enzo even learned to reload his own ammunition, a labour-intensive process that allows more experienced shootings to create customizable ammunition for a lower cost. The experience created a shared bond between the two. "We do it together as more than friends; like brothers." Enzo noted that though he enjoyed the hobby, it was the community that kept him coming back.[58]

Allison says her experiences within the gun community have been positive, especially compared to sports that she has competed in in the past.

I think that one of the one of the biggest themes that I see reoccur in the gun community is that there's a lot of togetherness ... I used to be a sprinter. So, it's a solo sport and I found I was way more lonely [sic].[59]

Participants noted that some of this community feeling came from the shared experience of stigmatization that many gun owners mentioned feeling about their sport or hobby. Annie summed it up like this: "We're an isolated community because we're so demonized publicly, especially in our media right now, and [by] our government. We basically have only each other right now to cling to, and I think that's bringing the community together even stronger."[60] Jack was more sanguine about it: "The nice thing about gun owners is you always have a common thing to start talking about, which is usually complaining about gun laws."[61]

The shared experience of belonging to a heavily regulated community can also create a bond among shooters. In some ways, going through the licensing process, and the heavy scrutiny that it involves, creates a shared sense of confidence in one another. Emily noted this when we spoke the sense of trust she feels towards other gun owners:

I think about the fact that people who are licensed to own firearms are law-abiding ... These people have gone through a process that I know is rigorous, and they've given up their freedom of information to be vetted every day, to have every part of their life exposed to a government agency.[62]

This feeling was echoed by Matthew, who noted the instant connection he feels with other gun owners, who he recognizes as accountable by virtue of having gone through the process. If you are a licensed gun owner, Matthew felt confident that "the government scrutinized your history; and you can feel safe with those people at the range. It's non-gun owners that you have to worry about, right?"[63]

Handshake Between Generations: Connections to History and the Past

For many owners, firearms represent a tangible link between the "past, present and future."[64] This was expressed most eloquently by Matt DeMille of OFAH:

I think that it's hard for society to understand the value of firearms ... When we talk about heirlooms, and firearms as something that we pass down from generation to generation, you're not just passing down the firearm itself ... When the firearm is passed down, it's passed down with stories of past hunts, and past harvests, and experiences with family and friends. And then you also get to use it, and hopefully build those same memories with the person that you're going to pass it down to. There's this, not just handing off of the firearm itself, it's like this handshake between generations.[65]

Since Rosensweig and Thelen's[66] famous study of the uses of the past, historians have established that ordinary people most often engage with the past as it relates to their family.[67] Firearms are no different. Sometimes, these objects are the key to connecting gun owners to a family memory, or family history. For Matt, firearms are a connection to his family lineage, but especially to his father, who had taught him to hunt using firearms passed down from his grandfather and great-grandfather. Matt spoke about the immense sense of pride he took in not just putting food on the table for his family but being able to do so "in the same way that generations before you did."

Matt's father passed away while he was studying at university. At that time, he had become disconnected from hunting by the rigours of the academic calendar.

When my father passed away, and my brother and I received firearms from him, it was something that shifted me right back into needing to do it more ... For me, hunting was something that I did with my dad, and therefore, I felt connected [to him]. But the firearm was an actual thing that he had touched.[68]

This history can stretch further back than the remembered past. Donal is a retired man living in the Yukon. A lifelong NDP voter, he writes often to his MP and to the NDP leader, frustrated with the party's increasingly anti-gun stance. For Donal, shooting is a hobby that he can continue to do as he ages, even as he watches more and more of his friends moving into long-term care or passing on. It is a way of connecting with his son, but also with his family history. Through his research Donal had discovered that his great-grandfather was a member of the Toronto naval brigade. When his great-grandfather died, he received a military funeral and was buried with his cap and his sidearm. Donal was interested in knowing which handgun his great-grandfather would have carried and travelled to a museum where he saw a representation of a militiaman from the same period, carrying an 1851 Colt Navy black-powder revolver. "And so, I thought, gee, I better have one of those. But now I have two. And it's kind of a connection to my great-grandfather."[69]

Donal noted that maintaining black-powder firearms is a lot of work, as they require frequent cleaning to prevent the highly corrosive potassium nitrate from damaging the firearm, and "it takes bloody forever to load." Many black-powder firearms predate the invention of the modern cartridge, and the powder, patch, and ball must be loaded one at a time. But the guns provide him with a tangible link to the past that makes these inconveniences worth it.

For others, firearms are connected to local and national histories, or certain historical periods of interest. Stefan lives on Canada's west coast. While talking about his interest in historical firearms, he took particular pride in a Browning handgun that he had recently acquired. The handgun had belonged to a Canadian soldier, Lloyd Thorpe of the Grey and Simcoe Forresters, who had carried the gun while serving in Europe during the Second World War. The firearm itself had even been manufactured in the suburbs of Toronto, something unheard of today.

Eager to return to civilian life after the war, Mr. Thorpe had returned to his job as a school principal and stuck the pistol in a drawer at home where it had gathered dust for some time before being passed on to a friend of his, who eventually connected with Stefan. For Stefan, owning the handgun connected his story to Mr. Thorpe's "It's weird because it's a weapon, but I feel very connected with humanity through that aspect of the hobby.[70]

Stefan's brother Wes, on the other hand, was more interested in the history of industry and technological developments than in any national history. After being introduced to guns late in life, he has since amassed a large collection.

> And of course, then it snowballed because you start getting into the history and the lore, you understand the technology better and what's going on. You gain capacity and confidence in disassembling and maintaining and reassembling these, in my case, very often quite old weapons. And I caught the bug, not the COVID bug, but that one [the collector bug].[71]

Gun enthusiasts drawn to the past can spend hours researching a given firearm. The gun, as a tangible link to the past, becomes a focal point around which gun owners learn about a myriad of different histories.

> Learning that background just introduces you to such a fascinating range of characters and crises and the early history of state-building, and state-society relations in early modern Europe ... And so it encourages me to delve deeper and is intellectually stimulating.[72]

For a particular subset of the gun culture, this connection to the past is taken even further, through participating in historical re-enactment, sometimes called "living history." Re-enactors generally belong to clubs, societies, and groups that re-enact particular historical eras. The Second World War is popular, as is the American Civil War for re-enactors in the United States. Re-enactment groups often have links to local history. For example, many re-enactment groups in southern Ontario focus on the War of 1812, given the importance of the region in that conflict. Much as American Civil War re-enactments are a cause of political controversy in America, Canadian re-enactors can sometimes become swept up in controversy if they touch on particularly charged periods of history. For example, in 2009 when the federal National Battlefields Commission decided to organize a re-enactment of Battle of the Plains of Abraham for the 250th anniversary, Quebecois nationalists took to the streets to protest, forcing them to backtrack.[73]

The intersection between historical re-enactment and firearm culture means that participants often move between the two hobbies. For Jack, collecting historical firearms is a big part of his interest in living history. He grew up watching his father perform in re-enactments, and as soon as he was old enough, he jumped into it. His eighteenth birthday present was the fee to cover his gun-licensing course, and working part-time jobs, he was able to slowly amass a historical collection. Now forty years old, Jack has an impressive collection of historical firearms, costumes, and memorabilia, alongside a library of historical texts, a testament to the intensive research that re-enactors put into their activity.

Jack participates in both public and private re-enactments:

> There's two types ... One is a dog-and-pony show. That's usually public commemoration events where you're either there in uniform as eye-candy, or you have a table set up with all kinds of kit for people to look at and talk to and ask questions. Then you have tactical events, which are generally not open to the public.[74]

These tactical events involve recreations of historical battles. Jack noted that one of his re-enactment groups even owns its own mock battlefield, complete with trenches and recreated buildings, and gathers twice a year to re-enact battles from the Second World War, including using historical tanks and aircraft. Jack said that re-enactors are so devoted to creating realistic costuming and props that they are sometimes used as extras in movies and documentaries. Jack himself had participated as an extra on a BBC documentary about the Second World War. Like many people involved in serious leisure pursuits, Jack always sought out ways to connect his passion to his work. Though he now lives in British Columbia, he grew up in the National Capitol Region and was able to work in several military museums during his teenage years, including the Canadian War Museum.

While Jack's interest in re-enactment led to a passion for firearms, Kane's trajectory into the gun culture moved in the opposite direction. Kane, a Chinese Canadian resident of British Columbia in his early twenties, first fell in love with black-powder shooting after being introduced to it by his uncle. "You go out and once you shoot it, you just, there's something about the smell, and the feel and the atmosphere, you just fall in love with it." Kane had been interested in history since high school, and the experience of shooting black-powder firearms allowed him to combine his love of guns with his love of history. Though relatively young, Kane is already on the board of his local gun range and involved in a historical re-enactment and traditional black-powder shooting group. He described to me a typical "rendezvous," as these groups call their events, a nod to the historical fur trade. Participants often stay several days, and camp out in canvas camps using period-correct equipment. They dress in buckskins and furs that participants take great pride in making themselves. The rendezvous usually feature powder trails, with targets set up in various places in the woods, which Kane finds more interesting than static target shooting at a range.

For many people, it might be hard to imagine someone in their early twenties so deeply involved in a historical re-enactment group. But for Kane, his involvement in the hobby is driven by passion. "I could go off on hours-long rants about things related to black powder. If you've never done it, I highly recommend you try it. It's addictive." Kane also discussed the joy he takes in introducing new shooters to the hobby, especially "the look on their face after the gun goes off, and that wisp of smoke lingers in front of them. It's just, it's a spark."

When thinking of the battle lines of the contemporary gun debate, one does not generally think of muskets or fur trade re-enactors as particularly controversial. But the ramifications of the May 2020 gun ban, or the handgun freeze, extend even to this small community of history lovers. When discussing the meetups of his re-enactment group, Kane noted that his group used to fire historical reproductions of cannons loaded with fruits like oranges and lemons, in order to balance historical accuracy and safety. This changed with the May 2020 Order-In-Council, which prohibited any firearm with "a bore of 20 mm or greater."[75] Given the hasty adoption of the policy, significant ambiguity surrounded these requirements that the government has only begun to clarify. For example, for a brief time gun owners feared that all 12ga and

20ga shotguns, the most commonly owned firearms for hunters, had been banned, until the issue was clarified in a statement by the Minister of Public Safety on Twitter.[76] Given the legal ambiguity surrounding historical firearms in Canada, there was considerable confusion as to whether the group could continue these presentations. They have opted to err on the side of caution and discontinue the practice. Though it took place after my interview with Kane, the handgun freeze brought in by the government in 2022 impacted these historical reenactors, as there is no exemption for flintlock, muzzle-loading pistols in the legislation.

While gun owners with an interest in historical firearms use them for hunting, sports shooting, and re-enactment, there is also a subculture of collectors who may even never shoot the firearms that they spend vast sums of money amassing. Firearm collectors vary on a spectrum from casual collectors to professionals. Claude, a retired government worker living in Quebec, has collected firearms since 1987. He took a strange pride in telling me that he had never fired a gun in his life, though he owned many thousands of dollars' worth of historical handguns. Claude's collection is built around three main elements: Civil War–era revolvers, Mauser Broomhandle pistols, and German and Japanese Second World War pistols.

For many collectors, their interest in guns is fully focused on the window they provide into the past. Claude described his guns as "witnesses of history." Eager to show me his collection, as well as his substantial library of books, Claude took me through some of the highlights during our one-hour virtual interview. Like many baby boomer gun enthusiasts, Claude's interest in firearms began as a young boy playing Cowboys and Indians with plastic guns, as well as seeing firearms in movies. After seeing *Lawrence of Arabia* at the local cinema, he was so enamoured by the Mauser pistol in the film that he ordered a book about the gun's history. In 1987, he finally purchased his first collectible handgun, a German Luger, and the collection grew from there. Claude notes that with collector-grade firearms starting at around $2,000, it is not a cheap hobby, but that it is very important to him. He describes it as "like holding history in my hand," and says the hobby makes him "feel a connection to history." The hobby has allowed him to make lasting friendships with collectors around the world through the various associations he is a member of. For Claude, the confiscation of firearms is not just about personal loss for the owners, but the loss of historical objects that he described as "cultural and historical vandalism."[77]

This sentiment was echoed by Bruce, whose most treasured possession is the first firearm he ever bought: a Walther PPK, likely recovered by a Canadian soldier from the battlefields of the Second World War. As a kid, he remembered shooting the gun on his parents' property, something forbidden since the 1995 Firearms Act confined the shooting of restricted firearms to licensed ranges. Bruce fears that with handgun bans looming, he may soon be forced to surrender this piece of history[78]: "They're heirlooms ... The day I'm going to have to turn in that Walther PPK (*pauses*). That's, you know, a piece of history that's never coming back."[79]

Firearms are tangible objects that allow users to connect with the past in the way that few other goods do, owing in large part to their durability. If properly taken care of and maintained, firearms can be used or stored for generations. They are often passed down as heirlooms by families or curated in personal collections. This allows users an experience that few other leisure pursuits offer. This connection, or sense of meaning that firearms give people, was cited by several participants.

> On the personal level it's a huge part of my life, huge part of cultural milieu, it connects me to other people, most immediately my neighbours and members of my family, but more broadly connects me across the country, and then backwards through history.[80]

Competition, Sport, and Empowerment

Projectile weaponry has been a part of human society going back at least 50,000 years and may have been a key factor into the spread of *Homo sapiens* from Africa around the globe.[81] There is something innately human about projectile weaponry that draws people towards not only the shooting sports, but sports like archery, darts, or javelin.[82] Like other sports, the shooting sports provide recreational benefits to participants. Caleb grew up in Vancouver, BC, in the 1960s, born to urban-Canadian parents who would never have imagined their son owning a gun. From a young age, however, Caleb had a passion for target sports. "The journey started with a simple thing: throwing a rock at a tin can ... I liken it to anything, a dart player throws a dart and if they get a bull's eye, it's pretty satisfying."[83]

Caleb would not be allowed to own real firearms until he moved out and found his own place, but the desire never left him. In 1973, he bought his first gun and has been an active participant in shooting sports ever since then. "Of all the people I've taken to the range, I can't recall a time when anyone said, 'Well, this is horrible.' They might not take the sport up, but they get it that it's fun to be able to, again, hit a tin can or knock something over."[84] Though he has participated in most of the shooting sports over the years, Caleb now mostly focuses on handgun competitions, as he finds them the most challenging. An active member of IPSC, he has been participating in practical shooting competitions for over forty years. These competitions are designed to mimic law-enforcement training and place competitors in dynamic shooting scenarios where they need to move around and shoot from behind cover or in changing environments. Shooters are supervised by a range safety officer, and accidents are very rare. They have grown exponentially in popularity on both sides of the border since the 1970s.

Participants noted that IPSC matches combined the cerebral challenge of target shooting with the athleticism of other sports: "I was explaining it to a friend saying, you know, it's like playing chess while running a 100-meter sprint."[85]

There is a long history in Canada of links between the civilian shooting sports and the military.[86] Given the value of firearm training to professions like armed security, law enforcement, and the military, shooting competitions often provide a link between these state institutions and individual target shooters. Hugh is an Indigenous Canadian resident of Ontario. He started shooting with his uncle, who would take him on duck and small game hunts. He got involved in competition shooting during his time serving in the Canadian Armed Forces and would shoot on his regiment's rifle team. Moving into civilian life, he has continued to compete in shooting sports. Before the 2020 OIC, Hugh participated in shooting competitions that pitted law enforcement, first responders, and military marksmen against civilian competitors. Hugh noted that these competitions were: "one of the only places that you'll actually see where policemen, military, and civilians are all shooting and learning from each other as we go." While the sports shooters were happy to learn the skills of experienced professionals, he noted that many soldiers and police officers also gained skills from the exchange that they would then bring back to their home units or detachments.[87]

For example, one of the competitions involved long-range shooting, an increasingly popular sport in the civilian world. Given the number of factors that can influence a bullet's trajectory when firing at long distances, from wind speed to humidity to the curvature of the earth, long-range shooting combines marksmanship and complex ballistic calculations. These competitions often feature shooters in pairs, with one person serving as a spotter and the other shooting. The combination of physical fitness, comradery, and mental acuity make these competitions highly dynamic. Further, the skills developed in this sport can be used by both hunters and marksmen in military or police units. Hugh said he knew Canadian snipers that had served in the former Yugoslavia and in

Afghanistan who had made use of the skills that they learned in these competitions.[88] The May 2020 OIC has meant that many of the events Hugh takes part in will have to be cancelled or rewritten, and Hugh fears the competition may never be the same.

Though many of the competitors I spoke to were men, women in Canada also enjoy the thrill of competing in the shooting sports. This is not without historical precedent. As one participant noted: "There is, going all the way back to Annie Oakley and beyond, a pretty good tradition of women who stood up the guys at their own game, you know. The Soviets in World War Two[89] is quite an impressive example of that."[90]

In our interview, Annie described the feeling of empowerment she got from besting large, muscular men at shooting competitions.

> It's the one sport that I could sit there next to a, you know, six-foot-three Marine and compete efficiently on the same level. It is a great equalizer, and it's very empowering for a woman to be able to do that.[91]

Annie had been a victim of domestic violence in her previous marriage. Her first husband had tried to run her over with his car. Annie was frustrated that her identity as a woman, and victim of abuse, was so often mobilized by advocates to justify the confiscation of her property, and the death of the sport she loved.

The theme of gender equality in the shooting sports was echoed by the CCFR's Tracey Wilson, an athlete before she became an advocate, who noted that being able to play a sport in the same league as men was a major draw for her.

> Anybody can play. I can't go join my local ice-hockey league or, you know, soccer league, and be on a competitive playing field with the men. Of course not; I'm going to get trampled, right? But I can join IPSC. And not only can I compete alongside men, I'm going to beat them. It's empowering.[92]

Emily, herself a former competitive trap shooter, now devotes a significant amount of energy trying to get women more involved in the shooting sports.

> If we look at women and girls, and, you know, there's all this concern about, you know, mental health, physical health and so on. And about 70 or 80 per cent of women and girls stop participating in any sport over the age of sixteen.[93] So when you think about a sport like sports shooting

discipline, this is something that has mental, physical, and social benefits. And it's something that you can do your whole life. I used to play basketball, but, you know, my competitive basketball days are over; but I can still shoot.[94]

Relaxation

Those outside of the gun culture might be surprised that a major appeal of shooting is the relaxation it brings. After all, guns are loud, and gun ownership is often portrayed in popular media as being associated with hypermasculinity, or even compensation for sexual dysfunction.[95] However, a large proportion of the participants I interviewed, without prompting, cited relaxation as a part of why they enjoyed hunting and sports shooting. Upon closer examination, however, this is not at all surprising. In an age of distraction, shooting provides moments of total focus. The shooter simply cannot be distracted, as the activity demands their whole attention. Further, being a successful target shooter or hunter involves activities that we associate with relaxation. Shooters must control their breathing and heart rate, as even a rogue heartbeat can cause their aim to shift. Shooters are trained to fire during their natural respiratory pause. This is what makes sports like biathlon, which combine intense aerobic activity with target shooting, so challenging.

Many of the gun owners I spoke to worked in high-stress professional jobs. Talia, for example, is a criminal lawyer in a big city. Growing up in an urban Jewish family, guns were never part of her upbringing. She went shooting for the first time on a date, but ended up falling in love with the sport, rather than the man. She now owns multiple handguns and long guns, and enjoys the opportunity to unwind from her highly cerebral career.[96]

Dirk, an immigrant to Canada from the Netherlands, and a loud, proud, liberal gun owner, owns a small bakery and works sixty to eight hours a week. "I measure my free time in hours per month, not in days." For Dirk, going to the range is a way of escaping that stress. "Going to the range, for me, is also a very personal, almost meditative moment ... You cannot think about anything else and shoot. It just doesn't work. So it's a really good way to get everything out of my head."[97]

This was echoed by Debbie, who similarly noted that the deep concentration required to shoot helped to drive away the stress of modern living. "I do find it very therapeutic. If I've had a bad day, sometimes it's just like, I want to go and I want to concentrate."[98]

Dawson was one of the youngest participants I spoke to. A so-called digital native, he would have never known a time without tablets, smartphones, and high-speed internet, where distractions are more available than ever. Dawson likened shooting to a form of meditation. "When I go shooting, I would sit down, I'd be working through whatever I'll be doing, and it was my downtime. So, it really would help me focus and just give me that couple of hours of that pure, singular focus. It helps you relax, and just have a good time."[99]

Still for others, this sense of relaxation was combined with the feeling of connecting with one's roots: "There's a sense of peace that you don't normally find in your day-to-day life in an urban centre. It's one of those few times where you can have some clarity. As weird as it may sound, it's very therapeutic."[100]

Fun, Joy, and Play

Those outside of the gun culture find it difficult to understand this, but guns evoke many positive emotions in those who own and use them. Though they were quick to emphasize their seriousness, the gun owners I spoke to also noted that guns are tools of recreation, used to pursue fun, joy, and play. Ava, a cowboy action shooter in her sixties, made this explicit in our interview:

> So, I'm going to use that word all the way through: *playing* with guns. And I know some people get very, you know, very ... [*participant trails off, looking serious*] but it is about play. It is. I mean to me, it's no different than somebody going out and (practising archery); I mean bows and arrows were at one point considered weapons. I don't think of it as a weapon, I think of it as a tool that I have to respect.
>
> My daughter is an arborist, and you should see her wielding a chainsaw around, but she is safe because she knows (how to use it). I wouldn't go near a chainsaw because I don't understand the tool, whereas I have no fear of guns whatsoever, because I know how they work.[101]

For Ava, her guns were just another tool, albeit a potentially deadly one, that she used to participate in an activity that she found fun.

While the average Canadian might be able to understand how dressing up like a cowboy and competing in western-style shootout competitions could be fun, the tactical shooting community is aware of the negative image the public has of their sport. Kevin, a Chinese Canadian former schoolteacher who retrained as a businessman, lives in a big city in Ontario, surrounded by friends and family members who do not consider gun ownership as normative social behaviour. Kevin's demeanour and behaviour read as urban, and he enjoyed showing off his knowledge of Jewish culture and Yiddish slang to me when we spoke, after I self-identified as Jewish. Yet, Kevin was also an avid participant in IPSC and 3-gun competitions, and was the owner of several handguns and an AR-15. He now travels extensively in the United States, where he can continue to train with firearms that are now prohibited in Canada. When we spoke, Kevin joked about the negative image of his sport: "Obviously I'm not doing it because I want to start a militia or you know, I plan a rise against the government. It's just more for fun and fantasy, I guess." Still, Kevin made sure to emphasize that he knew the difference between fantasy and reality. He joked openly about the Americans that he trained with, who he felt took that element too seriously, noting that they often fantasized quite vividly about the apocalypse and which weapon they would want to use. To him, this illustrated one of the big cultural differences between American and Canadian gun owners.[102]

Though he enjoyed the escape, fantasy, and the challenge of firearm training in the United States, Kevin mentioned his discomfort with American gun culture several times, and especially concealed carry. For Kevin, guns were a tool of recreation, not violence, and he expressed discomfort with the idea that someone would want to carry one with them while going about their daily business. He noted that many of the people he met while doing courses in the United States carried concealed handguns as part of their everyday lives. He told the story of feeling shocked when meeting an insurance agent who was told to take a concealed-carry course as part of his job training, as all of the insurance agents in his company went armed. "As much as I love gun stuff, I don't know if I feel comfortable living in that kind of society."[103]

Tammy was introduced to shooting in her sixties by her friend Wes, who suggested I speak with her. Though a new entrant to the hobby, Tammy was soon hooked and dove headfirst down the rabbit hole. She and Wes now produce a YouTube channel with videos of them shooting many of the historical firearms in their collections. The two adopted Russian pseudonyms, given their interest in historic Soviet firearms like the Mosin-Nagant bolt-action rifle, which was fielded en masse by Soviet troops in the Second World War, and is widely available on the surplus firearms market. For Tammy, her shooting channel was a way to share her passion for the hobby with a broader community.[104] Like Kevin, Tammy noted that for her, firearms were about recreation and enjoyment, not defence of self, and that she was happy to live in a country where firearms needed to be stored safely.[105]

Similarly, when gun owners I spoke to talked about the fear of losing their firearms to legislative changes, they did not speak of insurrection or a need to protect life and limb, but rather their fear of no longer being able to take part in activities that gave them profound fulfilment: "It would really make my life a lot less joyful than it is."[106]

Who Are Canadian Gun Owners?

Little data is made public on the demographic makeup of gun owners in Canada. Though the government collects this data through the RCMP Canadian Firearms Program, they do not release it to the public. As a result, I will use the demographic information collected from my Survey of Canadian Gun Owners, which was conducted during the summer of 2020. Given that the survey was distributed using a non-probability sample, the results should be taken with a grain of salt. In the absence of better data, however, they do provide a snapshot into the demographic makeup and behaviour of Canadian gun owners.

Despite having a fully translated survey available to participants, French-Canadians were underrepresented in my sample. While 21 per cent of Canadians speak French most often at home,[107] only 9 per cent of my survey respondents reported the same. Further, though 12 per cent of PAL[108] holders in Canada are women,[109] women were underrepresented in my sample, making up only 4 per cent of survey respondents. Canadians of Afro-Caribbean origin, who represent about 5 per cent of Canadians,[110] were also underrepresented, making up less than 1 per cent of survey respondents. This was true as well of Canadians of East Asian and South Asian origins. Indigenous Canadians, who make up 6 per cent of Canada's population, were relatively well represented, composing 4.7 per cent of respondents. This demographic distortion is likely explained by the rural nature of Canada's gun culture, as well as gender-related barriers that limit women's participation, despite recent efforts by the gun industry and gun rights movement to attract more women.[111]

The participants in my survey were also wealthier than the Canadian average. Comparing my sample to the GSS data from 2013, participants had a mean household income before taxes of $80,000–100,000, compared to a mean of $60,000–80,000 from the GSS data. This could be a result of the significant costs of gun ownership in Canada, including paying Firearms Safety Course fees, complying with safe-storage laws, purchasing a membership to a gun range, and buying ammunition.

I noted similar trends among my eighty-four interviewees. The overwhelming majority (93 per cent) were English-speaking, despite my recruitment material being made available in both official languages. They were geographically concentrated in Ontario (38.1 per cent), British

Columbia (27.4 per cent), and Alberta (15.5 per cent). Every province was represented in my sample, though only one territory. The majority identified as men (81% per cent), but given that only 12 per cent of gun owners in Canada are women,[112] women were overrepresented in my sample (19 per cent). This is likely due to my explicit efforts to recruit women and people of colour, and use of snowball sampling, to ensure that the perspectives of women and gun owners of colour would not be excluded from my interviews. Like Yamane et al.,[113] I felt it was important to look beyond statistical majorities and include the stories of those at the margins who are often written out of accounts of gun ownership in Canada and the United States.

On the whole, my interview participants were very well-educated, with 27.8 per cent holding a college degree or trade certification, 36.7 per cent a BA, and 13.9 per cent a master's degree. Like the survey participants, interview participants were older, with a median age of fifty-three, and wealthier, with a median income of $100,000. The majority were white (77.4 per cent); however, East Asian Canadians (6 per cent) and Indigenous Canadians (8.3 per cent) were well-represented in the sample. While my survey did not ask where participants lived, my interview questionnaires included a question about urban-rural location. Given that "ruralness" often has more to do with social identity than physical location, I allowed my participants to self-identify as living in rural, urban, or suburban Canada. A slim plurality of my participants identified as rural Canadians (34.9 per cent), with an equal number (32.5 per cent) identifying as suburban and urban.

Given what we know about the demographic makeup of both gun owners and Canadians who participate frequently in advocacy, this demographic makeup was not surprising. Research on participation in advocacy in Canada has demonstrated that well-educated, affluent, white men are more likely to engage in advocacy.[114]

Further, those sceptical of the gun culture often use the perception that gun owners in Canada are predominantly white men to dismiss the concerns of the community. For example, in the sole academic text published on the history of gun control in Canada, author R. Blake Brown titles his chapter on the early development of firearms advocacy "Angry White Men."[115] In contemporary Canadian discourse, where diversity and inclusion are rightly lauded as important values in a multicultural society, referring to something or someone as "white" implies that the activity or group is connected to privilege, or white supremacy. Old white men are seen as avatars of the old Canada, and all its faults. It is worth exploring, however, why Canadian gun culture has not undergone the same demographic shifts as American gun culture, which has seen an influx of diverse gun owners in recent years, especially during the gun-buying spree that followed the COVID-19 pandemic.[116]

The reality is that firearm regulation in Canada poses a significant barrier to the diversification of the Canadian gun community. First, Canadian firearm legislation establishes significant financial barriers to gun ownership. The most basic of these are the course fees, which cost $190 for a non-restricted licence, and $340 for a restricted licence, which allowed one to purchase handguns before Bill C-21.[117] The courses last an entire weekend, from Friday evening to Sunday afternoon. This does not include the licensing fees that one must pay after completing the course, which range from $42 to $80 depending on the licence.[118] This may not seem like a lot of money or hassle for a middle-class office worker, but a barrier to entry like this for a hobby could represent a significant stumbling block for young and low-income people, especially shift workers in the food service or hospitality industry, who may make most of their income on weekends.

For those seeking a restricted firearms licence in many provinces, the additional requirement of maintaining a club membership[119] further increases the financial barrier to gun ownership. Club membership fees range from $35 to $475 per year depending on where you live, with an average cost of $221[120] a year. Generally, clubs in urban areas tend to be more expensive, especially in Canada's largest cities like Toronto and Vancouver. This makes it difficult for young people, new immigrants, and lower-income folks to afford the privilege of handgun ownership. Safe-storage laws impose further financial costs, and firearms tend to be much more expensive in Canada, as the market is smaller and cannot generate the same economies of scale.[121]

Transportation laws in Canada mean that to be a gun owner, one must generally be an automobile owner. There is no provision in the Canadian Firearm Safety Course or Restricted Firearm Safety Course for transporting firearms on public transit, and some cities, like Toronto,[122] prohibit it. Further, gun ranges tend to be in suburban and rural areas. While some urban areas may have access to an indoor handgun range, these are often in out-of-the-way parts of town like industrial neighbourhoods, where rent is cheap and residents are less likely to oppose it. Most urban gun owners I spoke to mentioned travelling substantial distances to visit the range, something that is only possible with a car. These financial barriers mean that young people, those from urban areas without cars, and economically or racially marginalized folks may find it difficult to become licensed gun owners in Canada.

Getting a gun licence in Canada also requires social capital that many new immigrants may lack. Social capital at the individual level refers to certain resources that an individual can access by virtue of their social standing.[123] It includes things like trust or social networks. New immigrants may not have the social network required to fulfil the licensing requirements, or may be wary about interaction with the police. The Canadian Firearm Safety Program is administered by the RCMP. Racialized and marginalized communities, who may not have the same trust in police as white Canadians, could be uncomfortable with the invasiveness of the application process. Applicants for a firearm licence must provide two character references who have known them for at least three years, and cannot be a conjugal partner.[124] This could pose a barrier for new immigrants with limited ties to the broader community.

Further, in some communities, where the supply of gun ranges does not meet demand, membership can be restricted by personal connection. Rick, a Métis shooter, found this out the hard way. Rick had grown up hunting and shooting, including sustenance hunting since the age of twelve, but when I spoke to him he had recently become more involved in sports shooting. When he moved to Alberta, however, he found it challenging to find a gun range to shoot at.

> There aren't many (ranges) out there and they're getting less and less [common] it seems like every year, which means that waitlists are getting more and more [sic]. So, one of the things that I had to do when I moved here to Alberta, was the ranges around here require sponsorship. So I had to go and attend, you know, open-forum events, I had to meet people, I had to go through a couple events to show that I'm not a ... for lack of a better term like ... unrespectful, redneck kind of shooter that's just going to go out there and destroy the range.[125]

Luckily Rick, a well-educated professional, was able to connect with a club member who agreed to sponsor him. Others might not be so industrious, or lucky.

Issues of race and gender are also involved in determining who becomes a gun owner in Canada and who does not. Given that the gun culture in Canada remains largely rural, we would expect the majority of gun owners to reflect the demographics of rural areas, which tend to be predominantly white – with the exception of Indigenous Canadians, who were well represented in both survey sample and interviews. New Canadians moving to cities may not be exposed to gun culture in their home country, or after arriving in Canada, as gun culture tends to be absent or invisible in urban spaces. Those living in Canada's large cities, and in immigrant communities, may not know anyone who owns a gun and may associate gun ownership solely with criminality and deviance.

Given that marginalized and racialized communities often suffer the lion's share of gun violence in Canada, this is understandable. This prospect was raised in my discussion with an employee at the Office of the Chief Firearms Officer of Alberta. When asked about the diversity of the firearms community in Alberta, the employee responded that it largely reflects the diversity of the province, "but with a lag," as it takes new immigrants time after arriving in Canada to "get settled and think about leisure activities" or to "acquire the necessary wealth and legal standing and so on." Some who have come from conflict zones may also very understandably want nothing to do with firearms. The employee spoke of efforts their office had undertaken to ensure the diversity of firearms safety instruction, which might make new immigrants or women more comfortable with the licensing process:

> We do want to also make sure, for example, that the body of instructors, the core of instructors ... reflects the diversity that we need to have to be able to reach all segments of the potential firearms owning community. So, to put it bluntly, although there's absolutely nothing wrong with a seventy-year-old white man, we don't want every firearms instructor to be a seventy-year-old white man.[126]

Another major barrier noted by the employee was the lack of access to the Firearms Safety Test in languages other than English, French, and certain Indigenous languages. While the course can be offered in other languages with the help of a bilingual instructor, the licensing test cannot be translated. In the past, it was possible to use an interpreter when taking the test, usually a family member or acquaintance; however, this practice was banned due to concerns about cheating. This poses a significant barrier to new immigrants. "I had a conversation about this with an East Asian gentleman the other day, he actually had managed to pass it in English, but he had a lot of friends who were Chinese who found it very challenging to pass a test in English."[127]

The employee also referred to the "explicitly racist implications of Canada's firearms prohibitions." Since 1976, as Canada has experienced several waves of firearms prohibitions, the government has used grandfathering to avoid controversy and mute the protest from the gun community. As a result, older gun owners, who are overwhelmingly white, may have different classes of licence that allow them to own certain prohibited firearms. This is a particular concern to historical collectors, who may be denied certain firearms, even firearms from their home country, that white settler Canadians can own. "Why not? Because they are not just as law abiding as I am? Because they pose a threat to public safety? No, because they didn't happen to live here at the time when the prohibitions came and the grandfathering was decided."[128] The government's recent decision to "freeze" handgun sales, allowing established owners to keep them but banning new gun owners from purchasing handguns, is yet another example of this trend.

Why are women underrepresented in Canadian gun culture? There is a sizable scholarship on gender, masculinity, and firearms ownership in the United States that can be applied in some ways to Canada, given the cultural similarities between the two countries.[129] In Canadian society, young boys tend to be socialized in ways that make guns more desirable, from childhood games like cops and robbers to video games and toys. This plays a smaller role in young girls' socialization. Representations of gun ownership in the media, until recently, largely reflected this gender binary, explaining the lack of interest of many women to go to the trouble of acquiring a firearm.

Care-labour requirements may also make participation in hunting and the shooting sports more difficult for many women. In addition to financial cost, participation in the activities of gun culture often involves significant time commitments. A trip to the range is often a half- or full- day affair. Trips to a hunting camp can last days or even weeks. Given the gendered division of labour in many Canadian households, it is likely easier for men to devote time to these pursuits than women, who generally take on a greater burden of childcare and unpaid care labour.

The result is a self-fulfilling prophecy, in which the lack of participation of women, and especially women of colour, in the gun world makes it more difficult for women to get involved. Some women I spoke to noted the difficulties that they had entering the male-dominated spaces of the gun world. Allison, a mixed-race woman of Chinese and African descent who immigrated to Canada from Madagascar at a young age, is a passionate firearm enthusiast. She proudly stated that she "comes from a family of ranchers," and though her dad was a businessman rather than a shooter or hunter, she identifies deeply with her grandparents' agrarian legacy. When searching for a home, she and her husband made sure that the community would be firearm-friendly, checking local bylaws and even verifying the political affiliation of the local mayor. They purchased a piece of land large enough that they could hunt and shoot on it. Allison spoke highly of her neighbourhood in rural Ontario, noting that most people on her block owned firearms, and half were active hunters. She added that her race was an important factor when deciding to acquire private land to hunt on:

In Ontario it's easier that way, you know? There's a lot of Crown land, but you've got to make sure that there's nobody else there. Also, like I don't want to be that person, but as a person of colour I don't really fit in. So it was easier for us to just purchase property and just deal with it ourselves.[130]

Despite having land to shoot on, Allison and her husband are still members of a range. Like Rick, they needed a referral, which they were able to secure by chance when they ran into another French speaker while shopping at a popular sporting-goods store, who happened to be a member of the local range.

Despite the fact that most of the regulars at the range are "old white guys," Allison says that she was eventually able to connect and become a part of the community.

I would have never thought to meet them outside of their club because we don't like the same music. There's a generational gap definitely there. Sometimes there's a little bit of a language barrier, I don't always find my words. But because of the same interests and guns and shooting, we get along, and then you get to know someone that you aside from that would have never met.[131]

Despite this, being a gun owner of colour comes with its own challenges, like overcoming stereotypes of what it means to be a Black person with a gun.

If someone asks you if you have a handgun, then they're wondering immediately if it's drug-related. And I know that I've had some people say certain things to me that were a little bit racially conflicted ... I don't want to but I always feel like a little bit of a sense of responsibility. Not that I am a symbol of my community, but if I do something wrong, that it will reflect badly on a minority.[132]

For women or people of colour, going to the gun range for the first time can be a stressful experience.

Being a person of colour, I find sometimes I already know that I'm going to be out of place. And you just have to overcome that. And I know that for some other people, like I'm a very outgoing person, and I don't, I'm not easily intimidated. So for me, it's easier. But I know that there must be other people out there that don't feel as headstrong as I do.[133]

Despite this, Allison felt that the community overall was quite welcoming, though perhaps "lacking in representation." Advocacy groups representing firearm owners and the firearm industry have made efforts in recent years to broaden gun ownership and reach demographics that they have not necessarily reached before. All of the advocates I spoke to made special efforts to note their groups' work to expand gun ownership to new demographics, and especially to create new opportunities for women shooters. These include things like the CCFR's women's only range days, and women's outreach program. But structural barriers make this challenging.

Gun Ownership as Serious Leisure

The results of the survey and interviews support my claim that the activities associated with gun ownership fit Stebbins's definition of serious leisure. That is to say, the gun culture in Canada is made up of a community of gun owners rallied around a set of leisure pursuits. Serious leisure pursuits can be identified by six defining characteristics: durable benefit, effort, perseverance, careerism, ethos, and identity.[134] All emerged in my surveys and interviews with Canadian gun owners. This shared leisure culture makes it easier for advocates to rally the community to take action.

The gun owners that I spoke with and surveyed were deeply engaged in their chosen firearm-related activities. This engagement is demonstrated by high levels of spending and frequent participation. The average gun owner in my online survey sample spent $3,378.47 CAD on firearms, ammunition, accessories, and hunting supplies in 2019, with the median spending being $2,000 CAD. Further, participants were asked how long they had owned guns. The answers ranged from less than a year to eighty-three years. While many gun owners had acquired guns in the past decade, the average gun owner in my sample has owned guns for over twenty-six years, with a median of twenty-five years.

In addition to gauging participants' spending, and how long they have been involved in the hobby, participants were also asked how *often* they participated in their chosen firearm-related activity. The majority said they participated quite frequently, with 56 per cent of sports shooters reporting more than ten times per year. Similarly, just 3 per cent rarely participated in shooting sports. This provides support for the assertion that gun ownership is a form of serious leisure, in which

Figure 3.1 Years that Participants Have Owned Guns (online survey)

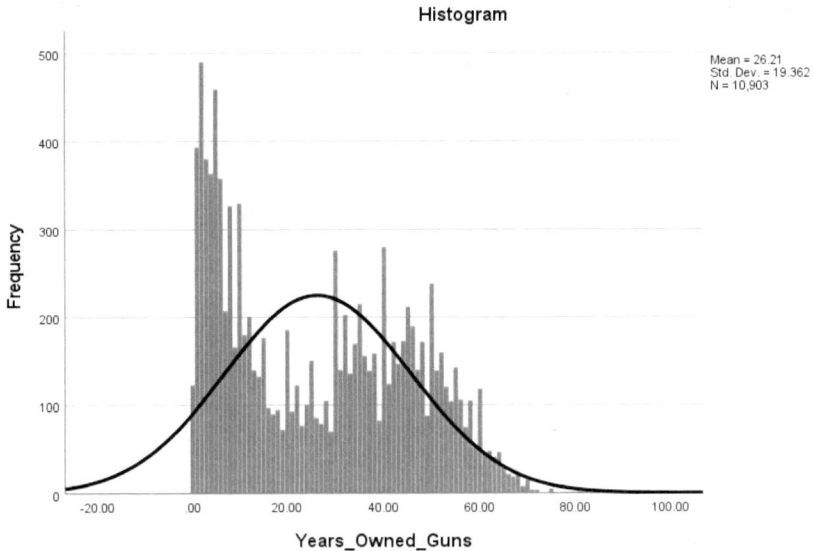

Histogram

Mean = 26.21
Std. Dev. = 19.362
N = 10,903

Years_Owned_Guns

Table 3.2. Frequency Hunting and Sports Shooting

		N	%
Hunting			
	Rarely	744	6.6
	Every few years	1,170	10.4
	Once per year	1,247	11.1
	2–3 times per year	2,627	23.4
	4–10 times per year	2,245	20
	10+ times per year	3,210	28.6
Sports Shooting			
	Rarely	462	3
	Every few years	322	1.9
	Once per year	372	2.2
	2–3 times per year	2,024	13.3
	4–10 times per year	3,576	23.5
	10+ times per year	8,465	55.6

Table 3.3. Pride and Importance of Gun Ownership

How proud are you to be a gun owner?		How important is being able to own guns to you?	
Very Proud	80.6%	Extremely Important	83.3%
Proud	12.1%	Very Important	13.7%
Somewhat Proud	2.8%	Moderately Important	2.5%
Not Very Proud	0.4%	Slightly Important	0.3%
Not At All Proud	0.4%	Not at all Important	0.2%
No Opinion	3.7%		

participants expend significant amounts of time and financial resources on their activity.

Serious leisure activities tend to become an important part of the identity of those who take part in them. When asked about how proud they were to be gun owners, 80.6 per cent reported being very proud, while 12.1 per cent selected proud. A further 83.2 per cent noted that being able to own firearms is extremely important to them, and 13.7 per cent reported that it is very important.

Despite acknowledging that the public image of gun owners in Canada is negative, several of my interview participants also expressed their pride in being a gun owner, or in being competent with firearms.

This pride can take many forms. For some, it is related to continuing family traditions around firearm ownership. When asked what values he associated with firearm ownership, Aaron replied: "It's also pride in owning these objects, like, my father's rifle that he gave me. They can make all the laws they want, I would never give that up."[135] For others, the pride is related to their prowess as hunters, shooters, or even collectors. During our interview, Claude spoke of his pride in his firearm collection, which he has worked since 1987 to assemble, and his ability to own objects that were "part of history."[136]

For others, especially some of the women I spoke to, the pride in gun ownership was accompanied by feelings of agency or independence. Annie, for example, regretted only getting into guns later in her life, but talked about the sense of pride she felt buying her first handgun. She got into the hobby through her husband, who eagerly took her to every gun shop in the region, but Annie stood firm that the final decision would be her own.[137]

At the same time, this pride was often contrasted with feelings of stigmatization, or being part of a misunderstood or even persecuted minority group. For example, Harrison noted that while he is "proud to be someone who's competent with guns," he is also aware that

Table 3.4. Acquired First Gun and Introduced to Firearms

How did you acquire your first gun?		Thinking of the first firearm-related activity you took part in, how did you get into this activity?	
Family member	28.8%	Family member	50.1%
Friend	1.2%	Friend	23.2%
Inherited	7.5%	Club/Organization	10.5%
Purchased	61.1%	Internet	2.4%
		Saw it on TV	0.6%
		Other	9.8%

"the paradigm is shifting a little bit."[138] When asked how it felt to be a gun owner in 2022, Lindsay responded, "I feel proud but angry." She described being proud of her community, but angry about how that community is perceived by the public.[139]

Another important element of serious leisure is the sense of community that serious leisure identities inspire. In the case of gun owners, family is an important concept tied to the collective identity of gun owners. This was demonstrated when gun owners were asked how they acquired their first firearm. Just over one-quarter of participants received it from a family member, with 7.5 per cent inheriting it. Though the majority of gun owners bought their first gun themselves, family and friends were major reasons why gun owners became involved in hunting, collecting, or sports shooting. Half of participants were introduced to firearms by family members, while 23.2 per cent became involved through friends. As I established earlier in the chapter, family, community, and friendship are important reasons why people participate in the gun culture.

I expect some readers may take exception to devoting so much space to exploring the Canadian gun culture, and the reasons why a small but vocal group of Canadians choose to own firearms. I assert that one cannot understand the gun debate in Canada, or the regulation of firearms, without understanding Canada's community of firearm owners in their own words.

> There is this relationship with firearms, it's not the way it's portrayed by people who don't have them and don't understand them. It has such a meaning and a value to people that when you start talking about losing it (*pauses*). It isn't about a hobby, it isn't about a pastime. When people say, "go out and do something different," you know, "get a different recreation." It's not like that. It's so much bigger than that.[140]

In this chapter, we have seen that Canadian gun culture is very different from its American counterpart, due to the political culture and regulatory environment in Canada. The early regulation of handguns, and the expansion of Canada's gun control regime in the 1970s and 1990s, meant that Canadian gun culture remains centred on the Gun Culture 1.0 model, unlike the United States, which has shifted towards a self-defence culture. As a result of this, and the regulatory hurdles involved in becoming a gun owner, the Canadian gun culture has failed to diversify as US gun culture has. Finally, I demonstrated that gun ownership in Canada fits Stebbins's model of serious leisure and explored why Canadian gun owners are so attached to their firearms.

As we will see, this leisure culture, and the interaction between the gun community and its regulators, have developed a unique conception of gun rights in the minds of Canadian gun owners: one based on the expectations that citizens have to fair treatment by their government.

4

The Canadian Pro-Gun Movement

Hunting isn't just a proud Canadian tradition, it's a way of life for communities across this country. Bill C-21 isn't about targeting hunters, it's about certain guns that are too dangerous in other contexts.

Former Public Safety Minister Marco Mendicino responding
to critics on Bill C-21

The path to victory in interest-group politics is not always clear. Sometimes, well-resourced movements with a large core of passionate members lose. To explain this phenomenon, scholars of social movements have come up with the term "political opportunity structure." This refers to structures external to a social movement or advocacy group that help to determine its success or failure in shaping policy. These environmental factors include institutions, the relationship of movements with elites, the interest-group system, and the public's view of the movement or the issue it seeks to advance.[1] Public opinion itself is often heavily shaped by institutions[2] and culture,[3] which can constrain social movements that seek to challenge or transform prevailing public opinion. Fleming et al.[4] demonstrate that the political opportunity structure can help us to explain policy differences between Canada and the United States with regard to firearm regulation. I build on this to demonstrate the impact of the political opportunity structure on the messaging, strategies, and outlook of the Canadian pro-gun movement, as well as the values of Canadian gun owners. As we will see, hunting in Canada enjoys considerable public support, to the extent that even politicians seeking to limit access to firearms must frame their policies in a way that avoids appearing to impact hunters. This is due to the influence and legitimacy that the conservation movement has built over more than a century of advocacy in Canada. Despite considerable resources and energy, sports shooters and collectors enjoy less legitimacy in the public sphere and face an uphill battle in pushing back against government policies.

Further, the political opportunity structure, and especially Canadian institutions, have had a significant influence on the goals and messaging techniques of the pro-gun movement in Canada. As a result, Canadian gun owners, and the groups that represent them, are fundamentally different from their American counterparts. This chapter aims to outline the contours of the gun debate in Canada. It begins by examining how various important institutions in Canadian politics have an impact on firearm policy, and thus shape the strategies the movement pursues. As we will see, the rules of the game that shape politics in Canada heavily favour the pro-control movement. The chapter then turns to consider public opinion and political culture in Canada, with a particular focus on rural alienation. Finally, it examines how the hunting and conservation movement have been successful at shaping public opinion by developing a strong and proactive relationship with their regulator.

To navigate the crucible of institutions and public opinion in Canada, the gun rights movement has been forced to adapt to survive. This has led to the development of a fundamentally different strategy from the American movement and a different conceptualization of rights and citizenship.

Institutions

Canadian institutions tend to be more adaptive than American institutions to prevailing public opinion. In many ways this is an advantage, as adaptable institutions are more relevant to the public they serve. This adaptation, exemplified by the Canadian Charter of Rights and Freedoms (1982), has allowed Canada's institutions to be used to protect certain minority groups from the tyranny of the majority and to win historic victories for 2SLBTQ+ people,[5] or the right to medical assistance in dying.[6] From the perspective of gun owners, this structure affords them little protection from the whims of non-gun-owning Canadians.

Charter and Courts

The Canadian Charter of Rights and Freedoms includes no explicit right to bear arms,[7] unlike the American Constitution.[8] The Canadian Supreme Court, in the case of *R. v. Hasselwander*, addressed this fact in their judgment: "Canadians, unlike Americans, do not have a constitutional right to bear arms."[9]

This has not stopped some advocates from claiming a right to gun ownership in the American sense. Bruce Montague, a gunsmith from Northern Ontario, for example, purposefully let his firearms licence lapse as a form of political protest. After having his firearms confiscated and facing multiple charges, including the possession of prohibited weapons like fully automatic firearms, Montague attempted to take his case to the Supreme Court, only to have his appeal dismissed.[10]

The claim to a legal or constitutional right to bear arms in Canada follows the same lineage as the American Second Amendment: the English political tradition. This dates back to 1181, when King Henry II issued the *Assize of Arms*. The law required common people to keep weapons that they could afford, mainly pole-arms, to be used in defence against attacks or raids.[11] It first established in written law the Anglo-Saxon tradition that ordinary citizens, at the time freemen, should be a part of the "defence of the realm."[12] Yet this duty of the people to keep arms was not unlimited. Like all arms-control laws, the purpose was to keep weapons in the hands of citizens considered desirable by the sovereign and out of the hands of those deemed undesirable or dangerous. The Assize sought to limit the number and type of weapons that common people could own, attempting to concentrate power in the hands of the aristocracy. Certain groups, like Jews, were forbidden to own weapons altogether.[13]

The laws surrounding arms-bearing were updated in 1242 by Henry III, who modernized the militia yet again, requiring those with greater wealth to present themselves for militia duty on horseback, and lower-income people with longbows.[14] The militia was further expanded by Edward I, who extended militia duty to all Englishmen in the Statute of Westminster. This ethos became reflected in English political philosophy, influenced by the writings of Machiavelli.[15]

The militia tradition in England persisted and would become enshrined in constitutional law following the English Revolution (1642–51) and Glorious Revolution (1688). During his reign, Charles II sought to solidify the power of the monarchy by banning the possession of firearms and bows from all Englishmen with less than £100 worth of land. The purpose was to avoid insurrection, but also to limit the ability of common people to hunt, and thus make them more dependent on the aristocracy. James II expanded this policy, focusing especially on disarming Protestants, since he was a Catholic king. These laws were struck down following the Glorious Revolution in 1688, when William and Mary took the throne and England fell once again under Protestant rule. Parliament created the English Bill of Rights to decrease the power of the monarchy and safeguard the rights of the growing merchant class and the common people. The English Bill of Rights would heavily influence the American Bill of Rights. A provision was thus added in the English Bill of Rights "That Subjects which are Protestants, may have Arms for their Defence suitable to their Condition, and as are allowed by Law."[16] As with the debate over the American Second Amendment, there is disagreement among sources about the original meaning of this bill. Charles[17] argues that the right to bear arms in England was "intimately tied to Parliament's powers over arming and arraying of the militia ... This right was controlled by the people, through Parliament, as a means to check a tyrannical sovereign, particularly one that maintained an oppressive or unlawful standing army."

Conversely, Hallbrook[18] and Malcolm[19] argue that the provision protected not only a collective right to arms, but an individual one as well. Hallbrook notes that the original version of this statement referred to "common Defence" rather than "Defence." The qualifier "common" was removed by the House of Lords. Hallbrook suggests that this indicates that the bill protected the rights of individual self-defence as well as collective self-defence.[20] Further, a group of prominent Whig politicians, who were themselves drafters of the Bill of Rights, later supplied further evidence that the bill was intended to protect individual rights. For example, Andrew Fletcher published *A Discourse of Government with Relation to Militias* in 1698. He considered arms to be "the only true badges of liberty" and supported an armed populace to protect that liberty.[21] The most oft-cited support for this interpretation of arms-bearing in the English Bill of Rights is found in the commentaries of William Blackstone, mentioned earlier.[22]

The second argument in favour of a right to bear arms in Canada derives from the concept of natural law. Natural law has origins in the Judeo-Christian tradition and refers to the belief in fundamental rights, such as the right to self-defence, that supersede the laws of man. In this case, given that human beings have a natural right to self-defence, the right to bear arms would operationalize that right. Proponents of this natural-rights view argue that without the right to possess an effective tool for self-defence, a right to self-defence is meaningless.[23]

In contemporary Canadian legal decisions[24] the courts have asserted clearly that they do *not* consider Canadians to have a right to possess firearms under either the constitution[25] or natural law.[26] Further, given the way that rights are conceptualized in Canada, even if a right to firearm ownership could be established, it would not be unlimited but, like all charter rights, would be subject to reasonable limitations.[27]

As a result of these limitations, Canadian pro-gun advocates have not enjoyed the same legal success as their American counterparts.

The American constitution famously contains a more explicit reference to the right to firearm ownership. While debates persisted for many years about whether the Second Amendment protects collective firearm ownership in the militia or an individual right,[28] the Supreme Court authoritatively sided with the individual-rights argument in *District of Columbia v. Heller*,[29] *McDonald v. City of Chicago*,[30] and later *NYSRPA v. Bruen*.[31] These cases have led to major breakthroughs for the American pro-gun movement, such as the expansion of the concealed carry movement.[32] Without constitutional protection, this avenue is closed to Canadian advocates.

Recently, pro-gun advocates have attempted to reframe a right to arms ownership in Canada using the language of property rights, in order to attempt to expand the scope of the conflict. Property rights, however, were explicitly excluded from the Charter, due to the fears of the provinces that it would limit their power to expropriate property for public projects,[33] and, as of the time of writing, the Federal court has rejected this argument.[34]

Parliament

Canada is a constitutional monarchy that uses the Westminster parliamentary system. This system has proven to be more amenable to change than the American presidential system. As a result, Canada's Parliament has had greater success in passing strong gun control laws at the national level.

Given the strong focus on separation of powers in the American constitution, power in American politics is diffuse, with multiple veto players that can block policies on divisive issues like firearm policy. First, in the American system, both Congress and the Senate can act as veto players, that is to say that each can stop legislation that it does not want passed. Further, with the presidential veto, the executive branch, which in the United States is distinct from the legislative branch, can also serve as a veto player.[35]

The Canadian system is more centralized. The legislative and executive branch in the Westminster parliamentary system are usually drawn from the same party. Further, while the Canadian Senate often suggests amendments or delays policies, it rarely uses its power to reject them outright. A government with majority control of Parliament thus faces few potential veto players to stop legislation from passing, as long as they can maintain party discipline.[36]

The representation of rural Canadians and Americans in institutional structures has also influenced firearm policies in both countries.

In both the United States[37] and Canada,[38] gun ownership rates are higher in rural areas. Though the relationship between support for gun control and living in a rural area is less robust in Canada,[39] much of the opposition to gun control in Canada is concentrated in the rural west.

In the American system, seats in the House of Representatives are allotted by population, while each state has an equal number of seats in the Senate. As such, the American Senate has strong rural representation, given that states like Wyoming or Idaho with small and largely rural populations receive equal representation as more populous and urban seats in states like California or New York.[40] Further, smaller states also receive a boost in the Electoral College. As a result, "rural Americans have the potential to influence national politics more strongly than do their urban counterparts, especially when those rural citizens are highly participatory," as they are on issues of gun control.[41]

Party and Interest Group System

Unlike the American two-party system, Canada has three major national political parties, as well as smaller and regional parties that have held the balance of power in Parliament at times in Canadian history. Differences in party systems, and the relationship between parties and groups in society, help to explain political outcomes.

Since the 1970s, the NRA in the United States has maintained a strong relationship with the Republican Party. This political relationship is so embedded that we forget gun control was not a highly partisan issue in the United States until that time. The Republican Party works hard to cultivate this alliance with the NRA, because they know that NRA members are reliable voters, volunteers, and donors that can help their campaigns. The NRA has proved to be very effective at mobilization, given its institutionalization and vast communications network.[42] There is a high level of party-group alignment between the NRA and the Republican Party.

Pro-gun advocates I spoke with alluded to a similar relationship with the Conservative Party. Though they all noted a willingness to engage with other parties, they admitted that they had an easier time talking to, and working with, Conservative politicians. As gun control has become absorbed into culture war and wedge politics in Canada, this divide has become more pronounced, with rural Liberal MPs who may have once stood up to party leadership on gun control beginning to toe the party line.

When I spoke to the CCFR's Tracey Wilson, for example, she noted:

The friendliest politician for a Canadian gun owner of any kind to speak to is, of course, a Conservative. Unfortunately, it shouldn't be that way ... For a lot of people, some of the other policies on the left, like the liberal policies, maybe on climate change, or environment or whatever, appealed to them ... The gun community, I would say, is probably 50 per cent right leaning, but I think the rest are left leaning on a lot of other issues. But they have no choice but to support a right-leaning party, because they're the only ones not wanting to come and confiscate your property for crimes you didn't commit.[43]

Strong party-group alignment does not always benefit an interest group. The danger of interest-group capture, when a group or movement's interests are so aligned with a party that they cannot credibly threaten to move their support elsewhere, makes close alignment with any party dangerous for an interest group.[44] Part of the NRA's effectiveness has been their ability to evade capture by the Republican Party. The same thing has not happened in Canada, and Canadian pro-gun groups recall a history of betrayal by the Conservative Party. For example, veteran pro-gun advocate Sheldon Clare, a college instructor and former president of the NFA, noted during our interview that he reserves particular resentment for Kim Campbell, who ushered in a sweeping expansion of gun control in 1991.[45]

More recently, during the 2021 election campaign, Conservative Party leader Erin O'Toole, who had campaigned as a "true blue" conservative during the leadership race, notoriously folded on his support for revoking the Liberal government's ban on assault-style weapons.[46]

Much is often made of the Harper government's revocation and destruction of the long-gun registry, but when set against the massive expansion of gun control laws in Canada since the 1970s, this action was relatively modest. The advocates I spoke to understood that while the Conservatives were likely their best bet, they could not always count on their support. Tony Bernardo of the CSSA joked about this during our talk when discussing misconceptions about gun lobbying in Canada, which observers often uncritically compare to the relationship between the NRA and the Republican Party. He expressed his frustration that, in his view: "The vast, vast majority of Canadians believe everything that comes out of Hollywood about the NRA having complete control over the US government. And of course, by corollary, that means the Conservatives are toadies to us."[47]

Canadian Federalism

In the fall of 2022, representatives of the government of Alberta announced that they would attempt to block RCMP officers stationed in their provinces from participating in the federal government's confiscation of "assault-style" firearms.[48] This strategy was soon echoed by Saskatchewan, Manitoba, Yukon, and New Brunswick. This was not the first time that western Canadian provinces had attempted to resist Ottawa's gun control efforts.[49] However, as critics noted, this move was more about expressing political solidarity than policy. Canadian provinces have little power to thwart the federal government's gun-control efforts, as the Canadian constitution places criminal law in Ottawa's hands. This was reaffirmed in the case of *Reference re Firearms Act (Can.).*[50]

This is another important distinction between Canada and the United States in this policy area. American states have significant leeway in shaping gun control policy,[51] which leads to a patchwork quilt of policies across the country. While states like New York, California, and Illinois have strict gun control legislation, more rural, southern or western, and red states like Wyoming, Louisiana, and Idaho have fewer restrictions in place.

Canadian provinces do retain a certain level of autonomy to regulate hunting, which has traditionally been managed by provincial natural resource or wildlife management agencies. The licensing, registration, and decisions surrounding the legality of firearms in Canada, on the other hand, are controlled centrally through the federal government and the RCMP Canadian Firearms Program.

This has a significant impact on the rules of the advocacy game in Canada. In the United States, pro-gun groups like the NRA have made significant gains in recent years at the state level,[52] especially with regard to the massive expansion of liberalized concealed carry laws.[53] Though public opinion in the United States has consistently favoured stricter gun control for some time, pro-gun supporters are more visible and audible.[54] State and local-level policy conflicts benefit grassroots movements like the pro-gun movement, which can count on its supporters to attend state- or county-level meetings where gun control is being discussed and to pressure policymakers. The pro-control movement, which suffers more from the free-rider problem,[55] has traditionally struggled to mobilize supporters as consistently. With gun laws in Canada concentrated at the federal level, there is less opportunity for the pro-gun movement to use its large number of passionate supporters to its advantage.

Treaties and Indigenous Rights

Firearms have been a part of Indigenous-settler relations since the first Europeans arrived on Turtle Island. Indigenous groups recognized the utility of firearms for hunting and warfare and sought to trade for them with European settlers and traders. Given that throughout their history, firearms have been both a symbol and tool of political power, many of Canada's early gun laws were aimed at disarming Indigenous groups resisting the government, or those that the government feared might rise up.[56] Firearms have been used by Indigenous groups throughout modern history to resist colonial power, from the Northwest Resistance of Louis Riel and Gabriel Dumont to the Kanesatake Resistance (Oka Crisis), in which armed protestors defended ancestral Mohawk territory from incursions by land developers intent on building a golf course and housing development.[57]

Firearms are also important tools for allowing Indigenous Canadians to exercise their treaty rights to hunting. Indigenous groups have used the courts to resist gun control efforts in the past, arguing that the Firearms Act violated their treaty rights.[58] Further, Indigenous gun owners who possess treaty rights under Section 35 of the Constitution Act of 1982 are covered by separate firearm regulations, which, for example, allow community elders to issue firearm licences.[59]

As a result, the very limited available evidence shows that Indigenous Canadians may be more skeptical about gun control efforts than settler Canadians.[60] For example, during parliamentary study of Bill C-21, Regional Chief Terry Teegee from the British Columbia Assembly of First Nations raised concerns about measures like red-and-yellow-flag laws, and how these might negatively impact Indigenous people, who are already overrepresented in the prison population, and rely on firearms to enjoy their treaty hunting rights. Further, Chief Heather Bear of FSIN, which represents seventy-three First Nations across Saskatchewan, also raised concerns about how these laws might be used to harm First Nations people, given tensions between settler land users and Indigenous subsistence hunters. She described the important role of hunting for First Nations in Saskatchewan, not just in providing food, but also in ceremonial practices, saying: "When you confiscate guns you are doing a whole lot more than just taking away a gun."[61]

As Bill C-21 made its way through the Senate, the Mohawk Council of Kahnawake submitted a brief to the committee studying the bill, arguing that Bill C-21 threatened the right of their community to self-governance, as well as the hunting rights that are central to the practice of Indigenous cultures and language.[62]

Some non-Indigenous gun owners that I spoke with saw Indigenous Treaty Rights as a "backstop," similar to the Second Amendment, preventing politicians from completely prohibiting firearm ownership in Canada.[63] Others speculated that the reason the 2020 Assault Style Weapons ban did not initially include the Soviet SKS semi-automatic rifle was because of its frequent use by Indigenous Canadians, though no evidence was offered to substantiate this claim.

Overall, Canada's institutions favour the pro-control coalition. Reliant on the Conservative party, with no explicit constitutional protection for gun ownership, operating in a political system with fewer veto actors, and unable to use their grassroots advantage at the provincial level, the pro-gun movement faces a daunting challenge. The prevailing Canadian political culture and public mood further complicate their efforts.

Public Opinion, Political Culture, and the Media

Political culture and public opinion in Canada are generally much more supportive of restrictions on individual liberties to secure collective goods than in the United States. While the United States was founded on the principles of life, liberty, and the pursuit of happiness, Canada's founding principles are peace, order, and good government. This is reflected in Canadian public opinion, which tends to favour the pro-control position. For example, the most recent polling data available at the time of writing demonstrates that a plurality of Canadians (44 per cent) believes that even the nation's stringent gun laws are not strict enough, with only 30 per cent saying that they are "about right," and 17 per cent too strict. A significant majority (67 per cent) supported a ban on civilian ownership of handguns.[64]

This is consistent with trends in public opinion in Canada over time. There is bipartisan support for many of Canada's gun-control measures. Women, young people, and those living in large urban areas and central Canada tend to be most supportive of expansive gun control, while men, western Canadians, rural residents, and Canada's Indigenous people tend to be less supportive.[65] This is a major impediment for the pro-gun movement in Canada. It provides significant incentives for Canadian political parties to propose new gun control measures and disincentives for friendly parties, like the Conservatives, to liberalize gun control. Further, it allows politicians seeking to enact gun control measures to justify them based on public opinion, despite presenting little evidence that they will improve public safety.[66]

While it is easy to provide robust evidence of the Canadian public's pro-control sentiments, it is more difficult to provide empirical evidence for why this is, given that almost all data on public opinion and gun control comes from the United States. Several explanations, however, are worth considering.

The most logical explanation is that there are fewer gun owners in Canada than in the United States. Research from the United States shows that gun ownership and use is negatively correlated with support for gun control.[67] Given that less than 6 per cent of the population is licensed to own firearms,[68] it is logical that the majority non-gun-owning population would support gun control laws that have little negative impact on their lives, or those of people that they know, but that they believe will provide for greater public safety.

The second is simple ignorance. The Canadian public does not seem to be very well informed about the country's gun control laws. For example, Mauser and Buckner found that less than 50 per cent of respondents in their study knew that a licence was required to purchase a firearm in Canada, less than one in five knew that a safety course was required, and only 13 per cent could name two or more of the requirements to purchase a firearm in Canada. The authors found that support for gun control was weaker than believed and easily influenced by information. For example, "Almost half of those who said they favoured registration [of long guns] changed their minds when informed of its possible costs."[69]

The pervasive anti-Americanism in Canadian politics, and the association of guns with American culture, especially in the post-Columbine era, likely also influence the pro-control sentiments of Canadian gun owners. The Canadian national image crafted in the post-war period explicitly sought to distance Canada from American cultural influence.[70] Canadian nationalism is, in many ways, centred on *not* being American.[71] It is possible that for many Canadians who regularly consume American news, and thus witness from afar the consequences of an overly liberalized gun control regime on a regular basis, gun control is a way to symbolically distance Canada from the United States. In my discussions with gun owners and pro-gun advocates, owners often expressed feeling negatively stereotyped by cultural images of American gun owners.

The media is another important actor shaping public opinion, and thus the political opportunity structure that movements operate in.[72] It does this both by priming audiences to be receptive to certain perspectives, selecting some issues as important and newsworthy by giving them attention while ignoring others, and through framing, that is, highlighting certain aspects of a problem or issue.[73] Claims of media bias are ubiquitous in contemporary culture-war politics. While it is important to treat these claims with a healthy scepticism, there is a widespread perception among Canadian gun owners that they do not receive fair treatment in the media.[74]

Little research has been conducted to substantiate claims of a gun-related bias among Canadian media outlets. Looking south, a small literature emerged in the early 2000s that demonstrates the ways in which the American media environment favoured the pro-control argument. One line of reasoning is that reporters come from a cosmopolitan world view unfamiliar with, and thus hostile to, gun ownership. As a result, the media emphasizes the use of guns by criminals and downplays positive aspects of gun ownership, like recreation, hunting, and defensive gun use.[75] A more parsimonious explanation is offered by Callaghan and Schnell, who argue that the use of guns in crime better fits the media's criteria for "newsworthiness," and thus is more likely to be amplified by media outlets.[76] As a result, the public is exposed almost constantly to the negative externalities associated with private gun ownership, but rarely to the everyday realties of gun ownership for most owners.

Given incentives in the media, Canadian public opinion, and a political culture with a built-in distaste of things considered too American, like guns, the pro-gun movement in Canada faces a serious public relations challenge.

Alienation

Gun politics in Canada is tied to a wider politics of rural resentment and western alienation: a belief that the needs of rural and western Canadians are underrepresented by Canada's political institutions. This urban-rural and east-west divides shape the political opportunity structure that advocacy groups operate in. As a result, the Canadian pro-gun movement must simultaneously cater to its rural and western base while also trying to establish a broader coalition with the largely urban Canadian public, especially in anti-gun Quebec.

It seems to be widely accepted in Canada that guns are rural objects: useful tools for hunters and farmers, but out of place in cities. For example, Minister of Public Safety Marco Mendicino, announcing the government's handgun freeze in 2022, went to great pains to emphasize that these measures were not meant to target farmers and rural Canadians who rely on firearms for pest and predator control.[77] This discourse was reflected in my interviews with both rural and urban gun owners. It was assumed that guns were something that rural Canadians understood and urban Canadians mistrusted. This narrative, of course, writes out of existence the many rural Canadians who do not own guns and who may be deeply against private gun ownership, as well as the many urban and suburban gun owners I spoke with.

Lindsay, who grew up in rural Prince Edward Island but went to school in Charlottetown, the province's largest city, often felt this tension in her friendships, where she was forced to defend hunting and firearm safety: "None of my friends growing up, none of their parents went hunting, none of them did any kind of shooting or archery. So, I knew that I was different." She felt her that her colleagues' disapproval of the activities were tied to a lack of exposure to the realities of the hobby: "That's all their experience has told them. And most things in the media about firearms are done with a negative connotation."[78]

Pierre, a Métis man living in Saskatchewan, also witnessed this tension between rural and urban in the culture shock his partner, a city person, experienced when they started dating. Pierre grew up in a community where guns were a normal part of life. He gave the example of a farmer he knew who kept a rifle in his truck when he was out on the farm mending fences to deal with the invasive population of wild boars that had that wreaked havoc. To his partner, who came from an urban area and had little experience with firearms before meeting him, firearms were objects of fear. "It took her a couple of years to even be in a room with me when I would be cleaning a firearm."[79]

As Pierre's anecdote shows, the centrality of firearms to certain aspects of rural life is certainly a major reason for the association between the two concepts. Farming, hunting, trapping, and employment in the natural-resources sector tend to be rural activities, taking place well outside of city limits. The unique dangers and nuisances that rural Canadians confront from predators or pest animals make guns useful tools. When discussing changes that he would like to see to Canada's firearms policies, Robert noted that open carry in remote areas would help him feel safer in the outdoors. In the United States, carrying a handgun for wildlife protection, and even hunting with specialized models of handguns, is a common practice. In Canada, however, handguns are tightly controlled, their sale or transfer now frozen, and only a select few people, usually those in natural-resource industries, are licensed to carry handguns in the woods, as rifles may be too unwieldy to use during an animal attack, or when the user's hands are otherwise occupied with tasks like mending a trap line, or field dressing a deer carcass.

> I would advocate for open carry out in the woods. I don't see a benefit to being able to open carry my Glock when I'm shopping at Walmart. But, we live our lives halfway up the side of a mountain. So, cougars and bears are our daily experience. Especially when we're deer hunting. It's primarily the wolves. As you're tracking something, they'll follow you. And it's been more than one hunter who's been chased away by a small pack of wolves after they've got their [deer].[80]

The connection between firearms and hunting has made firearms a key component of rural food systems and the rural economy. This was noted by several survey participants, who touted the nutritional and ethical benefits of hunting and consuming wild game over store-bought food. These participants saw urban Canadians as "disconnected" from their food, and their opposition to hunting motivated by urban ignorance of where their food comes from. This was one of the things Lindsay disliked most about having to move to the city for work. Most of her friends and colleagues saw meat as something that came packaged at the grocery store. "People are so disconnected from seeing where their food comes from that they shame hunters for killing animals, when I think that's way more ethical and sustainable than factory farming." Despite adopting a vegan lifestyle for several years, Lindsay said she still respected hunters like her father for being able to source their own meat: "I think that if you're going to be able to consume an animal, you should be able to kill it."[81]

Hunters often spoke of their connection to the land and the role that hunting plays in wildlife management. For them, rural Canadians have natural ties to the land, while urban Canadians are disconnected or alienated from it. At the core of this lies the ethics of hunting. Solomon, in his seventies, had lived in rural Ontario his entire life. He had hunted since he was a child, and though the realities of his ageing body and fixed retirement income limited the time he spent in the woods, hunting remained ingrained in his way of living. He often volunteered to give presentations at his granddaughter's school, teaching children about ecology and the role that hunters play in wildlife management. For Solomon, hunting was a rural tradition deeply tied to ethics and responsibility. To him, rural identity, linked to hunting, was so important that he even expressed a mistrust of other gun owners who happened to live in cities: "They're not all in the hunting community, and even some of those people don't understand the hunting community."

For Solomon, hunting was deeply intertwined with questions of ethics and morality. This ethic is tied to the land and to food production.

> When you're out there by yourself in the woods with a firearm you can't be unethical. Your ethics have to guide you through it, and it's not what do you do when somebody is watching what you're doing, but when somebody isn't.
>
> You take it upon yourself to take a life, right? So when you stop that other heart, it's something you have to contend with yourself. Some people can't do it. I understand that too. Some people won't do it. That's the part of the hunting I don't like. But to get the meat, you have to do it.

Like Lindsay, Solomon echoed the narrative that urban dwellers were unconnected to their food source, and thus distanced from the ethic of the hunter.[82]

Allison, who immigrated to Canada from Madagascar and settled with her husband in rural Ontario, also touted the health benefits of hunting. "We don't trophy hunt. I don't like that. We don't hunt for the looks of it, it's mostly to feed the family, right? And also, for sport." Allison noted that her sister had allergies to artificial hormones used in many factory-farmed meats. Unable to afford what she called the "Whole Foods" lifestyle, Allison set out to fill her sister's freezer. "So, once we started hunting, one of our goals was to make sure that we would have enough red meat for the family to share without having to go out of pocket." She described meat harvested by hunters as "good meat, clean meat" and "natural and free-range.[83]

The similarities between the thoughts expressed by Lindsay, a young white woman from Prince Edward Island just completing her undergraduate degree; Solomon, an elderly white man from rural Ontario; and Allison, an immigrant to Canada and person-of-colour settling in a rural area, speak to the shared code of ethics of the hunting community. Hunters see themselves as deeply connected to the land and environment in a way that "city people," who are presumed to be non-hunters, are not. This connection comes from the direct way that they source their food, taking it upon themselves to harvest an animal directly, rather than contract out their killing to farmers or slaughterhouses. In so doing, they take on the role of provider.

The association between rural people and firearm ownership transcended nationality. Mikael, an immigrant from Russia, remembered visiting his grandparents in their village in rural Russia, where he was first introduced to guns. At the time, he lived in the city but would visit his grandparents in their small village where, due to issues with local wildlife, gun ownership was so common that: "every single house has several."[84]

In addition to supplementing rural food systems, hunting is also tied to the rural economy through urban and suburban hunters. Hunters who live in the city must travel to have access to areas where hunting can be practised safely, and where game is abundant. This means spending money in the small towns or rest stops nearby. When we spoke, Darrell Crabbe of the Saskatchewan Wildlife Federation noted that hunting and angling generate around $650 million in the province each year.

> The really interesting part is that it's the only economic activity that actually moves dollars from urban areas to rural areas.[85] Everything else is the opposite flow, right? ... So maybe that's the other thing I would say is that, again, just the emphasis on the general public, especially in the GTA, and Vancouver areas, and Montreal, just don't recognize the societal benefits that come from a hunting and angling community.[86]

Beyond these practical considerations, for many of my rural participants, hunting and firearms use have become deeply tied to rural Canadian culture, masculinity, and social practices. Given that rural views of masculinity tend to be more traditional, recreational activities, such as hunting and sports shooting, were cited by multiple participants as key pillars of rural mental health. As has already been noted, shooting and hunting are activities that participants often find relaxing. They help them unwind and escape the daily grind.

In our chat, Pierre self-identified as an active member of the Liberal Gun Owners group on Facebook and noted that he is involved in Walk the Talk America, a charity that focuses on preventing firearm suicides by connecting gun owners with mental health resources. Pierre pointed to the stigma around firearm ownership as a reason that some shooters were uneasy about speaking up. "Firearm ownership is normal and normal people use firearms.[87] It doesn't really make someone crazy or whatever because they enjoy shooting." He also noted the importance of shooting as a social practice to rural men's mental health: "there's a lot of guys that this would be their mental health maintenance, for want of the better term. You shoot some guns, you shoot the shit with people, and you relax. Again, if you haven't been around it, you don't necessarily understand it."[88]

Annie also noted that the social practice of shooting was tied to the mental health of rural men. She felt that Canada's current gun laws, which allow authorities to revoke a firearms licence if they have concerns around a gun owner's mental health, created a stigma that made accessing mental health services more difficult for these men. When asked about how she felt about Canada's current gun laws, Annie noted she was mostly in favour of them, with one exception.

> I think there's a definite gap in terms of mental health. So right now, if a gun owner is going through any crisis at all, you think twice before approaching anybody for help, because they're going to take your guns away ... I think we really need to create a mechanism within current gun laws to allow individuals that do need help in mental situations to keep their firearms [and] to know that their firearms are not automatically taken from them.[89]

The association between rural people and firearms meant that for many of my rural participants, attempts by the Trudeau government to make changes to Canada's gun control laws were interpreted through the lens of rural social identity. Rural gun owners saw these changes as policy responses to events in the city, mainly gang-related violence, that ended up targeting primarily rural Canadians. In other words, urban problems resulted in rural punishment. This has been exacerbated by the feeling among gun owners that the NDP and Liberals have abandoned rural Canada. While it is difficult to empirically substantiate these feelings, political scientists have noted that the Liberal Party increasingly relies on urban ridings to win elections.[90]

Jack grew up in Ottawa, though he now lives in western Canada. His time living in the National Capital Region, and his interest in firearm politics made him a political junkie. He was quite sanguine when it came to describing what he sees as the disdain of urban Canadian "progressives" for people like himself. Jack felt that looking down on gun ownership had become "a point of pride for a certain political class" because of the association between gun ownership and the United States: "Canadians don't like guns because it separates us from the Big Bad Americans." He felt gun owners had only one viable political alternative, the Conservatives. As a result, however, Liberal politicians had few incentives to represent their interests. "Justin Trudeau – as much as I despise him; I really despise that man – he's no fool. Why bother catering to a group of people who are so hostile to them who are never going to vote for them (the Liberals) anyways?"[91]

Donal was among the most remotely situated of my rural participants, living in the Yukon Territory. A lifetime NDP supporter, he has been increasingly frustrated with the party's shift towards urban Canada. When discussing the 2020 OIC, Donal did not hide his disdain when noting some of the guns that had been placed on the prohibited list did not fit the government's description of assault-style rifles. "There's single-shot firearms, antique and collector shotguns and rifles, cannons and mortars. Come on. Are cannons and mortars a problem in Toronto?"[92]

This quote shows the symbolic status that Toronto, Canada's biggest city, holds as a stand-in for both urban violence and privilege, in that rural Canadians see politicians placing the needs of urban Canadians ahead of their own. Rural shooters often talked about the unfairness of them losing their serious leisure pursuit because of the failure of these large cities to control their gang problem.

Floyd was permanently injured in a car accident. Since then, he has struggled to adapt to his new limitations. One of the hobbies he was able to carry over from his previous life, however, was shooting. Floyd and his brother set up a specially accessible shooting range in his backyard, where they regularly practise target shooting. When asked what he would like to see changed in Canada's firearms laws, he immediately responded, "evidence-based policy." Like others, Floyd sees the Liberals' gun control platform as a strategy to pander to voters in key ridings urban Canada. "I mean, going after guys like you and me is not going to affect gun crime in Toronto and Vancouver."[93]

Harrison expressed similar sentiments. Like Floyd, he felt that politicians and the media privileged urban perspectives over rural ones, and felt frustrated that the gun control measures, which would largely impact rural Canadians like himself, were being used to try to assuage the fears of crime and gang violence of urban Canadians. Harrison felt misrepresented and stereotyped as a gun owner and did not want this used as an excuse to destroy the hobby he loves.[94]

The theme of loss emerged often in my discussions with rural gun owners. Not only the loss of their property, and the activities and communities that these objects allowed them to engage with, but feelings of a loss of rural Canada. For example, Robert, a former RCMP officer, when talking about changes in gun regulations, mentioned the deteriorating relations between police and the community in his rapidly urbanizing town. He mentioned that the gun range used to be a place where civilians and the police could practise a sport together and learn from one another. Most police officers received little marksmanship training, and the opportunity to exchange tips and knowledge with civilians helped boost their proficiency.

Robert sees this happening less and less now, leading to tensions between the police and civilians. "I mean, just the general, you know, attitude towards police officers now is changed. If you're a policeman, people don't want you around, much less trying to teach you something." He noted that this relationship between police and the community was worse in the United States, where he had friends in law enforcement, but was still happening here. He noted that when the town was smaller, this relationship was less tense and that police officers and gun owners would often shoot together at the range. "It was a great way of building bridges with the community." In a community with bear problems, this could also be a major asset. "When things got dodgy, as a policeman in a rural area, a lot of times we knew who in the community we could rely on."[95]

Teddy grew up on the West Island of Montreal when it was very different from the sprawling suburb of today. There were still farms and wooded areas then, and Teddy fondly remembered, as a child, hunting on the island of Montreal, something unthinkable now. This urbanization, he felt, was making gun owners a minority and thus hurting their political power.[96] While gun ownership is still normative in rural areas, many elements of it have changed, especially as a result of the moral panic surrounding children and firearms caused by school shootings, mainly in the United States.[97] Older participants from rural areas often talked about how normal it was, when they were young, to see children walk around with rifles, something that they acknowledge would be taboo now.

> My ex-husband will talk about, you know, when he was a teenager, his grandfather had property up in Uxbridge. So he'd go stay with Grandma and Grandpa for the weekend, and he'd put his rifle over his shoulder on a sling and go farm to farm saying, "Can I shoot your groundhogs?" And nobody said, you know, nobody called in the SWAT team because some kid was riding his bike with a gun slung over his shoulder on this rural road, right? So, you know, in that sense, we've really changed, you know, from viewing a gun as a tool, or as a piece of sporting equipment.[98]

The feeling that rural Canada was being lost, or was changing rapidly, was always raised in the context of Canada's changing gun regulations. These changes, especially those brought in by the Trudeau government, were seen as the victory of urban Canada over rural Canada, a symbol of the waning power and influence of rural Canadians in Ottawa.

What makes the gun debate such an informative case study of urban-rural politics in Canada is the extent to which the debate is permeated with meanings tied to this divide. The urban Canadian gun owners that I spoke to often struggled with what it means to be a gun owner in the city, despite the long history of urban and suburban hunters and sports shooters in Canada.[99] This suggests that due to the framing of the Canadian gun debate around hunting and farming, which are generally perceived as rural activities, gun ownership has become seen as deviant behaviour for "city people," so much so that the mayor of Canada's biggest city openly asks why anyone in his city would need a gun at all.

Zhi, a young, big-city professional from an immigrant family, summed this up when he said: "In Toronto, gun owners have to be kind of in the shadows. Obviously, there's the prevailing view that guns are bad and whatnot, right?"[100] Karl, born and raised in small-town Alberta, moved to Toronto and has lived in the city for decades. While he's made a lot of friends, he feels that being a gun owner, and being from a rural area, often opens him up to disdain among his friend groups. Gun owner-ship in some spaces carries a stigma attached to other markers of rural identity, like pickup trucks.[101]

These urban gun owners often noted that they struggled to recon-cile negative stereotypes of rural gun owners as "rednecks," "hicks," or "hillbillies" with their own gun ownership, adding to the sense of stigma they felt was attached to their hobby. Rowan, a well-educated veteran from the city, felt pigeonholed by the negative stereotype of the "gun nut." This image of gun owners as "rootin', tootin'" Yosemite Sam characters, or "rednecks from Alabama" did not fit with his personal experiences shooting alongside people he described as being from all walks of life.[102]

Sometimes, this negative perception of rural Canadians intersected with negative views about the United States. I connected quite easily during my interview with Ben, a left-leaning Jewish-Canadian tech worker from the city. As we spoke, we traded Star Wars jokes and talked about life in downtown Montreal, where Ben had attended university. During our discussion, Ben recounted a particularly irksome conversa-tion with his brother in law at a Rosh Hashanah[103] dinner before the 2016 election that he felt typified how gun ownership was understood by the non-gun-owning public. It all started when, during a discussion of Donald Trump's prospects in the upcoming election, his brother-in-law told him that "only rednecks with tattoos and guns vote for Trump." This irked Ben, who happened to have tattoos and guns himself, but described himself as "way more left-liberal than anybody in my fam-ily." Ben saw this as an uncritical projection of American culture onto Canada that misrepresented the community.[104]

The stereotypes and misconceptions that urban gun owners navigate when talking about their hobby with those outside of Canadian gun culture demonstrate the deep ties between gun ownership and rural identity, in the minds of both urban and rural Canadians.

Though less prevalent in my interviews than discussions of rural and urban Canada, discussions about west and east were certainly not absent. The divide, more precisely between central Canada and western Canada, goes back decades, but was exacerbated after 2015 due to the energy policies of the Trudeau government, which westerners felt prioritized the needs of central Canada, and especially Quebec. This divide is important for gun politics due to cultural differences between Alberta, interior British Columbia, and Saskatchewan, which have higher rates of gun ownership, and central Canada, where gun ownership is less prevalent on a per capita basis. As discussed previously, Western alienation emerges from feelings of exclusion from both political decision-making and dominant narratives of what it means to be Canadian. Ideas around Canadian identity have been heavily influenced by the historical and cultural experiences of eastern Canada. Recent changes to gun policy are thus interpreted from within this framework and layered into existing grievances against the federal government.

Amos was a well-travelled urban professional living in Alberta. Before our interview, he proudly showed off the artwork on his wall that his wife had painted. His home office, with all the modern furnishings, would not have looked out of place in downtown Toronto. Yet Amos identified strongly as a westerner and was upset with having his access to firearms limited by people who did not understand his way of life. He described his frustration with what he saw as people in downtown Montreal, with little knowledge of firearms or existing firearm laws, dictating gun policies. He saw the Trudeau government's approach to firearm policy as "pandering to the edges of the bell curve" and part of the broader political polarization dividing the country. This frustration has left him questioning the viability of the Canadian project.

> I don't know if you've ever heard about this, about the creation of Cascadia? No, so Cascadia is, you know, Alberta, Montana, Oregon, Washington, BC, Alaska, Northwest Territories, Saskatchewan, Manitoba. Right? If somebody said, well, these places are going to separate from Canada. I'm in Cascadia. Right? Because I know that I can relate to the people in Cascadia more than I relate to the people out east.[105]

Nicole, another well-educated urban professional from Alberta, also expressed this sense of cultural difference from central Canada. When asked about how it feels to be a gun owner in 2022, Nicole said, "Well, I live in (rural) Alberta. And I think that the general tone to Albertans is very, I wouldn't say Wild West, I'm not going to use that term, but I don't feel as constrained as if I were still live in Vancouver or Toronto or Montreal or even Calgary."[106]

Nicole's quote is particularly interesting, as it demonstrates the interconnections between constructions of rurality and the west. Vancouver and Calgary are excluded from this sense of western identity by virtue of being big cities. The authentic west, then, exists in the mind of westerners as a rural project. This came out in my conversations with Glen, who lives in rural British Columbia. When talking about changes he would like to see in Canada's firearm laws, he noted that the rules surrounding self-defence were not designed with rural and western Canadians in mind, although they faced both the threat of predation from wildlife and rural crime.

> I think we have this demented idea that there's always going to be somebody there to save us. Look at Canada: 35 million people rattling around in this gigantic landmass full of sharp things that are happy to eat you, both people and wildlife. I mean, BC is very different from Ontario ... You're not the apex predator out here.[107]

The gun debate in Canada is intrinsically tied to a broader sense that rural and western Canada have been left behind or are underrepresented by Canada's existing political institutions. In the eyes of many of my rural participants, gun owners, like rural Canadians in general, have been abandoned by Ottawa to win support in the vote-rich urban ridings of the GTA, Metro Vancouver, and Montreal. The continued attacks on gun ownership are integrated into a wider belief system about rural decline. This poses a challenge for the gun rights movement in Canada, which cannot count on rural overrepresentation in political institutions to shore up support, as their American counterparts can.[108]

Hunting and Conservation in Canada

As I have demonstrated so far in this chapter, the Canadian pro-gun movement faces an uphill battle when it comes to advocating for gun ownership in Canada. But that is not to say that the movement, or portions of the movement, have not enjoyed successes. The conservation movement has been the most successful wing of the pro-gun movement in Canada, which can sometimes lead to tension between hunters and sports shooters in the gun debate. In framing legislation, the government often goes out of its way to present its policies as unthreatening to Canadian hunters, as the opening quote from this chapter shows.

But how has the conservation movement succeeded in establishing broad support, or at least tolerance, for hunting in the minds of the Canadian public? What can this tell us about how movements navigate and shape the political opportunity structure? How can it help us to imagine a different and less antagonistic relationship between gun owners and the government?

Hunting seems to occupy a revered position in the Canadian gun debate, with even highly pro-control politicians seeking to frame their policies as avoiding targeting Canada's hunters. In a press conference announcing his assault-style weapons ban in May of 2020, Trudeau, for example, used the talking point, "You don't need an AR-15 to bring down a deer."[109] Later, when presenting Bill C-21 and the handgun freeze, Minister of Public Safety Marco Mendicino went out of his way to claim that the bill would not impact hunters.[110]

This likely has to do with the place that hunting holds in the public consciousness of North Americans, as well as the fact that the hunting rights of Indigenous Canadians are protected through treaties with the Crown. The clout that hunting wields can be tied to its long history in Canada, and the success that the conservation movement has had in integrating private, non-commercial hunting with wildlife conservation in North America.

While subsistence hunting was long practised by Canada's Indigenous peoples, and settlers often supplemented their diet with wild game through hunting, by the late nineteenth century, hunting was being transformed from a commercial or survival activity to a recreational one, especially among Canada's growing middle class.[111]

The European model of engaging with wildlife in North American post-colonization was extractive. Wildlife was seen as an abundant and inexhaustible resource, so European settlers saw no reason to protect it. This attitude led over time to the mass extinction of many wild-animal populations, and the destruction of the peoples that had relied on these resources for millennia. In the late nineteenth century, there was an "awakening," partially sparked by the destruction of the wild buffalo in the American West. At the time, a number of species were on the brink of extinction, including elk, wild turkeys, certain species of ducks, and even the iconic white-tailed deer.[112] This environmental crisis provoked a shift in thinking from the "citizen-conqueror" to the "citizen-steward."[113] The North American Model of Wildlife Conservation emerged as hunting shifted from a commercial to recreational activity based upon the ideals of "democratic access to nature, the sustainable use of wildlife," and "a European standard of fair chase hunting."[114] The model was developed in the nineteenth century by a community of American and Canadian sportsmen who founded hundreds of clubs and societies to protect wildlife.[115]

President Theodore Roosevelt was a major proponent of this model in the United States,[116] setting aside 148 million acres of land for national forests, creating the Forest Service to manage public land, and establishing five national parks, eighteen national monuments, and an extensive system of national refuges based on the policy principles set out by the Boone and Crocket Club, a sportsmen's group, in the late nineteenth century.[117] Canada, which faced some of the same problems, looked south for answers, and adopted the same model. Sir Wilfrid Laurier created the Canadian Commission for the Conservation of Natural Resources in 1909. The same year, Roosevelt hosted the North American Conservation Conference, attended by a significant Canadian delegation.

In Canada, much of the momentum behind the adoption of this model was provided by two different sources. At the federal level, bureaucrats in Ottawa pushed the Canadian government towards broader commitments to conservation by creating the National Parks Branch and committing Canada to treaties like the Migratory Bird Convention. At the regional and local levels, however, this work was done by local fish and game clubs, made up of enthusiastic middle-class sportsmen. In addition to undertaking conservation work locally, these groups formed local and provincial lobbies to push for conservation laws.[118] As a result, the North American model has been heavily institutionalized in provincial conservation bureaucracies, in the national and provincial parks systems, and in the regulation of hunting and angling.

The North American Model of conservation holds that wildlife "is owned by no one but held in trust by government for the benefit of all citizens." In Canada, this meshed with the idea of Crown stewardship. This is important, as it means that wildlife cannot be privatized and exploited for financial gain. It also establishes the role of the government in protecting wild species.[119] As a result, the model shut down or heavily regulated the exploitative practice of hunting and fishing for market and guaranteed democratic access to wild populations. "The objective became the pursuit of the animal and a profound engagement with nature, not the pursuit of profit."[120]

As a result, North America has a vast amount of public or Crown land that can be used by recreationists. This "anti-commercialization ethic" distinguishes the North American Model from Europe, where most land is owned by private entities and hunters must pay to access it.[121] It also means that the model places a significant focus on avoiding waste, a notable feature of commercial hunting. The pursuit of high-quality meat was the new guiding focus, and the model eliminated wasteful practices like hunting elk for their teeth.[122]

The ethic of "fair chase" emerged among the upper classes of Europe, where hunting opportunities were mostly limited to the privileged class. In North America, however, the democratic principles of the North American Model guaranteed that hunting could be enjoyed by a wider swathe of the population, who adopted the tenets of the fair chase model.

Finally, the principle of scientific management is key.[123] This emerged from the nineteenth-century fascination with the natural world. In the 1930s, Aldo Leopold, an influential professor of game management at the University of Wisconsin, established the modern scientific management of wildlife, and the field of wildlife science, which remains central to conservation practices.[124]

The North American Model has produced a unique set of institutions for the international management of wildlife across the continent. For example, in 1916, the United States and Canada signed the Migratory Bird Protection Act to protect birds that move between Canada, the United States, and Mexico. Under this treaty, conservation dollars are sent where they are needed, regardless of where the money originates. This means that American hunters fund conservation programs in Canada to protect Canada geese, ducks, and other migratory birds.[125]

It was American sportsmen who first championed the idea of national parks. Its first recorded proponent was George Catlin, a hunter, angler, and artist, who raised the idea in 1832. Anglers and hunters were major supporters of the national parks model, even though hunting and fishing would eventually be banned in these settings.[126]

The model has helped to restore many wild populations in North America and create a substantial tourism economy, effectively balancing the economic needs with the capacities of the ecosystem. Wildlife management is taught at over 500 schools across North America. "While appearing paradoxical to some, and unacceptable to others, the integration of hunting within conservation practices has been recognized internationally as a successful approach under specific circumstances, offering realistic long-term solutions to wildlife depletion and landscape impoverishment."[127] The ethos of the model has spawned a sizable advocacy network of hunters across the continent, who can be mobilized to defend habitat when it is threatened by commercial interests.[128]

For provincial governments in Canada tasked with managing natural resources, hunters are an important ally. Wildlife populations, when not properly managed, can have adverse impacts on human populations in fields like agriculture and transportation. Sustainable harvesting, based on the principles of scientific management, can help regulators to manage those risks. For example, rabbit populations can devastate crops. While most people think of hunting as occurring deep in the woods, much of it takes place on agricultural land and can help farmers to manage nuisance animals that would otherwise be detrimental to food production.[129]

Another negative human-wildlife interaction is road collisions. In Saskatchewan, there are between 30,000 and 35,000 collisions between wildlife and cars every year. While this seems high, without hunting, the toll could be substantially higher.[130]

As a result, research has shown that North American hunters and anglers are more likely to engage in wildlife conservation than the rest of the population. For example, research in New York State showed that hunters and anglers were four to five times more likely to have participated than the average resident.[131] In addition to providing tens of millions of dollars per year to provincial wildlife agencies through licensing, Canadian hunters volunteered more than one million hours annually for wildlife habitat projects and provided important biological samples for researchers.[132] In British Columbia, for example, the Habitat Conservation Trust Foundation, funded through taxes on hunting, angling, and trapping licences, spends $5–6 million a year acquiring new land for habitat protection.[133] Since the model's adoption, wildlife conservation groups, foundations, societies, and clubs have collected billions of dollars to put towards protecting wild spaces.[134] The conservation model has led to the restoration of Canada geese, white-tailed deer, pronghorn and bighorn sheep, and wild turkeys.[135] Further, some scholars have argued that hunters may be essential to building momentum on the political right to tackle the climate crisis.[136]

Hunters also engage in private land management for the purposes of hunting. In southern Ontario, for example, most land is private, not Crown territory. But this does not preclude wildlife management. Hunters on private land, eager to have habitat in which to hunt, are responsible for maintaining thousands of acres of habitat across the province.

> A lot of them (landowners) have forest management plans. A lot of them are considering those lands for not only their hunting purposes, but to responsibly manage those lands over long periods of time for the benefit of wildlife game and non-game species. So, when we talk about things like biodiversity and natural landscapes and all of these things that come into that environmental conversation, that becomes a really important factor in the kind of landscape for Ontario, and the protection of Fish and Wildlife Resources.[137]

This is not to say that the North American Model is without flaw. One of the largest challenges that the model will face in the twenty-first century is the need to include Indigenous partnerships in land and wildlife management, to abide by the commitments made to the United Nations Declaration on the Rights of Indigenous Peoples (UNDRIP), which make it an obligation to "share governance with Indigenous governments."[138] This will also include making room for Indigenous epistemologies in the scientific management of wildlife populations. Thus far, British Columbia has taken a leading role in this regard, with its *Together for Wildlife Strategy*, which created an advisory council including many Indigenous experts and leaders.[139]

Despite these challenges, the success of this model both in restoring Canadian wildlife and securing public buy-in, provides an important lesson: involving advocacy groups in the development of regulation can benefit all parties, creating a win-win situation. For example, hunter-conservationist groups receive both collective and selective benefits from the mandatory licensing of hunters, and thus are incentivized to work with the government to make these programs as effective as possible. Collectively, they benefit from the abundance of wild game populations created by these policies. Selectively, they benefit from a share of revenues from licensing fees. This has a positive impact on the rest of the community. According to Darrel Crabbe of the Saskatchewan Wildlife Federation, 30 per cent of all licence sales from hunting, angling, and trapping, are invested into the Fish and Wildlife Development Fund to pay for conservation projects. These projects impact land used by thousands of people across the province, not just hunters and anglers.[140]

By allowing hunters, trappers, anglers, and the groups that represent them to be actively involved in the regulation of their sport or hobby, the system gains built-in buy-in. Most hunters I spoke to were deeply proud of their conservation work and the role that hunting plays in protecting Canada's wildlife. Involving hunters in the political process and having an open dialogue between the regulator and regulated helps to develop strong policies and institutions.

The conservation movement has also leveraged this model to secure wide public buy-in for hunting across North America. In the United States, Responsive Management and the National Shooting Sports Foundations have found consistent and widespread support for hunting among Americans since they began monitoring public attitudes in 1995. A recent 2019 study found that 80 per cent of Americans approved of regulated hunting.[141] While this data is harder to find in Canada, a 2022 survey from a polling company in Vancouver found that 62 per

cent of Canadians approved of hunting animals for meat.[142] Further,
a survey of Canadians conducted in 2017 by Nanos on behalf of the
Ontario Federation of Anglers and Hunters found that 90 per cent of
Canadians agreed that wildlife management should allow for "regulated sustainable activities" like hunting, fishing, and trapping.[143]

Influence of the Political Opportunity Structure on the Movement

There are many factors that influence the success of a social movement
or advocacy group. While some are within its power to control, many
are not. This political opportunity structure influences not only how
movements act, but how they imagine themselves and make rights-
based claims.

The political opportunity structure in Canada is hostile to the wider
pro-gun movement. Canadian courts have been unwilling to read any
rights to firearm possession into the Canadian Constitution or Charter,
or to accept the natural-rights argument to own guns for the purpose
of self-defence. The structure of the Canadian Parliament makes it easy
for parties to pass laws limiting gun ownership, without the multiple
veto actors present in the American system. Parties and interest groups
work against the movement, which has largely been captured by the
Conservative Party, without any reasonable prospect of defection –
barring a rise of support for the People's Party of Canada, which at
the time of writing seems unlikely. Further, the Canadian system lacks
the built-in protections for rural communities in the American system.
Canadian federalism means that the pro-gun movement struggles to
bring its greatest advantage into play: its substantial grassroots membership across Canada.

At the same time, hunters have enjoyed considerable advocacy success, given the accomplishments of the conservation movement and
the integration of hunting with the country's wildlife-management
framework. By institutionalizing the movement, they have been able
to protect hunting and fishing in Canada from the rise of hostile coun-
termovements like the environmental movement or animal rights
movement.

The relationship between hunter-conservationist groups and provincial governments also points to a better way of doing gun politics,
characterized by compromise and cooperation. It demonstrates that
relationships between regulator and regulated can be quite fruitful for
both parties, if both sides engage in good faith.

5

From Pastime to Politics

I just, I believe I'm a good Canadian citizen and I respect the laws of the land. Why do I keep having things taken away, or potentially taken away, from me, when I and 99 per cent of my fellow Canadians have done no wrong?[1]

Gun owners in Canada are a highly regulated population. Despite this, we know little about what Canadian gun owners think about gun control. In the public debate, the voices of gun owners are rarely heard. We may hear, briefly, from groups that speak on their behalf, and sometimes from the owners of gun-related businesses; but rarely are the voices of ordinary Canadian gun owners quoted in media or recorded by public opinion polls. As we will see, adding the voices of gun owners to the conversation injects important nuance into the discourse on guns in Canada. Rather than sabre-rattling extremists, my data shows that many gun owners in Canada are broadly supportive of the gun-control measures that existed prior to the election of the Trudeau government in 2015, such as licensing and safe-storage laws. At the same time, gun owners expressed intense levels of frustration with policies that they see as motivated by political machinations rather than a genuine concern for public safety. These policies lead gun owners to feel targeted by their own government. Among conservative, western, and rural gun owners, these grievances layer into feelings of alienation, rural decline, and anti-Trudeau sentiment that can be observed in other policy areas, such as environmental policy. For urban, liberal, or left-leaning gun owners, the experience of becoming a policy externality leaves them feeling alienated from the broader political or social groups to which they belong.

This chapter begins by presenting two key findings from my survey of Canadian gun owners. These themes are then further unpacked using data from my semi-structured interviews with members of the gun-owning community in Canada. As we will see, the political opportunity structure discussed in the last chapter has led to a unique Canadian model of gun rights, distinct from the American conceptualization. Gun owners in Canada see themselves as being targeted by politicians, the media, and the law. Their secondary, and as we will see, sometimes direct experience with this mistreatment motivates much of the advocacy among gun owners in Canada.

Citizenship and a Canadian Model of Gun Rights – Between a Right and a Privilege

Is there a space between a right and a privilege? Supporters of the CCFR proudly display shirts declaring that "Firearm Rights are Human Rights." At the same time, Canadian officials, and many of the gun owners I spoke to, noted that gun ownership is a privilege in Canada, not a constitutional right.

While the phrases "firearm rights" and "gun rights" immediately conjure an image of the American Second Amendment, I contend that an alternative model of gun rights has emerged north of the border. It is shaped not by Jeffersonian Republicanism and the fear of a tyrannical government, but instead by the very Canadian expectation that law-abiding citizens deserve fair and reasonable treatment by their government.

Two key themes emerged from my survey of Canadian gun owners. First, gun owners are broadly supportive of Canada's gun laws as they stood before the election of the Trudeau government. Second, Canadian gun owners feel marginalized by the popular discourse. They believe that the public image of gun owners is skewed and that the media rarely gives gun owners a fair shake. From these two trends, we can observe the formation of a distinct gun-rights ideology in Canada: one that does not position firearm rights as absolute for the purposes of individual or community self-defence but is centred on the idea that the government should deal with its citizens in a fair and just manner.

Gun owners who completed my online survey were asked about how they perceived the efficacy of certain policies at reducing crime involving firearms. Gun owners' support for different firearm policies was mixed. Handgun bans and assault-weapon bans, measures proclaimed as policy priorities by the Trudeau government at the time of the survey, were the least popular, with 91 per cent and 89 per cent of respondents, respectively, believing them to be "not effective at all." Support was higher for licensing and safe-storage laws. Most participants felt that firearms licensing was either moderately (19.4 per cent), very (18 per cent), or extremely (17.5 per cent) effective at combatting gun crime.

Table 5.1. Perceived Efficacy of Firearm Policies by Gun Owners in Online Survey

	Not Effective at All	Slightly Effective	Moderately Effective	Very Effective	Extremely Effective
Licensing	30%	15%	19%	18%	18%
Registration	58%	16%	12%	7%	8%
Authorization to Transport (ATT) for Restricted Firearms	64%	11%	9%	7%	8%
Magazine Limits	71%	11%	8%	5%	5%
Safe-Storage Laws	22%	15%	24%	21%	18%
Handgun Bans	91%	4%	2%	1%	2%
Assault-Weapons Bans	87%	5%	3%	2%	2%

Similarly, safe-storage laws received strong support, with a significant majority of participants answering that these laws are moderately (23.7 per cent), very (20.9 per cent), or extremely (18.2 per cent) effective at combatting gun crime (See Table 5.1).

These results were surprising given the sampling method, which involved using the mailing lists of pro-gun groups. The idea that around 60 per cent of gun owners involved in, or at least connected to, firearm-related advocacy in Canada approve of licensing and safe-storage laws is noteworthy.

The gun enthusiasts I surveyed did not feel well-represented in the public discourse or mainstream media. A majority (50 per cent) of participants stated that the public image of gun owners in Canada was very unfair, with a further 38 per cent describing it as unfair. Only 3 per cent felt that gun owners were well represented in Canada. The data on the media was even more troubling. A larger majority (62 per cent) of participants felt that gun owners are portrayed very unfairly in the media, while another 32 per cent felt they were portrayed unfairly. Less than 2 per cent of respondents felt that gun owners were portrayed either fairly or very fairly in the media.

The survey also asked respondents about the values that they attach to gun ownership. While American gun owners often associate firearm ownership with self-protection or political values like freedom, Canadian gun owners were less likely to mention this association. While completing the survey, participants were asked "When you think of gun ownership, what values come to mind?" Rather than present participants with a list of values, they had the chance to write them in themselves. The answers were analysed and grouped into categories. The most common cited values were variations of responsibility (9.47 per cent), freedom (3.92 per cent), safety[2] (3.81 per cent), and respect (2.27 per cent).

Table 5.2. Values Associated with Gun Ownership

Value	Occurrences	Weighted Percentage (%)
Responsibility	5,181	9.47
Freedom	2,143	3.92
Safety	2,081	3.81
Respect	1,243	2.27
Family	1,139	2.08

N = 13,596

Examining the full text of some of the answers provides context, as participants reported associating their hobby with: "heritage, responsibility, love of outdoors and wildlife" and "honesty, integrity, self-control, discipline" alongside values like "freedom, independence, self-sufficiency." Sometimes the two values were cited together: "freedom and responsibility that comes from ownership." The results are particularly interesting for two reasons. First, they reaffirm findings in the existing literature that compares Canadian and American gun owners, demonstrating that while firearm ownership in the United States tends to be associated with an American civic religion that places liberty and freedom at the apex of its hierarchy of values, Canadians value firearms as tools of recreation and enjoyment.[3] The fact that participants cited "responsibility" more than twice as often as "freedom" lends credence to this observation, though a significant number of gun owners do associate firearms with freedom and liberty, suggesting that this may not be a solely American phenomenon.

Second, the findings point to the influence of key actors like the government and gun rights organizations in framing the values that participants attach to gun ownership and disciplining the hobby. This need emerges from the unique nature of firearm ownership as a form of contested serious leisure. While sports like triathlon, or hobbies like dog-showing, may elicit confusion, derision, and bewilderment in people outside the community, they are generally seen as socially acceptable and harmless. Gun ownership, on the other hand, has been heavily scrutinized in Canada since the 1970s, when the contemporary battle lines on gun politics were drawn.[4] This stems from the fact that firearms are potentially deadly tools. But it also points to the politicization of the issue of gun control in Canada. In the post-Columbine era, depictions of gun owners in the news media have also been stigmatizing, especially given the efforts of politicians like former Prime Minister Trudeau to frame the debate in American-style language.[5]

The image of the "responsible gun owner" thus emerges from two opposite forces. On one hand, it is a way for regulators to discipline the community. These values are inculcated into new gun owners by the CFSC/CRFSC process, which all gun owners in Canada must pass through to acquire their licence, as well as by hunter education courses, which are necessary to procure hunting licences and game tags. These courses go to great lengths to stress the themes of safety and responsibility to prospective gun owners. While the class is ostensibly about the skills needed to own and use firearms, or to hunt safely and ethically, substantial time is devoted to instilling a shared ethos of responsibility in participants and to emphasizing the consequences of irresponsibility.[6]

Advocacy and conservation organizations also work to instil this ethos. The gun-owning community is highly self-policing, as participants are aware of the high level of scrutiny their serious leisure pursuit is subjected to by outsiders. It is not uncommon at gun ranges to see gun owners berating others for relatively minor safety infractions. The ethos of responsibility and the image of the responsible, law-abiding gun owner that is central to the movement's messaging are ways of managing the relationship between insiders and outsiders, as well as drawing boundaries between the lawful use of firearms and their unlawful use by criminals.

During my longer Zoom interviews, I also asked participants about the values they associated with firearm ownership. The most common values mentioned were responsibility (46.4 per cent) and community (46.4 per cent). Freedom/liberty was a distant third (23.8 per cent), with sport (9.5 per cent) and conservation (9.5 per cent) also being mentioned.

The centrality of responsibility to the ethos of the gun-owning community in Canada supports the assertion that gun owners see themselves as highly regulated, responsible citizens. Even those who cited freedom and liberty as important values went to great pains to distinguish themselves from American gun owners. For example, Steffan expressed support for George Orwell's assertion that firearms were an important signifier of a democratic society, while at the same time distancing himself from the American model of gun rights.

> Politically, I'm not a survivalist or a Second Amendment type freak, but I do kind of subscribe to the caution, as it was expressed by George Orwell, who is as left as you can get, who said the "shotgun hanging on the wall of the English cottage is the essence of liberty."[7] When it's gone, we will no longer be a free people.
>
> I really love living in an *unarmed* society, but I would hate to live in a *disarmed* society. I really like going to the grocery store and knowing

that the people I'm interacting with are highly unlikely to be armed. That would be a crappy way to live. I'm big on gun control and keeping things in your safe at home. But you don't have to look further than our history to see what happens with methodical disarmament. Acadians were disarmed before being expelled. There was a very concerted effort over decades to disarm Indigenous people in this country before residential schools became mandatory. The two are not explicitly connected, but one wonders whether had the Indigenous people not been so thoroughly disarmed, whether they would have stood for the RCMP coming and dragging off children. I don't want to be alarmist about it, but I think that a population that is responsibly armed is the sort of society that I want to live in.[8]

Steffan's distinction between an unarmed and disarmed population bears highlighting, as it demonstrates a key fault-line between the American and Canadian model of firearm rights, and a middle ground between a gun-free society and the dangerously unregulated reality south of the border. It also shows that Canadian gun owners do not conceive of this right as unlimited or beyond regulation. Steffan expressed support for safe-storage laws, and his desire for a "responsibly armed" society. This sentiment was echoed by others. Many participants, like Robert, reiterated the sentiment that gun ownership in Canada is a privilege. "Not everybody should have firearms, so there needs to be a vetting process. I'm not convinced that the one we've got is a bad thing."[9]

Once again Robert's answer demonstrates the idea that gun owners conceive access to guns as a privilege, and one that should come with reasonable limitations. Mani expressed a similar sentiment: "I know it's not a right in Canada. It's a privilege and a privilege can be taken away. But I believe as long as you're following the law, and you're not hurting anybody, I believe the government should not be attacking us in any way."[10]

Conceding that access to guns is a privilege comes with the expectation of fair treatment and that limitations on this privilege should be based on sound evidence. This explicit demand for evidence-based policy was echoed by almost one-quarter of my interview participants, who felt that the Trudeau government was making policy based on "knee-jerk reactions" to criminal violence.[11]

Not all of the gun owners that I spoke to shared the view that Canada's existing gun laws were a good thing. This was especially the case among older gun owners, or people who had been part of the community since before the major legislative changes of the 1990s. Sheldon Clare, former president of the NFA, felt that the very purpose of his organization was to "attack the essence of the Canadian gun control program, which was the Liberal firearms licence." He argued that gun licensing was "the absolute worst thing about this [gun control]. The licensing of firearms owners is not a badge of honour. It is a chain. It is an albatross. That is the worst part of the legislation."[12] Clare, and others I spoke to who shared his view, felt that licensing was a step on the road to compromise that would only lead to other restrictions.

At the same time, several participants I spoke to did subscribe to the "badge of honour" model of gun ownership. Several expressed the trust they felt in other members of the community, all having been vetted by police. In a sense, having a gun licence was seen as an elite form of citizenship: a guarantee of a person's trustworthiness. Rod, a law-enforcement professional, typified this view: "If you are a licenced gun owner in this country, I feel like there's a certain amount of trust that I have in you ... I know that you've been vetted, I know you've gone through the process."[13]

While there are disagreements within the community, the majority of the gun owners I spoke to and surveyed were broadly supportive of Canada's existing gun control regime. While they spoke of gun rights, they envisioned these rights not as an absolute, inviolable principle, but rather the right of citizens to fair and honest treatment by the government. They were deeply angered by changes made by the Trudeau government, which they saw as motivated by politics and culture war dynamics rather than sound evidence. They felt targeted.

Targeted

Canadian gun owners feel strongly that the public image of their community is skewed. Participants in my online survey were asked whether they felt that "the public image of gun owners in Canada is fair." The results were stark. Only 3.6 per cent felt that the public image of gun owners in Canada was either "very fair" or "fair." Another 7.1 per cent felt that this image was "neither fair nor unfair." At the same time, 33.4 per cent of participants felt that this image was "unfair," and 44.1 per cent "very unfair."

I sought to probe this feeling further in my qualitative interviews with Canadian gun owners. My participants expressed feeling unfairly targeted by three main groups. The first was progressive politicians, with former Prime Minister Justin Trudeau and former Public Safety Minister Bill Blair being mentioned most often. But gun owners also felt targeted by the "mainstream" or "legacy" media, typically the CBC, and by the inconsistencies and administrative burdens in the Canadian gun control system.

By Politicians

Given the former prime minister's frequent statements and legislative changes regarding gun ownership in Canada, Justin Trudeau became a symbol of what many of my participants felt is a concerted attack on Canadian gun owners. This is not unique to the gun-owning community, but is prevalent across the political right, on issues like oil and gas, western alienation, and other culture-war issues.

Trudeau was particularly unpopular in the west. This is partially a legacy of his namesake. Trudeau's father, Pierre-Elliot Trudeau, had also been a polarizing figure during his time as prime minister, angering western Canada with his decision to create the National Energy Program. Like his father, Justin Trudeau enjoyed little support in Manitoba, Saskatchewan, Alberta, and the interior of British Columbia, even at the height of his popularity in 2015.

Trudeau's environmental policies angered western Canada. His opposition to pipeline construction was seen as an attack on Alberta's oil sector. The Federal Carbon Tax was viewed as disproportionately impacting rural Canadians, who could not easily switch to public transit, and western Canadians who could not take advantage of western Canada's comparatively dense network of rail connections.

Scandals like the SNC-Lavalin affair, in which the prime minister was accused of interfering in the justice system to secure preferential treatment for a Quebecois business, and the prime minister's lack of willingness to call out xenophobic policies like the infamous Bill 21 in Quebec, gave westerners the impression that the Liberals were the party of central Canada.

Pandemic restrictions, which were deeply unpopular in the west, and the decision to use the Emergencies Act to disperse Freedom Convoy activists in Ottawa, further raised the ire and tenor of the debate. That these restrictions were put into place at a time when the government was creating policy to expand the role of government in regulating misinformation on the internet was viewed with deep suspicion among Conservatives.

The gun owners I spoke to felt targeted by the policies of the Trudeau government. Some accused former Prime Minister Trudeau of deploying "misinformation and disinformation" about guns and their owners to justify his proposed firearm policies, such as the ban on "assault-style weapons" introduced by order-in-council in 2020.[14]

The use of the term assault weapon, or "assault-style weapon," is a major point of contention in the gun debate. The term, originally used as a marketing technique by gun manufacturers, was picked up by pro-control advocates in the United States, frustrated by the lack of progress in regulating handguns, which are responsible for the overwhelming majority of gun deaths in America.[15] American advocates noted in publicly available documents that the use of the term "assault weapon" was a deliberate attempt to confuse the public: "The weapons' menacing looks, coupled with the public's confusion over fully automatic machine guns versus semi-automatic assault weapons – anything that looks like a machine gun is assumed to be a machine gun – can only increase the chance of public support for restrictions on these weapons."[16] The term is perhaps even less appropriate in Canada. While it may be reasonable to cast aspersion on the need for a thirty-round magazine in a semi-automatic rifle, Canadian gun laws have prohibited high-capacity magazines since the 1990s, limiting detachable magazines used in semi-automatic rifles to five rounds, half the capacity of the strictest state-level American legislation at the time of writing.

Donal's frustration with the prime minister's framing techniques was shared by others, like Roger, a retired electrician living in northern Canada, who noted that while usually wary of political participation, he could no longer keep quiet about the gun issue: "They are creating a lot of fear in people; a lot of rhetoric, a lot of it misleading. I'm a union electrician, okay? And one of our mottos was in the union you keep your eyes down, your mouth shut, and you'll go home at the end of the day. I can't keep still for this Trudeau stuff."[17]

Similarly, Ava accused the prime minister of using misinformation to buttress his firearms stance. "Every time that Justin Trudeau opens his mouth, I wish someone would come up and say: 'Here's what he said, here are the facts.' Because as a gun owner, you just sit there and you listen, and you get so angry."[18]

Another common refrain among gun owners was that the government's announcements regarding changes to gun laws were a convenient distraction when the government was facing a crisis, such as the scandal in 2019, when several photos emerged of Trudeau wearing blackface.[19] Bruce used the term "channel changer" to describe the government's pattern of announcing changes to firearm policies in the wake of major scandals: "When the government has nothing good to talk about, or they're getting slammed by another scandal, the channel changer is always, 'hey, let's talk about guns.' It distracts people; it's a very emotional subject."[20]

Some gun owners I spoke to learned to shoot in the military or law enforcement. During their careers, or following their retirement, they became interested in hunting and sports shooting. Those who had served their country now expressed feeling betrayed by their treatment at the government's hands. Rowan, who owned rifles now prohibited by the OIC, expressed this during our interview.

> I signed up to serve my country. I signed on the dotted line. I gave the government a blank cheque; they could do with my life whatever they wanted to. And they trained me how to use firearms safely, probably the best training you can get in the country. And now it's like "you can't have that rifle anymore. Because we think it's dangerous, and you're a criminal. And so, we're going to take it away from you."[21]

Joe, another veteran, expressed a similar feeling of betrayal by his government:

> I stood up for my country, I put my life on the line for this country. And I put my life on the line based on the ideals that were in place when I served. I would not serve under this Liberal government. I followed all the rules, all the regulations, I've jumped through all the hoops. And still, I'm branded as a criminal. I'm branded as a, what was it that Bill Blair called us all? Extremists? Because we own guns.[22]

Here, Joe references comments made during a Liberal Party conference by former Public Safety Minister Bill Blair, which were widely shared in gun-owning circles. When discussing red flag laws, the minister was quoted as saying, "Not every person who is in the gun lobby is an extremist, but anybody extremist is in the gun lobby,"[23] a strange take on a deeply Islamophobic and ahistorical saying that was often repeated during the war on terror: that "not every Muslim is a terrorist, but every terrorist is a Muslim." No mainstream media outlets reported these comments. For gun owners, this statement typified the vilification to which they have become accustomed and which has gone largely unreported to the Canadian public.

These feelings of vilification were often the most emotionally tense parts of the interviews. Claude, a gun collector from Montreal who had never actually fired a gun in his life, described the bureaucratic entanglements involved with having a collection of his size. These included allowing the RCMP to inspect his home and to conduct interviews with his wife to assess his character.

> But Christ, leave us alone after that. Stop using us to drum up votes amongst people who don't know, in urban areas, who are afraid of the gun shootings and the violence of the gangs. Gun collectors and target shooters, we have as much relation to those criminals as a Martian with somebody from Uranus.[24]

Claude was far from the only participant to express feeling hated and misrepresented by his own government. Enzo also spoke along similar lines: "I don't think the Liberals realize, you know, Justin Trudeau realizes that as much as he hates us, we're actually very good people, because we understand what we could lose if we screw up."[25] Here, of course, Enzo is referencing the vetting and licensing that gun owners like him went through to enjoy their hobby. Like Claude, Enzo and others felt they had complied with more than their fair share of bureaucracy, and did not appreciate being continually attacked.

> Could you imagine any other identifiable minority group in Canada be treated in such a way? Now I understand my involvement in this minority group is voluntary. Nay, I paid and applied to be in this minority group. But you searched my background, you know? So, to be treated like how we are treated in Canada, it's appalling.[26]

By the Media

The gun owners I surveyed and spoke to were highly critical of the media, and especially the CBC, which is a common target of ire on the right in Canada. They saw the media as complicit in the circulation of misinformation about gun owners and accused media outlets of uncritically parroting the government's soundbites on gun control policy.

Participants in my online survey were asked: "Do you think the public image of gun owners in Canada is fair?" Participants' answers gave a strong indication that gun owners feel maligned in the mainstream media in Canada. Only 1.4 per cent of participants felt that gun owners were presented either "very fairly" or "fairly" in the media, and 4.1 per cent felt the media's coverage of gun owners was neither fair nor unfair, while many felt that gun owners were treated unfairly by the media (28.3 per cent) and a majority very unfairly (54.1 per cent). These feelings were echoed in my qualitative interviews with gun owners. My participants' criticisms of the media fell into three broad categories. First, that members of the media often do not possess the requisite knowledge to talk about firearms. Second, that the conversation in the media lacks nuance and often fails to present both sides of the story. Finally, that the media often participates directly in the vilification of gun owners.

The first complaint, that the media often presents misinformation on firearms, is in my opinion valid, with some notable exceptions. As an expert on firearm policy, and someone who through the course of my research has become reasonably familiar with the functioning of firearms, I am also often frustrated by the way that guns are depicted in the media, though this is slowly changing. Given the status and symbolic and emotional significance of the AR-15 in the gun debate, participants often complained about the way this gun was discussed in the media. "I heard one CBC guy saying that you shouldn't have an AR-15 to go hunt deer because you can blow the heads right off? Well, in most provinces, you can't even hunt with an AR-15. The calibre is too small."[27]

The commonly heard refrain that the AR-15 is inappropriate for hunting combines three popular misconceptions: first, that hunting is the only legitimate use for firearms; second, that deer hunting is the only type of hunting; and third, that the AR-15 is a uniquely powerful firearm. As we have already discussed, sports shooting, including the modern action sports like Three-Gun, were considered for decades a legitimate purpose for gun ownership by the RCMP and Canadian Government. AR-15s are most often used by sports shooters in Canada. Further, there is little difference between an AR-15 limited to a five-round magazine, and other semi-automatic firearms. The weight of the literature demonstrates that it is bans on high-capacity magazines, which Canada has had in place since 1991, that save lives, not bans on specific types of firearms.[28]

The .223-calibre round that most AR-15s use is simply not powerful enough to ethically harvest larger animals like deer. In fact, modern intermediate cartridges like the .223 were developed because they are *less* powerful than older military rounds like the .30–06, commonly used by hunters to harvest deer, elk, and moose. Armies simply did not see the sense in providing their rank-and-file soldiers with ammunition that could fire accurately at long distances, when most firefights occurred within a few hundred yards. Thus, smaller rounds that weighed less and could be produced more cheaply won the day.

AR-15s, or other rifles chambered in .223-calibre rounds, are commonly used for hunting in the United States and Canada, but not for deer hunting. Predators like coyotes, for example, can cause significant problems for farmers. Some hunters also take part in predator hunting to harvest furs. Given the speed of predatory canines, quick follow-up shots are sometimes needed. Further, given that some predators, like coyotes, are best hunted at night, hunters will often use technologies like illuminated scopes or even night-vision accessories. The AR-15 lends itself well to both purposes, given the ease with which accessories can be attached to the platform and the semi-automatic mechanism.

Gun owners also felt that reporters either were not familiar with, or did not make enough effort to stress, the differences between American and Canadian gun laws. Debbie, for example, felt that the media often presented the Canadian gun problem using the same lens as the

American issue. "They constantly say that we are the US, which we are nothing like. The US *does* need to get stronger gun laws. I totally disagree with how they do it. But I don't live in the US. I live in Canada."[29]

Similarly, they felt that the media made little effort to distinguish between crime guns and those owned by licensed firearms owners. To gun owners, this created the impression in the minds of the public that licensed gun owners were the ones committing gun crimes in large Canadian cities, or that handguns diverted from them through theft or illegal sales were supplying the arsenal for criminals. Talia, who lives in Toronto, took up shooting sports later in life, not having been raised in an environment where guns were present. Now working in the legal system, she noted that she felt there was a "conflation between legal and illegal firearm use and possession in Canada," propagated by the media, which made it difficult for her to have conversations with friends and family members about guns.

> That's the problem when you start talking to people about firearms in general: they get their back up, and say why does anyone need a gun? Why should you have a gun when all these people are getting shot, you know? I understand that's a concern. But those shootings are not involving legally possessed firearms 99 per cent of the time.[30] That's the reality ... I know when I have conversations and explain what the difference is, as well as like the socio-economic factors that go into illegal gun use or possession and why that's happening, it's a whole different conversation.[31]

Harrison, a middle-aged veteran, hunter, and sports shooter living in Alberta, felt that the major news organizations in Canada were failing to ask the Liberal government hard questions on gun issues, especially the assault-style weapons ban, which led to a skewed perception among the general public. When asked about the media environment in Canada, he noted: "It's unbalanced. I mean, the media bias is, it's pretty evident. You tend to know which news organizations lean in which direction, but there's not a lot of them out there actively supporting gun owners. We're an easy target." Harrison could empathize with ordinary Canadians living in cities who were worried about criminal gangs and violence, but felt that focusing on legal gun owners was a "smokescreen" or a "misleading scare tactic" to avoid tackling the real issues causing crime. "Clamping down on legal, licensed firearms owners does nothing to solve the gang problem and the smuggling problem and the illegal importation and all of that."[32]

Other gun owners, like Mani, a South Asian Canadian sports shooter from Ontario, echoed this sentiment. He felt that the media were not living up to their responsibility to fact-check misinformation being put forward by politicians. Further, he felt that the media failed to share the stories of the community of gun owners that he was a part of. "It's a joyful experience going to the range and shooting ... I don't think I've ever had a negative experience with a fellow firearms owner. They are really nice people. They're down to earth. You don't hear these stories in the news media, and it's really troubling."[33]

Others felt that the media deliberately ignored the pro-gun movement when the story did not fit their narrative. Jerry, a middle-aged white man from suburban Ontario, marched in Ottawa in the summer of 2020 to protest the assault-style weapons ban. Labelled the Integrity March by the organizers, the CCFR, the march attracted a large group of gun owners who travelled to the nation's capital. At the same time, the march failed to capture much media attention. Jerry felt that this was not an accident and that the media had deliberately downplayed the number of people in attendance.[34]

Other gun owners felt outright vilified by the Canadian media. This is connected to larger feelings within the Canadian conservative movement that the media tends to reflect the views of urban and eastern Canadians in big cities like Toronto and Montreal. Some gun owners compared the Canadian media to a "schoolyard bully" that never misses an opportunity to "get a dig in" at the expense of gun owners and never gives them "a fair shake."[35] Nikolasz, a small-business owner in Alberta whose livelihood has been directly threatened by Liberal government policies, did not mince words when talking about the CBC, which he felt purposefully misled Canadians on the country's gun laws: "I believe that right now, we are fighting a propaganda battle against the CBC and other left-wing media ... The CBC is doing nothing to educate the public. They're doing the opposite."[36]

Others felt that the media fed into misconceptions and stereotypes about gun owners. For example, Adrian, an African Canadian veteran living in Alberta, did not feel well-represented in the media's portrayal of gun culture in Canada:

> Well, I think one of the biggest misconceptions [presented by the media] is that most gun owners are, excuse the term, what they may call redneck or illiterate, or people that just want to kill things or shoot up things or whatever. You know, most gun owners are professionals, whether you have a police officer, military, there's some lawyers, doctors, we're just not just one specific type ... And as you can see, I'm visible minority.[37]

This was a common refrain among gun owners of colour, who expressed that they did not fit the image of gun ownership held by the majority of Canadians and perpetuated, in their view, by the media. Allison, for example, felt that the media's stereotyped portrayal of gun owners writes gun owners of colour like her out of existence. A biologist specializing in vaccine development, she felt her story was missing from the media's portrayal of gun owners as "right wing, very racist" and "closed-minded." "I'm sure that they exist, like, for 100 per cent I'm sure they exist, but I don't think that that's the majority." Allison felt that this media portrayal pushed people into corners and fostered division. "I think that the portrayal that we have in the media isn't as nuanced as I would like."[38]

Mireille, who lives in Quebec, felt the situation was even worse for gun owners in French-speaking Canada. She felt that given the large pro-control sentiment in the province, she had a hard time making inroads when discussing her hobby: "I feel like people are stuck in their opinions and closed off about them. It's sad, because they read the mainstream media, and they listen to what happens, and they make their ideas based on that. And it's hard to break through."[39]

By the Law

The large majority of Canadian gun owners I spoke to were broadly supportive of many gun regulations. However, they reserved a tremendous amount of antipathy for the complexity of the administrative system. Canada's gun laws are principally governed by the Firearms Act (1995), a dense and complicated legal patchwork. For example, firearms in Canada are prohibited by make and model rather than function, sometimes leading to legal ambiguity over which guns are legal and which are not. Confusion over important terms, like what constitutes a variant of a particular rifle, make life complicated for gun owners and firearm businesses: legislators will prohibit variants of certain firearms without providing a robust definition of what does and does not fall under that category.[40]

Further, Canadians choosing to own firearms expose themselves to considerable legal liability, given the ease with which one can run afoul of the strict requirements for gun storage and transportation. Add to this local bylaws that limit where firearms can be discharged, for those target shooting on private land, as well as hunting regulations, which span federal, provincial, and municipal jurisdictions, and owning a gun in Canada becomes a complicated venture. It can also involve inviting the government into very intimate moments of their lives.

Emily noted that she often talks to non–gun owners about this little-known element of gun ownership in Canada:

We have to tell this government agency our personal life, like who's our husband, who have we had relationships with in the past five years, our financial health. Have we ever declared bankruptcy? Have we ever had problems with our mental health? Have we been fired from a job? So when I renewed my licence, which I had for thirty years at the time, I was going through separation and divorce. That raised a red flag, not with my application, but with my ex-husband's application. He was interviewed twice by the RCMP because at that time we were separating. It wasn't a contentious separation. But that flagged. So where else do you apply for anything where you literally have to expose all aspects of your life to a third-party licensing agent?[41]

The complex, invasive, and sometimes arduous requirements surrounding gun ownership in Canada make many gun owners feel targeted by their own laws and government. Warren, a young, white professional living in British Columbia and a self-identified left-wing gun owner, understood that participating in a potentially risky activity should carry consequences. "We are partaking in a regulated activity, and we understand that there are responsibilities associated with that. I think that Canadian gun owners respect that. I respect the fact that you need qualifications to own a firearm ... I don't think everyone should own a gun." At the same time, he expressed frustration at the bureaucratic complexity of the current system and felt it was intended to be overly burdensome in order to create the appearance that it contributes to public safety. "There's way too much bureaucracy. I think it's confusing. I think it's not based on logic but based on emotion."[42]

Hugh, an Indigenous hunter and sports shooter from rural Ontario, felt exasperated with the complexity of the current system. "Canada's gun laws are overly complicated to the point where legal experts, the courts, and judges cannot understand them. So, with that kind of complication, what hope does a private citizen have a being in compliance with those laws?"[43]

Applying for and holding a firearm licence in Canada also requires applicants and licence holders to sacrifice a considerable amount of their personal privacy. For example, Section 55(2) of the act gives the chief firearms officer the ability to conduct an investigation of applicants and interview anyone they consider to be relevant to determining whether an applicant is eligible to hold a licence. Applicants must disclose to the government any breakups of significant relationships within the past two years.

Further, having a firearm licence could open individuals to the risk of having their home searched by police. Sections 102 and 104 authorize firearms officers to search a home that they suspect contains firearms or a firearms collection, though they must obtain a warrant or the consent of the occupant. One is left to wonder how many people would possess the legal knowledge or wherewithal to say no to a police officer asking to search their home.

Even when police obtain a warrant, these searches have the potential to be deadly. While I was conducting research for this project, Ontario gunsmith Roger Kotanko was killed by Toronto police during a no-knock raid on his workshop,[44] leading his family members to launch a lawsuit against the police force to try to clear his name.[45]

While this is an extreme example, even cordial interactions with the police can end up leaving gun owners feeling stigmatized. Claude is a gun collector. While, as noted, he has never actually fired a gun, he has a large collection of antique firearms, which he is prohibited by law from taking out of his house, with limited exceptions. A collection of this size requires that Claude keep a Collector Handbook, similar to those maintained by a gun business. He must also submit to searches by the RCMP, in which police officers inspect his firearm storage setup, check each firearm against his registry, provide copies of articles he has published as a registered collector, and conduct interviews with his spouse.[46]

Gun ownership exposes people to significant legal liability, not just from potential accidents or the misuse of their firearms, but through the complexity and ambiguity of Canadian regulation towards firearms. For most Canadian gun owners, this legal liability never results in any sanction, though it may weigh heavily on their heads. Others are not so lucky. Two men I spoke to understood all too well the cost of violating Canada's firearms regulatory regime.

Roger lives in rural Ontario, far away from the city. An older man, he has lived alone for years. Roger was able to build his own electrical grid using his skills as an electrician, and he is almost completely self-sufficient. As a result of his work, Roger developed osteo-arthritis, for which he now has a medical cannabis licence. Prior to legalization, however, Roger had self-medicated with cannabis for some time, growing his own supply on his property. After getting caught smoking marijuana in public, the RCMP raided Roger's house, confiscated his firearms and licence, and fined him for unsafe storage. "So when I went to court, I got a $250 fine for improper storage, and I lost all my firearms. I'm so sorry. One of them was my father's. My mom gave it to him in 1948." Roger had long used hunting as way of supplementing his food supply. He had to turn to using a crossbow for a decade, making hunting much more difficult, before he was able to reapply through the courts to have his licence restored.

Chris Levesque would also face a decade-long legal struggle as a result of an administrative offence, though he would end up losing much more than just a licence and family heirloom. I met Chris[47] through his daughter Lindsay, who was a student in one of my classes. When she heard about my research, she asked if she could take part. During our interview, she mentioned her father's story, and his willingness to participate in my research as well.

Chris grew up as an avid hunter and shooter. He was heavily involved in the board of his local shooting club, eventually becoming president of the Charlottetown Trap & Skeet Club, and worked with hunting-related charities like Delta Waterfowl, which seeks to preserve habitat for migratory birds like duck and geese. He was also involved in historical re-enactment, which involved the use of historical firearms. Professionally, he had worked as a driver for an armoured-car service, which required him to maintain proficiency with a handgun, and then as a mechanic. In 2003 Chris was asked by an old friend, Alan Baker, to take over his gun business. He saw the opportunity to finally make a living from his passion for the outdoors and the shooting sports. He opened Island Guns & Gear in August of that same year, moving the previously rural business to downtown Charlottetown.[48]

At the same time, the Liberal government was under fire for problems with the long-gun registry, brought in with the 1995 Firearms Act. The registry was already significantly over budget, and with the amnesty period running out, Solicitor General and PEI MP Wayne Easter was warning gun owners to register their firearms or face the consequences. In June of 2003, on the eve of the amnesty's expiration, CBC News's *The National* interviewed gun owners voicing their displeasure with the registry. One of them was Chris Lévesque.[49]

Chris described the segment as one of the few "fair shakes" the CBC ever gave gun owners, but he felt that participating in it placed a target on his back. He says his hunch was confirmed when he says he received a call from the chief firearms officer for PEI, Eric Goodwin,[50] whom he knew through organizing permits for his reenactments. Chris claims that Goodwin warned him that Easter was not happy with his decision to open the gun shop. "I can remember, you know, Eric Godwin sitting me down and saying ... 'Easter called me and said he really can't believe I'm going to issue you a licence.' And I go, 'What do you mean?' He said, 'Well, I mean you're on the news, telling everybody how rotten the gun registry is, and now you're gonna open up a gun shop as well?'" Goodwin warned him that he would be under a high level of scrutiny, but Chris was unfazed.

The shop was a success, despite the complexity of managing gun registrations. Chris said that he worked with the chief firearms officers' (CFO) office as a verifier. When he asked the CFO what the business should do with any unregistered firearms brought into the shop for repair or consignment, he says he was instructed to bring the guns in and register them. With numerous firearms being registered during this period, the process was chaotic, and the CFO enlisted Lévesque's help in registering the firearms that came into the shop.

> They made us a dumping ground for all the unregistered guns out there. We'd have thirty or forty at a time coming in, you know, people would trade them in. Now, at the same time, if somebody came in to get a gun gunsmithed, it wasn't our job to make sure it was registered. Right? You know what I mean? Like, and we weren't the authorities to say whether it should be registered or not. Obviously, if we brought it in on trade, we would have to register it.
>
> So then, with all this influx of guns, we were trying to figure out, working closely with Miramichi,[51] how do you register these guns online? How do we bring them in? What if the individual doesn't have a licence? Because there was all kinds of that, and one of the prescribed legal ways to get rid of a gun if you don't have a licence is to give it to somebody that has a licence.[52]

Because of the well-documented challenges with the registry infrastructure,[53] Chris said he often had to find workarounds. One would end up getting him in trouble. Many gun shops allow patrons to bring in guns on consignment. The patron leaves their firearm with the business, which agrees to sell it for a pre-arranged price. The business then takes a share of the sale, and the patron is saved the hassle and liability of a private gun sale. Due to problems with the national registration system, Chris says he was instructed by the employees working at the National Firearms Centre to register any firearm that was dropped off for consignment to himself or one of his employees. The employees took turns registering the firearms in their names, as the Firearms Centre had warned them that if one individual registered too many firearms in a short period of time it would raise a flag in the system.

This complex system of firearm registration would lead to trouble down the line, after two important incidents. The first involved a lever-action rifle turned in to the store for consignment. When Levesque went to register the gun in his name, per the procedure he said he had been instructed to follow, he was informed that the gun had been reported stolen. This triggered an investigation by local police and the RCMP, which ended up being inconclusive, as well as a few visits to Chris's shop by the authorities. The firearm was eventually returned to its original owner.

The second incident involved the theft of a handgun from Island Guns & Gear, which turned up buried in a quarry nearby. Once again, this triggered an investigation, and recommendations from the Charlottetown police to increase security, though Chris noted that he had already met the stringent security requirements for all gun shops.

Around this time, the National Weapons Enforcement Support Team was conducting a series of raids on firearms businesses. Alan Baker, the man from whom Chris had bought Island Guns & Gear, was raided and charged. Rather than fight the charges, Mr. Baker, who was ageing and in poor health, decided to plead down the charges. A few months later, Chris was called in to talk with the city police.

He showed up at 9 a.m. on a Friday morning, 8 April 2005.

> When I came through the door, they took me down, sat me in a room and said: "hey, you're under arrest. We got a search warrant. We're going through your house where there's a team at your house right now. There's a team at your business" ... It was life-altering, you know. I'm thirty-five years old and I got twenty cops in my kitchen. The police are rifling through my wife's panty drawer. Like, all my kids' toys at the house.

In the search warrant, Chris says the RCMP cited the two incidents, including the lever-action rifle he had registered in his name. "Yeah, the charge that got them the search warrant was the saying that I was knowingly in possession of a firearm obtained in the commission of an offence." Chris's legal team fought this charge in court, and without needing to provide a single piece of evidence, got the charge dropped.

Following the search, the police charged Levesque with several counts of possessing a firearm without being the holder of the registration certificate.[54] Levesque noted in our discussion that these were firearms that his employee had taken in for gunsmithing. The prosecution attempted to paint Chris as an irresponsible shop owner, deliberately flouting the government's registration regime. Chris saw himself as a victim of an overly complex and chaotic system.

Chris was sentenced to six months of house arrest and a ten-year prohibition from owning firearms.[55] After a lengthy legal battle involving two Charter challenges,[56] and two appeals,[57] the firearm prohibition was reduced from ten years to three. During his trial, the Harper government was in the process of dismantling the very registry under which Levesque was charged, and granting amnesties to individuals charged with violations of the registry – though Justice Campbell noted this amnesty did not apply to businesses.[58]

In an ironic turn of fate, during this same period, RCMP officer Jeffrey Rae Gillis, who Levesque says worked on his case, was himself amassing a collection of contraband firearms. Between 2009 and 2016, Gillis falsified documents stating that he destroyed firearms confiscated by the RCMP. Rather than destroying them, he kept them in his home, where a raid in February of 2016 turned up seventy guns.[59]

The legal battle left Chris emotionally scarred and financially ruined. He attempted to keep the shop open during his almost decade-long legal battle, but pressure from his creditors and declining sales caused by the incident eventually forced him to close. "In Canada, you're innocent until proven broke."[60] Chris noted that the legal battle cost him a quarter of a million dollars. He lost his business, spent his inheritance, and was forced to sell his home and many of his possessions. He describes his time under house arrest as trying.

> I had a five-year old kid that has autism and a ten-year-old daughter that, you know, wanted to go outside. And every time I had to take the kids out in the yard, I had to call the jail and tell them I was doing it. I had to call the jail to go and feed my dogs. I mean, I'm not your career criminal guy. I have to sympathize a little bit with my probation officer, because she didn't really know what to do with me. I was just Joe Blow. Never had more than a speeding ticket ever in my life.[61]

The incident left a lasting impact on Chris's family as well, especially his daughter Lindsay, who now studies political science.

> It made me really question everything, and the motives behind why people do things. And it really made me just not trust any system or institution that we have. Any time I'm exposed to law enforcement I just think it's a joke. I don't know. I don't trust them. I don't. I grew up learning that these people are supposed to serve and protect, you know, I just don't believe it.[62]

Chris's case is complex: a mix of small-town politics, administrative snafus, and legal ambiguity. The case demonstrates the legal risks that gun owners and businesses in Canada expose themselves to and the consequences of overly complex regulations for the real people behind these stories.

As we have seen, the gun owners I surveyed and spoke to feel targeted by many powerful Canadian institutions, from politicians to the media to the law. Ultimately, this sense of being targeted leaves many Canadian gun owners feeling like lesser citizens, as Warren summed up during our chat:

> It feels like I'm a second-class citizen. It feels like I'm being blamed for things that I have no control over and I haven't contributed towards [gun crime]. It feels like my opinion doesn't really matter. It feels like nobody's listening. It feels like everything, even though I follow all the rules, it's never good enough. And it feels like my property can be taken away from me at any moment.[63]

The Political Behaviour of Canadian Gun Owners

Annie's husband was a long-time sports shooter and a devoted supporter of the CCFR. When he passed away, the undertaker asked for personal items of significance to dress him in for his cremation. Annie knew immediately what to contribute: "The first thing that came to my mind is what he would wear trapshooting.[64] So, I pulled out all of his trapshooting gear, his hat, his shirt, his best jeans, and I gave it to our undertaker to dress him in that.[65] She also included his CCFR T-shirt.

Serious leisure pursuits become an important part of the identity of those who participate in them. Passion drives advocacy. The CCFR reached out to Annie when they saw the photographs of her husband's memorial posted on Twitter. She has since become involved with the group, marching on Parliament Hill, and helping them with their 2021 election ad campaign by handing out flyers around her neighbourhood, among other things.

A nascent literature in the United States has demonstrated how gun ownership can influence political behaviour. Joslyn[66] convincingly establishes the existence of a widening "gun gap" in political behaviour and opinion between gun owners and non–gun owners, which first appeared in the 1990s, and expanded following the increasing salience of gun control in public debates after Columbine High School. Joslyn shows that gun enthusiasts are a unique "group" in American politics, with "distinctive political behaviour or beliefs that differentiate members from nonmembers" and "the distinctiveness of the behaviour or belief increases with attachment to the group."[67] In the 2016 election of Donald Trump, gun ownership represented a stronger predictor of vote choice than education and income. While non–gun owners had a 0.44 probability of voting for Trump, those who owned a single gun had a 0.49 probability, those who owned two guns a 0.54 probability, those who owned three 0.6, and those who owned more than four

0.64.[68] Further, gun ownership has been proven to be associated with higher levels of political participation. Gun owners, including gun-owning women, are more likely to vote, contact their representatives, or give money to a political cause.[69] This is especially true for rural Americans.[70]

Large national Canadian surveys do not ask about gun ownership, and thus it is very difficult to establish whether the same trend is present in Canada, though evidence from my survey of gun owners does support the assertion that at least a strong core of Canadian gun owners are very politically active.[71] Unsurprisingly, given my sampling methods, the gun owners I spoke to tended to be very involved in political activities. What this data can help us to better understand is the *type* of activism that gun ownership inspires and *how* and *why* gun owners become politically active. As we will see, the shared experiences of feeling targeted by major Canadian institutions and misunderstood by the broader Canadian public drives gun owners to take action.

Evangelism

The gun owners that I spoke with were highly active political participants. In my online survey, participants were presented with a list of political activities and asked to select from a list of sixteen categories the activities they had participated in related to gun ownership during the past twelve months (See Appendix A). Activities included things like contacting an elected representative (45.7 per cent), donating money to an advocacy group or political party (49.4 per cent), or talking about gun politics with family members (75.8 per cent). This was used to assign each participant a participation score, based on the number of activities they had been involved in. The mean was 5.33 activities, with a standard deviation of 3.35 (n = 16,880).

Participants in my Zoom interviews were also asked about a narrower range of political activities. The most common activities that they participated in were talking about guns with friends, or taking them to the range (76.2 per cent), contacting an elected official (65.5 per cent), and signing an e-petition (58.3 per cent). Volunteering (21.4 per cent) and talking about guns online (25 per cent) were less popular (n = 84).

What emerged from the data was evidence of a sort of gun-centred messianism among gun advocates in Canada. This evangelism has certainly been encouraged by pro-gun groups on both sides of the border[72] who feel that the more people get involved in the hobby or sport, the more supporters they will have. But the extent to which it has been incorporated into the personal politics of my participants was surprising. The gun owners I spoke to saw talking to friends about guns, or taking a friend or family to the range, as a political act. They felt strongly that the negative perception of their hobby or sport discussed in the first half of this chapter stemmed from ignorance and that the remedy to this was to show others, one at a time, the true face of their hobby or sport. This theme came out in the majority of my interviews, where participants mentioned talking to friends about guns or taking friends to the range to experience the shooting sports.

Annie was not a professional or paid activist but saw herself as an advocate for her sport, especially since the passing of her husband. For Annie, the advantage of talking to someone face-to-face was the ability to humanize a hobby that she felt had been maligned by the media and politicians.[73] She felt that this human connection helped to overcome people's inbuilt scepticism about guns and gun culture.

Many gun owners I spoke to felt that this scepticism was born of ignorance. Mani noted that he felt educating his friends and family members on Canada's gun strict laws was a good way to dispel this misinformation.[74] Mani has also taken friends to the range in order to demonstrate first hand how safe the hobby is. This is another common tactic among advocates seeking to overcome negative stereotypes surrounding gun ownership. Dawson, a white man in British Columbia in his early twenties, had been involved with firearms since high school, before he and his family immigrated to Canada from New Zealand. He noted that people were often shocked to hear of a high school student being involved in the shooting sports, but after explaining the regulations around it, and his reasons for owning a gun, his conversations often "kind of opened up their perspective on it." When the people he spoke to learned that Dawson was involved in organized and supervised target shooting sports, they tended to soften their views.[75]

As a Métis Canadian, Rick finds it easier to frame gun ownership through the lens of his traditional hunting rights when talking to those outside the gun community. By emphasizing the connection between gun ownership, food, the land, and heritage, he says he is able to cut through the partisan roadblock that could make conversations about guns with colleagues and friends deeply uncomfortable.[76]

Of my survey participants, 76.2 per cent reported talking to friends about guns, or taking them to the range, as a political activity that they engaged in. Participants saw this as a way to grow the movement. This evangelism provides leisure-based movements with a unique method of swelling their ranks. Whereas movements like the 2SLBGTQ+ movement, movements for racial justice, or the environmental movement can engage people as allies and concerned citizens, the pro-gun movement can bring in converts.

Admittedly, this is something that pro-gun advocates south of the border are better poised to take advantage of, given that the barriers to entry to gun ownership in the United States are much lower than in Canada. The pro-gun movement in the United States, for example, recruited heavily in the wake of the great pandemic gun-buying spree of 2020–1, with groups like the National African American Gun Owners Association (NAAGA) growing exponentially.[77] In Canada, while a friend or family member might become curious about gun ownership after a chat or a trip to the range, the institutional barriers to becoming a gun owner impose a higher cost on following through with that curiosity, once again muting the grassroots advantage of the pro-gun movement.

Talking to Politicians

Talking to elected representatives was the second most popular political activity among my interview participants (65.5 per cent). Jack was fairly typical of the gun owners I spoke with: "I've written letters to the prime minister, the minister of public safety, before that the minister of justice. I've written to various other MPs, my own MP, that sort of thing. I put my money where my mouth is." Others, like Lowell, a retiree and British immigrant living in Alberta, confessed to being constant gadflies in their communities: "I'm known as the grouchy old guy of the local newspaper. I'm quite capable of firing off scathing emails to both our federal MP or provincial MLAs and any other chucklehead that raises my ire."[78]

Many of the gun owners I spoke with reported that before the election of the Trudeau government and the 2020 ban, they had not been particularly active. The ban, however, served as a catalyst for many to start participating more actively in the political process.

Francis, a middle-aged Indigenous man from British Columbia, used to see himself as the "silent majority type," usually taking the "whatever, this will sort itself out" view of politics. After the OIC he started paying attention and became more active politically.[79] Francis has now not only written to his MP and the prime minister, but even volunteered for his local MP during an election campaign.

Donal, a die-hard NDP supporter from Canada's north, has written and even hand-delivered messages to his Liberal MP when the latter failed to respond. He has also tried to shift his own party away from its increasingly anti-gun stance and expressed his frustration at trying to reach the NDP leadership with his concerns, only to receive a letter soliciting donations as a reply.[80]

Zhi, a Liberal Party member and self-described political moderate, is passionate about gun policy in Canada, given his strong feelings about the importance of individual liberties. He wrote to his MP and even spoke to her a few times on the phone, offering to take her out to the gun range to see for herself, though nothing ever came of the offer. As a backbench MP, however, he did not think she had much influence within the party.[81] Even when reaching out to more influential MPs, participants reported that it was difficult to be taken seriously when partisan considerations intruded. Archie is a middle-aged suburban white man who lives in the riding of then prominent Liberal MP Pam Damoff. As Parliamentary Secretary to the Minister of Public Safety, Damoff was a member of the House of Commons Standing Committee on Public Safety and National Security (SECU), and thus wielded considerable influence on firearm policy in Canada. Archie described his efforts to reach Damoff, who he noted eventually agreed to speak with him. "I know she didn't want to have that conversation with me, but she still did. I was allowed to book a phone interview with her. She didn't offer a lot of opposition to my comments. Then she went in to the SECU hearings and did her thing. She's got her votes to get."

Since then, Archie has volunteered for the Conservative Party in several elections and reported donating hundreds of dollars a year to the party.[82] He was not the only person driven to be more involved in Conservative politics by the government's policies.

Emily was so galvanized by what she saw as political attacks against her community, and her concerns about public safety, that she decided to run for the Conservative Party in the 2021 Election. "I'm not a politician, that's for sure, and this was never in my plan. I guess the turning point for me was when we had the order-in-council gun ban and two firearms bills, C-71 and C-21."[83]

Not all of these chats with policymakers happened at the national level. The provinces in Canada are in charge of wildlife management and hunting regulations. Because these governments are closer to the people impacted by their decisions, it is easier for individuals to impact policy. Leo, a thirty-something white hunter from rural Saskatchewan, was born with spina bifida and requires a wheelchair to get around. This posed serious problems for access to hunting opportunities, given that travelling through forested areas with limited road access is often necessary for big-game hunting. Leo's problem was solved when an American company launched an all-terrain wheelchair, aiming to make the outdoors more accessible to differently abled people. The problem was that at the time, it was illegal to hunt while seated on an all-terrain vehicle (ATV) in Saskatchewan, as part of the province's efforts to ensure fair-chase hunting and hunter safety. The province considered Leo's chair to be an ATV. Leo contacted his local MLA in September of 2019. By June of 2020, the government had amended the regulations so that Leo could hunt using his wheelchair. The chair has allowed Leo to access hunting opportunities he would not have had previously and even launch his own YouTube channel to share stories of his trips with the online community of hunting enthusiasts.[84]

Community Activities

Though some participants may not have been active politically, they were certainly active within the gun community, volunteering or holding positions in their local gun clubs, fish and game associations, or sports-shooting leagues. Caleb, the former president of his local Fish & Game Club in British Columbia, noted the time he put into his leadership work, growing his club from nienty members to 350, even though this was to the detriment of his own practice time. "When I was club president, I spent hundreds of hours a year on administrative issues, and not much time shooting because I was all in."[85] Archie worked with his handgun club to raise $25,000 for a local hospital.

Others volunteered their time as instructors, helping to bring new people into their sport. Rod, a former police officer, spends his spare time as a firearm-safety instructor, donating any proceeds from his classes to the CCFR.[86] Lowell has been a constant fixture at his local Alberta gun club since he took up sports shooting in the 1980s. For years, he taught the Canadian Firearm Safety Course in order to grow the sport he had come to love.[87]

Memberships in gun or hunting clubs, or recreational shooting sports leagues, are a pro-social activity that forms the basis for a community. In an era where a sense of community is seemingly harder to access than in the past, these activities bring together a group of passionate enthusiasts.

The Canadian gun-owning community is centred around a leisure pursuit, and a uniquely Canadian vision of gun rights, one tied to citizenship and the right to fair treatment that citizens expect of their government. This community perceives itself as under attack by major institutions: politicians, the media, and the law. It sees the gun-control measures introduced by the Trudeau government not as tools to improve public safety but as politically motivated attacks, preying on the ignorance of Canadians, and perpetuated by a hapless or nefarious media. These feelings of persecution motivate high levels of activism in the community, giving the pro-gun movement its grassroots strength. Gun owners are highly motivated to do things like engage in gun evangelism, contact their elected representatives, or do related work within their community.

6

Formal Pro-Gun Advocacy

We laugh together and we cry together. Right now, the culture is hurting very much. We're battered, and bloody, but we're not broken by any stretch of the word. We will be hanging on until the very last muzzleloader is gone, because we love it so much. And because it really is more than just a sport, it makes us who we are. That's what a culture is. It shapes you.

– Christine Generoux[1]

It was late at night, and Tracey Wilson was standing alone by the side of the highway watching the black, white, and gold *Sûrété du Québec* police car drive off into the night. Beside Tracey's truck, her infant daughter was crying, and her dog barking frantically. She looked around at her possessions, everything one would need for a relaxing weekend at the hunting camp, which were strewn along the side of the highway. This was not the first time she had been pulled over and searched by the police on this stretch of road. While Quebec's provincial police force was rumoured to favour pulling over cars with Ontario licence plates, Tracey felt it was the pro-gun bumper stickers on her car that had made her a target. In that moment, she vowed to do something about it, though she likely could not have imagined that in a few short years, she would become one of the few voices for gun owners on Parliament Hill.

This chapter looks at how the pro-gun movement has translated the serious leisure identity of gun owners into formal political activism. It sketches the contours of contemporary pro-gun advocacy coalition in Canada, which is composed of groups representing a variety of interests, from sports shooters to hunters and trappers to businesses.

The chapter will survey the tactics and resource mobilization techniques of the pro-gun movement, highlighting the schisms and disagreements within it and its vision of firearm rights in Canada. As we

Figure 6.1. Pro-gun Advocacy Coalition in Canada

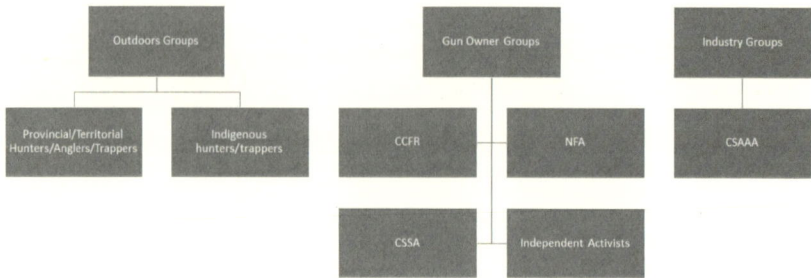

will see, examining this uniquely Canadian vision of firearm rights allows us to better understand how the collision between ideas and institutions produces ideological variation across political communities. When most Canadian advocates talk about gun rights, they are not talking about an absolute right to unrestricted firearm ownership, the use of firearms for self-defence, or the Jeffersonian Republican militia ideal. Rather, the Canadian vision of gun rights is one of fair treatment for citizens by their own government, in line with the Canadian vision of peace, order, and good governance.

Who Are the Advocacy Groups?

The National Rifle Association (NRA) is synonymous with firearm advocacy in the United States. Perhaps one of the most famous advocacy groups in the world, the NRA's notoriety has increased over its more than 150 years of work. No such behemoth exists in Canada. While American gun owners are represented by a relatively permanent and well-funded advocacy network, headed by well-established groups like the NRA and Second Amendment Foundation, the Canadian pro-gun movement is much smaller and operates with a tiny fraction of the funding.

The movement can be subdivided by area of focus. The three largest groups focus principally on the interests of gun owners: the National Firearms Association (NFA), the Canadian Coalition for Firearm Rights (CCFR), and the Canadian Sports Shooting Association (CSSA). The Canadian Sporting Arms and Ammunition Association (CSAAA), on the other hand, is an industry group that represents the small-arms and ammunition industry in Canada. Finally, there are provincial or Indigenous hunting and trapping organizations, such as the Saskatchewan Wildlife Federation or the Cree Trappers Association, that focus primarily on conservation and hunting issues but can be mobilized to assist the wider movement when their own activities or members are threatened by legislation.

The National Firearms Association (NFA) was formed in Ottawa in 1978 as an amalgamation of several of the older firearm rights groups. The group began with only a few thousand members, but its ranks swelled after each crisis it confronted, first opposing Bill C-51 in the late 1970s, then the gun control efforts of the Progressive Conservative and Liberal governments in the 1990s. By the turn of the twenty-first century, the group's membership had grown to almost 30,000 members, and it now claims almost 72,000 members. Of the three gun-owner groups, the NFA is known for its fiery rhetoric, adopting the motto "No Compromise," and taking a hard stance in opposition to gun control. The organization's leadership feels that policy battles over firearm policy are not won or lost in a single moment but are part of a gradual erosion of rights. According to the NFA, the history of gun laws in Canada shows that when gun owners give in to compromise, they will inevitably be asked to compromise again in the future. The pro-control coalition, on the other hand, has nothing to lose or give up; it can only win.

Further, in the eyes of the NFA, its no-compromise attitude is really about no one being left behind. Each subsequent wave of legislation tends to target specific groups within the gun community, as pro-control advocacy coalitions use divide-and-conquer tactics. In 2020, for example, Justin Trudeau's Liberal government was very careful to frame its "assault-style" weapons ban as something that would not impact Canadian hunters, in order to try to divide the community of sports shooters from the larger gun community. In the 1970s, the same strategy was followed with regard to the small community of collectors who enjoyed acquiring machine guns, which came to be banned at that time.[2]

Alternatively, the Canadian Coalition for Firearm Rights (CCFR) has adopted what it sees as a public relations approach to firearm advocacy in Canada, using more moderate and bipartisan language and taking what its leaders consider a more measured stance on firearm legislation. During its first five years, the group grew quickly to over 30,000 members. The CCFR originated as a splinter group from the NFA in 2015. Several members of the NFA board felt that the group's no-compromise attitude alienated ordinary Canadians and played into the hands of pro-control advocates and politicians seeking to frame the movement as extremist. They argued that a public-education approach was the best way to advocate, rather than an exclusive focus on lobbying. This was based on the idea that politicians change more quickly than public opinion on certain issues. The group's founders felt that: "you can have politicians and politics and you will *never* stop working on this. Like, every four years politicians change, there's going to be rollover. So, you're always working.[3]

The group faced opposition led by the NFA's director, Sheldon Clare, who argued fiercely that a focus on lobbying was the best way for the organization to attain its goals. Clare had been elected president in 2010 and had a strong vision of how the group should focus its efforts:

> What I did is I set out certain goals for the organization ... I wanted to build a professional organization with a modern staff, grounded in sound administrative procedures. I set out a vision for the NFA as allowing no compromise in the fight for firearm rights, and my no-compromise vision meant that no firearms owners would be left behind. There'll be no group of owners that were segregated or ridiculed because of the class of firearms that they owned.

This led to a schism on the NFA's board of directors, with five of the ten directors supporting Clare and the "old guard," and the other five supporting the reformers. The schism paralysed the organization, and as lawsuits started to fly around, the reformers decided to go their own way.[4] Searching for a figurehead to represent them, the group approached YouTube star and firearm instructor Rod Giltaca in August of 2015 to be their first president. The group asked Rod what he thought was missing from firearm advocacy. He wrote a short four-page document laying out his ideas, which was eventually adopted by the group as one of the CCFR's founding documents.

> I still have it today. And it's exactly what the CCFR is. It was all about educating non-gun owners. Because that's where the reward is for political parties. If people don't know anything about gun control, you can show them, you know, silhouettes of so-called assault rifles, and they'll respond [positively] to slogans like "more guns equal more death." If they're savvy on the topic, then that stuff won't work anymore. So that's why we started the CCFR.[5]

Since the split, the CCFR and NFA have engaged in a sometimes-heated rivalry. Meanwhile, the CSSA has quietly continued its advocacy efforts. Founded in 1960 as the Ontario Revolver Association, the organization has gone through a few name changes. While not originally a political organization, the legislative challenges of the late 1970s pushed the group into a more political role. Amalgamating with the

Ontario Smallbore Association and the Canadian Institute for Legislative Action, the CSSA was born. In 2021 the group claimed to have 37,000 members.[6]

A common misconception about pro-gun advocacy is that the pro-gun groups in Canada represent the interests of gun companies. Groups like the CCFR, NFA, and CSSA instead represent the firearm community, or the "end users" as they are known in the industry. Firms in the small-arms and ammunition industry are represented on Parliament Hill by the Canadian Sporting Arms and Ammunition Association (CSAAA). Founded just over forty years ago, the CSAAA represents Canada's manufacturers, importers, wholesalers, distributors, retailers, and gunsmiths. Membership is reserved solely for those with a firearms business licence, with the exception of a few firms that specialize in firearm-related accessories. The group sees itself as a voice for the industry, separate from that of the consumer. This helps the group to remain non-partisan with the "goal to have open dialogue with whatever government is in power to provide expertise, which we find very lacking in the development of firearms policy."[7]

Given the special relationship that Canada's Indigenous peoples have with the land, hunting and trapping are an important part of maintaining their traditional lifestyle and cultural practices. Indigenous peoples in Canada enjoy constitutional protection for their treaty rights to hunt outside of provincially mandated hunting seasons and without the quotas that settler hunters must operate within.[8] Navigating the practical use of these rights can be complex, however, given the legal ambiguity surrounding concepts like "traditional territory." As such, political organizations representing Indigenous people in Canada will become involved in advocacy when firearm policies threaten treaty hunting rights.[9]

Provincial groups that primarily, though certainly not exclusively, represent settler-Canadians include the Ontario Federation of Anglers and Hunters (OFAH), the British Columbia Wildlife Federation (BCWF), the Saskatchewan Wildlife Federation (SWF), and the Quebec Federation of Hunters and Anglers (FQCP). These groups comprise alliances of outdoor enthusiasts, including recreational anglers, trappers, and hunters. Firearm rights are not their primary purview; they focus mostly on advocating for conservation. They emerged out of the conservation movement of the late nineteenth and early twentieth centuries, a time when human expansion and industrialization were devastating the natural landscape and when unregulated commercial hunting led to the erasure of many species from the landscape. Based on the principles of scientific management, the conservation movement has restored many formerly endangered or extinct species, like wild turkeys, which were successfully reintroduced to the eastern United States and Canada thanks to the efforts of conservation groups.[10] Advocates working for these groups are often trained biologists.

Due to their experience working with governments, and their high levels of professionalization, these conservation groups were more likely to use insider tactics, like lobbying and puzzling,[11] and to work with government on outreach efforts like public education, even when governments were implementing policies that the groups disagreed with. Since talking to the federal government as a provincial organization can be challenging, the groups created a national body, the National Fishing and Hunting Collaborative, composed of the twelve non-partisan, non-profit, provincial and territorial conservation organizations. Collectively, the groups represented 375,000 Canadians in 2021.

The OFAH is one of the largest conservation organizations, with 725 affiliated clubs, including fifty-eight shooting clubs that operated 125 licensed gun ranges across Ontario in 2021. Their mission is to "ensure a future that includes healthy lakes and forests, bountiful fish and wildlife, and accessible opportunities for all Ontarians to share our passion for fishing, hunting, trapping and conservation."[12] Given its proximity to Ottawa, and its considerable size and resources, OFAH often takes the lead on advocacy efforts at the federal level on behalf of the other groups.[13]

The FQCP was established in 1946 to protect hunting and fishing in Quebec. The organization operates two foundations that help to fund wildlife conservation projects and deliver firearm safety courses across the province to over 20,000 Québecois/Québecoise each year. For decades, the organization has been a leader in advocating for firearm safety, and the Canadian Firearm Safety Course was based on the course developed in Quebec.[14]

Farther west, the SWF has just under 33,000 members, and 124 different branches across Saskatchewan. It was founded in the 1920s by three men concerned by the decline in the population of migratory birds, such as Canada geese. The group prides itself on having contributed to the restoration of several species, including the whooping crane, which the group adopted as their logo.

Because these groups hold charitable status, they were limited under Canadian law from engaging in the sort of partisan advocacy that gun-owner groups do, such as explicitly supporting candidates or parties. The groups believe that this non-partisan approach, however, is a feature rather than a bug, as it allows them to work with parties across the political spectrum.

Who Are the Advocates?

Given that the logic of collective action[15] dictates that groups pursuing collective goods, such as firearm rights, face challenges in mobilizing due to the free-rider problem, policy scholars have had to create new concepts to explain the proliferation of advocacy groups. One important concept is that of the political or policy entrepreneur.[16] Since then, the concept of policy entrepreneurs has been important for explaining change within policy process theories[17] like the Multiple Streams Framework[18] and Advocacy Coalition Framework.[19] Broadly speaking, policy entrepreneurs are individuals who are willing to make significant investments of their own time, energy, and resources in support of a political cause. Like business entrepreneurs, policy entrepreneurs generally possess the ability to relate to and motivate others, build strong teams, and take risks.[20]

Policy entrepreneurs play a substantial role in the pro-gun movement, providing much of the blood, sweat, and tears needed to drive the movement forward. The Canadian pro-gun movement is small compared to its counterpart to the south, and most groups lack the funding for a large team of full-time staffers. The advocates I spoke to described the heavy personal sacrifices they and their colleagues have made to build the movement.

Bill Jones, the original founder of the NFA, almost bankrupted himself fighting Bill C-51 in the 1970s, selling his three farms to be able to travel across Canada and take part in debates.[21] Reflecting on this sacrifice, former NFA president Sheldon Clare noted: "That's the hallmark of people who are committed in this, you know, like people I've served with on the board of directors. My own story is one of personal hardship and sacrifice. To do this ... I mean the telephone calls, emails, threats, all of that kind of thing comes with it."[22] This leads naturally to the question: what kind of person would become a gun advocate? What drives these policy entrepreneurs forward?

When asked how they became advocates, those I spoke with told compelling personal stories of the events that launched their journey into activism. I labelled these "origin stories," a nod to the comic book genre, which often spends significant time exploring the roots of their central character's or antagonist's personal journey.

Tracey Wilson describes having been a gun owner for over half her life. Despite this, she had not been politically active until the fateful night on the side of a Quebec highway described earlier. Others were spurred to act after being impacted by changes to legislation.

Christine Generoux is an environmental technician in western Canada. Before the May 2020 OIC that banned many of her favourite firearms, she would have never imagined she would end up self-repre-senting in a Charter challenge against the Canadian government. Chris-tine cited her upbringing when noting her motivation to become an advocate. Describing her younger self as a "troubled youth," she said that she had felt disillusioned and had trouble finding where she fit into society, until she discovered her passion for the outdoors. "What kind of got me back on the right track in life was learning about the outdoors, like taking camping trips with my family. And then that kind of sprung a passion for the environment and nature, and wilderness survival, you know, independence and hunting."[23] This passion was stoked by an important relationship in her life with a family friend. "My mom's best friend's husband was a firearms advocate for the NFA. He's very involved in the firearms world. He's a collector, and so I was lucky enough to have access to him as kind of a mentor to take me out. You know, shoot my first gun with me."

After six years of hunting and sports shooting, the gun ban prohib-ited one of the firearms she owned, and several of her mentor's.

> I acquired this property lawfully, with their [the government's] permis-sion. I've done everything that's been asked for [sic] me. I pay for this. I work hard for this. And now you're just trying to take it away from me? I realized that we were dealing with something that didn't have to do with public safety. It didn't have to do with certain firearms being more danger-ous than other firearms. It was an attack on all firearm owners as a group, and that the objective was in the future to ban as many as possible. So that's when I decided that I would go to court to try to defend my culture and my rights.

Generoux sought to pursue a legal case against the government, but encountered difficulty finding legal counsel. Unable to afford what one lawyer called the "Cadillac" of legal battles, and with no civil rights groups willing to take up her cause, Generoux took on the challenge of self-representation in her Charter challenge. Still, Generoux feels that what she is doing is important to defend what she describes as her cul-ture. "I feel the most satisfied and the most at peace and myself when I'm alone in the woods hunting or focusing at the range on improving my skills. I feel really in the zone. Firearms, and belonging to a culture of likeminded people ... Our lives centre around this culture of sports shooting and hunting. And everything that goes with it."[24]

For other advocates, their journey into advocacy was less dramatic. Jamie Elliott, the president of the CCFR, works for the organization on a volunteer basis. While Elliott grew up with guns in the home, he was never passionate about gun rights or involved in the broader community of gun owners. "It [guns] was just like your fishing-rod-in-the-closet type thing. It was just there." As casual gun owners, his parents considered getting rid of their guns once the Firearms Act was passed and licensing requirements became stricter. "That actually really hit me, because one of the guns is my grandfather's shotgun." After getting his PAL licence, Elliott became more and more involved in hunting and shooting. Elliot formed strong social bonds to the community, which prompted him to get more involved in online advocacy, educating people on Facebook and Twitter. "I found that very quickly, a small amount of education didn't necessarily turn people pro-gun, but it showed them that what they were hearing wasn't necessarily the whole truth."

The reception to his online advocacy was not universally positive. "I had one friend that actually posted on my Facebook page that: 'I liked you better before you had guns.'" This shocked and hurt Elliot, who described this as another stepping-stone on the pathway to advocacy. "I'm like, wait a second, this is what people actually think? These are people that I've known, that I've had dinner with, hung out with, you know, partied with, and everything like that, as soon as they find out I have guns, it's like, well, we don't like you anymore." Elliott became more and more involved in firearm advocacy after that moment but never forgot the friendship he lost. "You can brush it off at the time, but it does ... it sticks with you."[25]

A latecomer to the gun world, Rod Giltaca was middle-aged by the time he got into firearms, but he hit the ground running. Already a successful businessman, Rod went on to become a firearm instructor and YouTube star before becoming involved in advocacy. He was prompted to get involved when a legally registered rifle that he owned, the CZ 858, was reclassified as a prohibited firearm by the RCMP without him being notified. It was only through social media that he discovered that the rifle was now illegal to take to the range, despite the fact that the long-gun registry was still in place at that time and the government knew he owned one. Rod was frustrated and worried by the legal liability that opaque government decision-making exposed him to as a gun owner:

> I found myself in a position that I could have been out in the forest shooting using that rifle to shoot cans, and should a conservation officer roll up, I could have been [*pauses*] ... at the time there was a mandatory minimum of three years in prison for an unauthorized possession of a firearm.[26]

Before this event, Rod had kept his politics and his YouTube channel separate. After the incident, however, he decided to become more involved in advocacy, first through his videos. He made a video to raise awareness about the reclassification of the CZ-858 and was able to use his platform to launch his advocacy career.[27]

The advocates that I spoke with were all motivated by a similar sense of injustice and by experiences of feeling mistreated by their own government and stigmatized by the wider society.

Tactics

Scholars studying advocacy groups note that groups can use a variety of tactics to achieve their goals. The tactics they choose are influenced by their access to policymakers, resources, and the institutional environment they work in.[28] These tactics are sometimes classified as "insider" and "outsider" tactics. "Insider" tactics generally refer to lobbying and puzzling, strategies that are largely invisible to the public. "Outsider" tactics include visible strategies for advocacy, like using the court system or conducting public relations campaigns.[29]

The groups that I spoke with differed in their approach to advocacy, placing emphasis on the importance of different tactics. While the more established gun-owner groups, the NFA and CSSA, as well as industry representatives, professed a preference for insider lobbying, the newer CCFR favoured public communication, though it still engages in some lobbying activities. This represents a truism in advocacy: older groups prefer insider tactics. What is interesting is the way the mission is articulated by the CCFR, however, as more of a deliberate choice or philosophy. The provincial conservation groups, given their experience working with governments on issues unrelated to guns, show a propensity for insider tactics like puzzling and lobbying.

Lobbying

Lobbying involves direct communication between advocacy groups, or individuals, and government officials.[30] In Canada, lobbying is regulated under the *Lobbying Act*, and paid lobbyists must register and report their meetings with public officials to the Office of the Commissioner of Lobbying. Despite the relative transparency of lobbying in Canada, the term is quite charged, conjuring images of backroom deals and corruption. The advocates I spoke to were aware of the baggage that comes with the term and, as such, tended to talk about this aspect of their work the least.

Despite being proud of her job as a gun lobbyist, even going so far as to place a "#gunlobby" sticker on her car, Wilson notes that the term is loaded, so to speak: "It conjures up these images of this sort of dark, seedy person in an alley with a trench coat making backroom deals with politicians or, you know, the sort of dirty, negative images." Wilson noted that the reality was far more banal: "a grandma from the suburbs, showing up to speak to politicians of all stripes. And I'm asking them for fair and effective legislation for gun owners and credible work on crime".[31]

Bernardo agrees, noting that the popular image of lobbyists lying to or bribing politicians is more Hollywood than reality: "You have to go to the government, and you have to rationally convince them why your side is correct. Being an advocate/lobbyist is an educative role. It's not a persuasion role. You are never going to persuade a politician to do something that's against their best interests."[32] According to Bernardo, the most important part of lobbying is providing accurate information to policymakers in a way that does not compromise either party or make anyone look stupid.

> When you're dealing with the government, let's face it, Noah, 99 per cent of the stuff happens in backrooms. And governments need to find out information and act upon the information ... They have to do that in ways that never compromises them. Because at the end of the day, of course, a politician's real jobs: number one, get elected; number two, get reelected. Right? ... So we tend to be more reserved in our public aspects. We don't blow our horn as much, and in fact, we've come under criticism from many of our members for sometimes not loudly taking credit for all the things that we do. In real politics, you want to give the credit to the politicians, because that's how they get reelected. Remember mandate number two, right?[33]

Bernardo argues that his organization's lobbying-focused strategy has borne significant fruit. Among the lobbying successes that the CSSA claims is writing the bill that dismantled the long-gun registry in Canada,[34] one of the principal successes of the pro-gun advocacy network during the last thirty years.

Former NFA president Sheldon Clare noted that for most of its history, his organization engaged in grassroots lobbying. This involves lobbying by unpaid volunteers. Given that they do not draw salaries from their work, grassroots lobbyists do not need to register with the commissioner. Over the years, the NFA relied on committed volunteers among their membership to engage in lobbying. This, of course, could exact a personal toll. Clare worked as a professor at a community college in Alberta, and the regular travel to Ottawa did not permit the group to be as agile as he liked. So in 2013, the NFA hired a professional lobbyist.[35] It touts a number of successes in its lobbying efforts, including several classification victories for popular firearms like the Ruger Mini-14 and AR-15, though these were later prohibited by the OIC.[36]

The flip side of lobbying as a strategy, however, is that politicians must be willing to listen to and meet with you. This can be a problem for pro-gun advocates, who can end up shut out from the halls of power when more pro-control governments are in charge: a function of the interest-group capture noted in previous chapters. As noted earlier, Tracey Wilson of the CCFR says that she works most often with Conservative MPs and senators. "I mean, of course, probably the most friendly politician for a Canadian gun owner of any kind to speak to is, of course, a Conservative. Unfortunately, it shouldn't be that way."[37] Wilson noted that she used to have good relations with some rural Liberal MPs, like TJ Harvey, who was the chair of the Liberal Outdoor Caucus before being removed for his opposition to the Liberal's Bill C-71, which brought in several measures unpopular with gun owners.[38]

For example, while Bill C-71 was working its way through the Canadian Senate, Wilson expressed her frustration that Liberal senators would not even meet with her. As a result, she was relegated to trying to help Conservatives attempt to "shave off the rough edges" of legislation to make it less harmful for gun owners. This included helping Conservative senators connect with expert witnesses, or consulting with them on firearms issues. Wilson also affirmed that the lobbyists' subject-matter expertise is their most important tool.

At the same time, the greatest challenge that lobbyists reported was gaining access. The gun-owner groups discussed the challenges of losing and gaining access to decision-makers depending on which party held power. For the manufacturers, however, the greatest threat was more systemic: access to their regulator.

> I think the main point we'd like to make is that, you know, like any other industry, our main goal is to insist on having a working relationship with our regulator. No other regulated industry operates in a vacuum. We have no appeal process. We have no formal outline of how we interact with our regulator, which is the RCMP, meaning they can decide anything. We have no recourse, we have no opportunity to present evidence, and we have no rules around timing.[39]

This poses major challenges to the industry. For example, the approval and categorization process for new firearms often takes up to two years. This is challenging for gun shops, which will often sign distribution agreements with American or other foreign gun manufacturers that can last up to a year. This means that by the time a firearm is approved for sale in the Canadian market, the distribution agreement may have expired, and another company can profit from the work that the firm has done struggling through the regulatory process. "A competitor comes in, grabs the distribution contract, and the investment of two years getting the firearm through the RCMP vetting process that the original distributor made is wasted."[40]

The uncertainty around the classification system for firearms in Canada has also made the work of outdoors stores challenging. Since the 1990s, Canadian firearm classification has been based on the make and model of the firearm, not necessarily its characteristics. For example, before being banned, the infamous AR-15 was a restricted firearm in Canada, requiring the same licensing, storage, and transportation laws as handguns. The AR-15 could not be used for hunting, despite being a very capable firearm for varmint and predator control on farms and in rural areas, and could only be transported to federally regulated ranges. Countless functionally equivalent though less famous firearms, like the IWI Tavor or Ruger Mini-14, which fire the same round from a removable magazine in a semi-automatic fashion, were classified as non-restricted, meaning they could be used for hunting or fired on backyard ranges by rural Canadians.

This created a regulatory quagmire for businesses, making it challenging for them to survive while also keeping up with the ever-shifting regulations. "It's impossible for a business to understand how to operate its supply chain without clear specifications on what it is and isn't allowed to import. We are having trouble complying, because compliance is undefined. Our businesses want to operate in compliance with the law."[41]

While most firearm policy is crafted at the federal level, the advocates I spoke to mentioned working at the provincial and municipal level as well, given what they saw as a multi-pronged attacked on gun ownership in Canada. Bernardo noted the challenge of dealing with municipal political battles, in addition to working with other levels of government: "We do it in the provinces, we do it in the federal government, we do it in municipalities, should the need arise ... As a matter of fact, municipalities can be sometimes the hotbed, because you're playing whack-a-mole with eight, or nine, or ten of them at a time."[42]

At the municipal level, a major issue for the gun groups is zoning laws. Gun ranges in Canada face a dilemma. They must be far enough away from city limits to avoid noise complaints, but close enough to be convenient for urban patrons to access. Given that many of the ranges in Canada are decades old, city boundaries have shifted significantly since they were built. As suburban sprawl continues, many gun ranges face anew the threat of being shut down by noise complaints, some of which Bernardo argues, are politically motivated. The CSSA works to support gun ranges dealing with these complaints.[43]

While the NFA, CSSA, and CCFR represent gun owners, firearm manufacturers have their own representation on Parliament Hill, such as Alison De Groot of the CSAAA. De Groot noted, however, that the reach of the firearms industry in Canada was quite limited, as many firearm businesses were reluctant to engage in advocacy. The Canadian gun market is simply not big enough to be a priority for gun manufacturers, leaving Canada's small- and medium-sized retailers to fend for themselves. While some businesses would reach out to MPs on their own, De Groot was the sole voice representing the firearms industry: "Federally, I am the only voice in Ottawa, much to the disappointment of the anti-gun movement. This is Canada, it's not the United States. These are all small-business owners who pay their membership out of their pocket. We don't have big gun manufacturers in Canada."

Like the CSSA, the CSAAA advocates at all levels of government, albeit with varying degrees of success. De Groot highlighted that her role as a lobbyist was to provide her expertise, a difficult task given that "Very often public policy is made emotionally and politically, without regard for the technology or the technical definitions." De Groot remembered attending a meeting of the Toronto City Council Public Health Committee held to discuss banning handgun ammunition. "I was there to explain that there's no such thing as handgun ammunition." De Groot's argument was that ammunition is not classified by "handgun" or "rifle" but by calibre. While some calibres are used more often in handguns then in long guns, few are exclusive to a single type of firearm. For example, the popular .22 LR cartridge can be fired from both handguns and long guns; 9mm, perhaps the most famous handgun cartridge, can also be fired in several popular rifle platforms. Much to De Groot's frustration, "They [city council] have very little understanding, and they passed it anyway."[44]

Sometimes, firearms advocacy happens even in international organizations. Clare noted that his group, the NFA, had been recognized by the United Nations as a non-governmental organization (NGO), allowing it to participate in talks regarding the Arms Trade Treaty. Though the treaty was nominally aimed at controlling the flow of small arms to conflict zones, elements of it threatened the interests of civilian recreational gun owners. Pro-gun activists worried that this was an attempt to impose civilian disarmament from above.[45]

While lobbyists very rarely reported major successes, they noted that lobbying sometimes helped them to smooth the rough edges off policies that, without their input, could have been highly destructive to the community. The Harper government abolished the Canadian Long-Gun Registry in 2012 with Bill C-19 and ordered the records destroyed. After Quebec lost a lengthy legal battle to retain its records,[46] the province established its own provincial firearm registry. While popular in urban centres like Montreal and Quebec City, the bill was deeply unpopular in rural areas. When the deadline for registry expired, 75 per cent of long guns in Quebec had still not been registered, and fifteen municipalities had passed resolutions expressing their opposition.

The FQCP originally fought against the registry. Though it was unsuccessful, the group believes that it managed to get it softened. For example, gun owners in Quebec no longer need carry a physical copy of a registration certificate, as the firearm's serial number can be looked up in the system. This eliminates the onus on firearm owners to show documentation to a police officer or conservation officer when approached, and protects them from potential legal liability from a paperwork infraction. The FQCP sees the registry as wasted money that could be better spent on things like public education, noting that the system is rarely used, and records are incomplete and poorly managed. That said, the organization still works to educate its members on the importance of following the law and how to comply with the new regulations. For example, some gun owners thought that their firearms were still registered in the federal system, not knowing that they had to re-register them in the new provincial system.[47]

Public Relations

Though talking to politicians is an important part of advocacy, and a major focus of two of the three principal gun owner groups, the advocates I spoke with acknowledged that engaging with the Canadian public was also necessary, albeit to different extents. A common refrain among advocates and gun owners was that their community was misrepresented in the Canadian media and that an important job of firearm advocacy was to correct popular misconceptions about them. For the lobbying-focused CSSA, the purpose of what they called "media advocacy" was to correct what they called "Hollywood" myths perpetuated by politicians, pro-control advocates, and the media. One example is the myth that the NRA operates in Canada, despite the fact that its charter forbids it from working outside of the United States.[48] The NFA also engaged in public relations work through media interviews with major outlets like the CBC and CTV, social media, postcard campaigns, and its own firearms magazine, the Canadian Firearms Journal. Clare also touted the NFA's work sponsoring shooting-sport athletes, including Olympic athletes and biathletes. The group provides scholarships for student athletes and pays for them to attend international shooting competitions like the Commonwealth Games.[49]

For the CCFR, however, public relations work is central to its mission and approach to advocacy. Executive Director Rod Giltaca noted in our interview that he saw the role of the group as tackling misinformation, or misunderstandings that the public has about the community.[50] The founders of the CCFR felt that gun owners in Canada had an image problem, that the "entire firearms community had suffered from thirty years of bad branding," and that the only way to address this was to approach firearm advocacy from the perspective of marketing.[51]

The advocates I spoke with understood that representing the community could sometimes be a challenge, given public perceptions. For example, the CCFR felt that past advocacy had been "preaching to the choir" and no one had been reaching out to the public. "What you're saying makes sense to the people who understand the topic. But the topic is incredibly complex."[52] Wilson gave the example of the GSG-16, a small, semi-automatic rimfire rifle. While the rifle has a "tactical" appearance, and would likely draw the ire of those unfamiliar with firearms, the gun fires the anaemic .22 LR cartridge, which is usually reserved for target shooting or hunting small game like rabbits or gophers. When it comes to creating legislation, however, the public perception of a firearm can have a greater impact than the technical realities. In their 2020 ban, for example, the government used the term "assault-style firearms" rather than the more popular "assault weapon," in essence ceding the point that these firearms were banned for their appearance rather than their function.

CCFR advocates felt that their efforts to correct negative public perceptions of gun owners was challenging, given the willingness of the media and politicians to profit from scaring the public, or from spreading misinformation.[53] To get their message across, the CCFR has taken full advantage of traditional and digital media. The organization has a large YouTube presence, releasing campaign-ad-style videos alongside "explainer" videos, to try to break down the complexities of the gun debate in a way that is accessible to ordinary Canadians. The organization sees this as empowering its members to take advocacy into their own hands.[54]

Social media like YouTube allow the group's messaging to have a relatively large reach. One of their most popular videos, the ironically named "Ban the AR 15 – It's Just Common Sense," has reached almost 700,000 views on YouTube[55] at the time of writing. The CCFR sees these videos as a way to interject facts in a debate that is dominated by emotion, in order to cement their image as the "reasonable gun lobby." They recognize that once they lose that credibility, they will cease to be taken seriously.

The CCFR engages extensively with the mainstream media, regularly doing interviews with reporters, and even consulting on documentaries like Vice News's "How to Buy a Gun in Canada: Armed and Reasonable," which has been viewed over 2.5 million times on YouTube.[56]

The CCFR has also ventured into television, producing several shows which have aired on a Canadian outdoors television network. These attempt to introduce the public to the Canadian gun-owning community. For example, the group's first major show, *Canada Downrange*, travelled across Canada to showcase firearm clubs and competitions.

One of the greatest victories of the modern intersectional feminist movement has been the discursive power now vested in concepts like "diversity" and "inclusion." Movements, even those based in conservative politics, understand the need to showcase their diversity, or risk being labelled as "too white" or "too male." This is a problem for the pro-gun movement, which has traditionally been dominated by older white men.[57] The CCFR has broken ground in Canada by creating explicit diversity and inclusion programs, especially those geared towards women.

Wilson notes that breaking away from the "old boys' club" image was one of the reasons for founding the CCFR. "You know, I'm a pretty cheerful, vibrant grandma from the suburbs. And I'm literally one of two registered lobbyists for gun rights in the country. So, it's not, this isn't your granddad's gun lobby ... and women play a really huge role in our organization."[58] To support this claim, Wilson cites the CCFR women's program, which has given over 7,000 women across Canada the opportunity to experience the shooting sports firsthand in a safe environment. The CCFR also hosts women-only retreats.

The funds for these efforts comes from the CCFR *Gunnie Girl Calendar*, an initiative that Wilson devised despite initial resistance from Giltaca. Giltaca feared that if not done tastefully, the calendar could be used to reinforce traditional images of gun owners as misogynists. Wilson persisted, however, and now the *Gunnie Girl Calendar* raises over $50,000 annually to help fund the women's program. The women who appear in the calendar are not professional models but ordinary gun owners who volunteer and are given a weekend retreat in exchange for their labour. Wilson takes great pride in the calendar, and her efforts to "keep it classy" and focus on women's empowerment: "There's nothing better for a woman's self-esteem than to take your average, you know, Canadian hunter, bird shooter, and turn her into a supermodel for the day."[59]

The advocates noted that a focus on women is especially important in the Canadian context, where discussions of women's safety, intimate-partner violence, and misogynist terror have been central to the gun debate since the École Polytechnique shooting in 1989. The advocates felt that making space for women was their way of showcasing that women are gun owners too and do not want to lose their property any more than men do.[60]

The women I spoke with who had worked on the calendar project spoke highly of the initiative. Allison noted that as a young mother, finding time for herself can be a challenge. The prospect of a weekend away from the family shooting guns and getting to know other women with similar interests was a boon. Allison notes that she connected very quickly with the other women due to their shared experience as women in a male-dominated hobby.[61]

Beyond their efforts to engage women, a centre of gravity for the CCFR has been its ability to mobilize the online community of gun owners. It uses tools like its closed Facebook group to share information with members and followers, encourage donations, and get people involved. Elliott, who has taken a leadership role in moderating the Facebook page, noted the importance of inclusivity to maintaining the CCFR's online presence. He stressed that the group is completely open to 2SLBGTQ+ folks and people from different backgrounds, and that his moderator team takes a zero-tolerance policy to any racist, sexist, or homophobic comments. "If you're a gun owner, you're a gun owner. To us. That's it, end of story. Everybody's welcome. That pulled in an entire strata of society that felt very ostracized from the community as a whole."[62] This included centrist and left-wing gun owners that the CCFR felt had been left in the cold by other pro-gun groups that catered mostly to the Conservative Party base.

In the summer of 2020, the CCFR took its public relations approach to the streets, organizing an "Integrity March" on Parliament Hill. It was the first time that gun owners had marched in significant numbers on Parliament Hill since the "Fed Up" rallies of the 1990s, and it was a risky strategy. The march took place in the first summer of the COVID-19 pandemic, and the CCFR risked a public-relations disaster if the march turned into a super-spreader event. Further, the risk that the movement's message might be tainted by extremists infiltrating the protest was real. In the end, the protest proceeded peacefully, with thousands of supporters gathering on Parliament Hill and marching down Sparks Street in downtown Ottawa.[63] The march itself garnered some media attention, but the news cycle at the time was dominated by COVID-19 headlines. The CBC, for example, reposted a short article from the Canadian Press on the march, the narrative of which was largely driven by pro-control activists interviewed in response to the protest.[64]

The conservation groups I spoke to also engaged in public relations campaigns, although mostly relating to hunting and fishing rather than firearms. For example, in 2008 the FQCP launched a campaign to promote a positive image of hunting in the province and "demystify" hunting for the general public. It also carries out public relations campaigns such as donating meat from hunting to food banks.[65]

The advocates were quite sanguine about the challenges of a public relations approach to an issue as technical and emotional as firearm policy. The reality of the twenty-four-hour news cycle is that detailed discussions of policy are often sacrificed in favour of talking points and soundbites. Matt DeMille of OFAH noted the challenges of getting heard in the current media environment: "You only have a little bit of time to unpack a complex problem." The lack of public education on the issue compounded this problem: "but you're not just unpacking a complex problem, you're unpacking a complex problem with a society and media who don't understand the complexities of that."[66]

Coalition Building

Scholars since Schattschneider[67] have noted the tendency of winning and losing coalitions to seek to expand or constrict the scope of a conflict. According to this logic, coalitions that perceive themselves to be on the defensive will seek to expand the scope of the conflict to attempt to bring in more allies. Actors that perceive themselves to be winning on a policy issue will try to limit access.

Given that the pro-gun coalition has been on the defensive since the election of the Trudeau government in 2015, it is natural that it would try to broaden the scope of the conflict. What is interesting is the way it has gone about this. The coalition has used two key strategies: first, reaching out to victims of gun violence, long seen as natural allies for the pro-control camp, and second, positioning firearm rights as property rights.

The CCFR has made efforts to enlist the help of gun-violence victims and reframe the conversation on guns around the social determinants of violence. This is a game-changer in a gun debate that has long been dominated by stagnant and predictable rhetoric. In our talk, Wilson

discussed this approach at length. "You can't oppose gun control without suggesting something else, right?" Rather, the CCFR has worked to
shift the conversation towards a discussion of the sources of crime guns
and the social determinants of crime.[68]

To that end, the CCFR has found unlikely allies in victims of gun violence and advocates working on the front lines of the gang-violence crisis in many of Canada's large urban centres. While gun-control debates
in Canada are dominated by discussions of highly publicized mass
shootings, it is people of colour in big cities like Toronto and Indigenous people who bear the brunt of violence that involves a firearm in
Canada.[69]

Evelyn Fox lost her son Kissinger to a stray bullet outside a Toronto
nightclub in 2016. Her grief and outrage prompted her to get involved
soon after with the Zero Gun Violence Movement. Fox began as an
advocate for stricter gun control, speaking in support of Bill C-71,
which she felt would help address the problem of straw purchasing;
when a licensed gun owner purchases guns to sell on the black market.[70]
She found herself often sparring online with the CCFR, and Wilson in
particular. After a particularly heated Twitter exchange, Fox extended
an olive branch and ended up meeting with Wilson in a room in Toronto
City Hall. Since then, the two have been friends and allies. Wilson has
marched alongside Fox with other mothers who have lost sons to gun
violence, while Fox has gone to the gun range with Wilson to experience
gun culture for herself.[71]

The two managed to find common ground around their shared frustration that the government was not addressing the social determinants
of gun crime.

> At some point in time, we have to look at why a person picks up a weapon
> in the first place, and that hasn't been done. So, after I started advocating,
> I found out that in 2008, a report was done called the Review of the Roots
> of Youth Violence report,[72] after the 2005 "year of the gun." And it has all
> of these recommendations outlined in it for how to deal with prevent-
> ing youth from getting involved in gang violence and committing violent
> crime. All of those recommendations, every single one of them, there has
> been [government] cuts. Every single party at every single level has cut
> from those recommendations, every one of them since that report was
> released, and then they expect that things will get better?[73]

Fox found herself frustrated by the lack of investment in communities of colour and Indigenous communities in Canada, and by the dis-
proportionate emphasis on gun-control measures in this debate.

Every life is precious. I think that ever since I've started advocating, I've really noticed how black and Indigenous lives are not valued by the government. It's been an extreme eye-opener. Like, it's, it's deplorable how uninvested they are in the communities that are predominantly impacted by violence.[74]

Fox also feels that the focus on gun violence, rather than taking a holistic view of violence in general, is more a political strategy than an honest attempt to intervene in these at-risk communities. She feels that the focus on guns distracts from honestly examining the reasons youth turn to weapons to solve problems in the first place: "How can we prevent these children from picking up weapons, period? Because the stabbings far exceed gun violence numbers. I support mothers whose children have been killed by stabbings, and the pain is not different. It's the same."[75]

Fox acknowledges that her perspective sometimes places her at odds with the more established gun-violence victims' groups, or the groups representing doctors. Though she is grateful to them for fighting to create Canada's strong gun-control infrastructure, she feels that their differences of opinion stem from their different socio-demographic positions and experiences of violence. "How do you rationalize spending a billion dollars or more to ban firearms when you're throwing chump change across Canada to the communities that are impacted?"[76]

Another rhetorical strategy that the CCFR has employed to broaden the scope of the conflict is framing the ban of assault-style weapons in Canada as a broader attack on property rights. The group lays out its perspective in a YouTube video posted on the website that they created to share news about their lawsuit, purchasing the domain name propertyjustice.ca. The principal argument of the video is that if the government can confiscate lawfully acquired property from ordinary gun owners under the auspices of public safety, then similar initiatives could be launched against non–gun owners during emergencies. One example they provide is the confiscation of pickup trucks, using the excuse of the climate emergency.[77] As a legal strategy, this has proven challenging, given that any guarantee of property rights were explicitly left out of the Canadian Charter due to provincial concerns that this would diminish their governments' powers.[78] As a rhetorical strategy, however, it is a useful way to try to expand the coalition and try to show non–gun owners what they feel is at stake in the debate. Once again, we can see the movement framing gun rights not in relation to self-defence or resistance to tyrannical government, but in the expectations that citizens have of fair treatment by their government.

At the same time, holding together the coalition of gun owners can sometimes be a difficult task, give the divisions between hunters and sports shooters. Since the debates over the long-gun registry, hunters in Canada have enjoyed greater social legitimacy than sports shooters. Hunting is seen by most Canadians as a legitimate activity that justifies firearm ownership. This is also because the firearms that hunters use are generally less controversial than the handguns or semi-automatic carbines favoured by sports shooters. As a result, sports shooters often have a difficult time mobilizing hunters' support, something that the government has exploited with its messaging.

Matt DeMille noted that the government's communications around policies like the assault-style weapons ban often specifically disclaimed an intention to target hunters. He noted that the controversy around the long-gun registry changed Canadian discourse on guns, making governments wary of appearing to unfairly target hunters and farmers.[79]

As a result, the firearms groups representing the sports shooters must invest energy and resources communicating not just with the general public but within the community as well. For example, the CCFR has created several series and television shows on the hunting network WildTV to try to attract hunters to the group.

The Courts

Unlike the United States, it was quite rare for advocacy groups in Canada to make use of the legal system before the 1980s. This changed in 1982 with the adoption of the Canadian Charter of Rights and Freedoms.[80] Since then, the courts have been an essential tool for advocacy groups like the Gay and Lesbian Rights movement in Canada.[81] The courts have looked less favourably, however, on the pro-gun movement. The Canadian Charter does not include a right to bear arms, as the US Constitution does. This has not stopped older iterations of the pro-gun movement from looking further back in Canada's history to try to establish this right – for example, citing the English Bill of Rights, which avowed a right to bear arms for Protestant men and was the precursor to the American Second Amendment.[82] Despite these faint hopes, in 1993 the Canadian Supreme Court of Canada declared that there is no right to bear arms in Canada and that gun ownership was a privilege granted by the Crown.[83]

The 2020 OIC changed this, as advocates saw an opportunity to challenge the ban in the courts. These advocates did not, however, rest their arguments on establishing a constitutional right to bear arms, but on the right of Canadians to be free from unfair government interference and on cultural rights.

On the advice of their lawyer, Solomon Friedman, the NFA's approach to the lawsuit was to find a plaintiff who had been personally impacted by the ban. Cassandra Parker, owner of K.K.S. Tactical Supplies in Prince George, BC, stepped forward.[84] Like many small-business owners in the firearm sector, Parker's business had been severely impacted by the OIC, leaving her with $75,000 of merchandise that she could neither sell nor return to the manufacturer.[85] The NFA funded her case, with Friedman becoming her representative. At the time of writing, the case has not yet been heard.

While the NFA case has been a relatively quiet affair, the CCFR used it to underpin a major fundraising drive, and as a way of getting the community further involved in the fight against the government. The CCFR's legal case was grouped together with several others fighting the ban, including Indigenous activist Laurence Knowles, who died before the case could be heard; professional competitive sports shooter Ryan Steacy; and firearm-related businesses like Wolverine Supplies.

As previously mentioned, the CCFR launched the website propertyjustice.ca, where it has published affidavits and documents produced by the court. It has also launched a legal fund, crowdsourcing money directly from clubs and individual members. The group has used its Twitter page to showcase the clubs that raised money for the legal challenge, and in the first four months after the OIC, journalists used the website to estimate that the group had already amassed over $300,000.[86]

After a three-year fight in Federal Court, Judge Catherine M. Kane ruled that the OIC was within the scope of the government's authority and did not represent a violation of the Charter or Bill of Rights.[87] An attempted appeal was also rejected by the courts in 2025.

For the CCFR, however, the court case was not just about winning. They saw it as a way to hold its opponents accountable. The group often challenges pro-control advocates to debates, even going so far as to promise to donate $10,000 to both Big Brothers and Sisters Toronto, and the charity of their opponent's choice, if the Doctors for Protection from Guns[88] engaged them in an organized debate.[89] The Doctors refused. The lawsuit, however, offers the group the opportunity to publish statements by their opponents on the stand.[90]

Christine Generoux, who first launched her case as an independent Charter challenge, had her case combined with the CCFR's, a common practice in Canada's legal system. Generoux's approach, however, was somewhat unique. Rather than frame her case around due process, she argued that the 2020 OIC would irreparably harm gun culture in Canada, which like other cultures, she argued, should be protected under the Charter. She contended that the damage to businesses from the ban would eventually destroy the gun culture in Canada, noting that "if you destroy places to buy firearms, and places to shoot firearms, like shops and ranges, then the culture itself will be irreparably harmed." She believed strongly that gun culture fit the definition of culture set out by the Canadian government, which she argued defined culture not in terms of race or ethnic/national origin, but rather around belonging to: "a group of people who believe and can demonstrate that our history and heritage has included firearms for hundreds of years, that our use of the firearms is focused around safety, independence, and law-abiding behaviour."

Generoux believes that these cultural rights establish a right to own firearms in Canada, albeit on very different terms than the American Second Amendment.

> I would argue that just because we don't have a Second Amendment in Canada, doesn't mean that there are no firearm rights. And if the courts don't think that there is [sic] firearm rights, that still doesn't mean that firearm owners have less rights than other people, or that we don't have the same equal benefit and application of a law, that the fundamental principles of justice do apply to everyone in Canada, whether or not they own firearms.[91]

Generoux's conception of gun rights captures the major difference between the American vision of this concept and the focus on procedural fairness that underscores the Canadian conceptualization.

Puzzling

Puzzling occurs when groups work with the government towards the creation of better public policy.[92] It is an important function of advocacy groups in a democratic system and helps to incorporate diverse views and interests in the public policy process. The advocates I spoke with engaged in puzzling with government officials to greater and lesser degrees, depending on the issue.

Gun-owner groups worked with the government on several policy initiatives. A major victory for the NFA was its intervention on the revision of the Explosives Act. While this does not seem like something that would impact the gun community, it was a big issue for reloaders[93] and muzzle-loaders[94] who store different types of gunpowder in their home. For example, many hunters prefer to hunt with muzzle-loading firearms, similar to the frontier rifles and muskets that their ancestors used. Provinces often have expanded seasons for those who hunt with muzzle-loading firearms, given that it is much more complex and involves getting closer to the animal. Shooters thus have to store black powder or black-powder substitutes, like Pyrodex, in their homes. These substances fall under the Explosives Act and could have been regulated out of existence were it not for the NFA's intervention on behalf of such hunters. Clare argued that storing these substances did not pose any more of a risk than a family storing propane tanks on their deck.[95]

On the other side, a major frustration of the industry group, the CSAAA, was the government's unwillingness to work with the firearms industry, which De Groot noted was eager to open a dialogue with its regulator. De Groot expressed the industry's frustration that the May 2020 OIC continued the practice of banning firearms by make and model, rather than by technical designation.

De Groot highlighted the frustration of the industry with the OIC, noting that many stores were now stuck with stocks of firearms that they could neither sell nor dispose of, with storage fees piling up. To make matters worse, the government continued to add firearms retroactively to the list of banned models. Owing to American law, the firearms cannot be reimported to the United States, leaving gun businesses, most of which are small and medium-sized enterprises in rural communities, in a difficult spot. De Groot argued that this example highlights the lack of dialogue between the industry and their regulator: "No industry can operate without technical terms and an open relationship with their government that allows for supply-chain issues to be addressed when regulations are coming into place." She noted that this leads to problems such as orders from suppliers being banned while they are in transit, which forces businesses to pay to store the firearms, which cannot be re-exported.[96]

De Groot notes that the actions of the politicians, and the lack of technical designations in determining which firearms should and should not be banned, has created chaos on the ground for both regulator and regulated.

> These regulations come into effect without prior notification to the industry, but also without prior notification to our service agencies. So, all of a sudden, CBSA[97] does not know how to conduct business with us, Global Affairs does not know how to conduct business with us. The RCMP does not know how to conduct business with us.[98]

Given that provincial hunting groups work with the government on more issues than just firearms, puzzling was central to their approach to influencing policy. By virtue of their charitable status, hunting groups cannot engage in partisan advocacy. Their non-partisan approach, however, is more of an advantage than a hindrance when it comes to working with government.

Given that these groups work with governments on a broad range of issues, from land management to invasive species, they are better placed to find common ground with governments less friendly to the gun-owning community. This allows them to build trust and respect with policymakers through "evidence and logic." Rather than focusing solely on the political level, the groups also noted that they considered the entire policy system and worked with staffers and people in the civil service with whom they had built relationships.[99]

Cooperation between provincial conservation groups and the government on gun-safety legislation has a long history in Canada. After witnessing a rise in hunting accidents in the post-war period, provincial governments began working to regulate hunting. Taking a similar approach to the regulation of automobiles during this period, they began experimenting with mandatory hunters' safety courses. The provincial conservation groups, like OFAH and FQCP, encouraged these developments and worked with the governments to develop and deliver the curriculum to hunters. Mandatory hunter-safety training was associated with a sustained decrease in hunting accidents in Canada.[100] During my talk with Alain Cossette, director general of the FQCP, he spoke proudly of the impact of mandatory hunters' safety at reducing hunting accidents in Quebec, and his organization's record in designing and implementing the safety training. In 1966, for example, sixty people were hurt or killed in hunting accidents in Quebec. Now zero to three people die in hunting accidents in Quebec annually, and these are often not firearm-related, but involve falls from hunting blinds, raised tree platforms that conceal hunters from their quarry. According to the FQCP, there has never been a non-hunter shot in a hunting accident in Quebec.[101] The FQCP also works to conduct campaigns among members that help to promote the safe storage of firearms and campaigns on mental health and suicide prevention.

Resource Mobilization

Early scholars of group politics, called pluralists, argued that when confronted with legislation that threatened their interests, people would naturally turn to advocacy to have their concerns addressed.[102] This assumption was dealt a crushing blow by Olson's famous counterargument. Olson reasoned that involvement in advocacy was not a natural human response. Rather, it was rational for people pursuing collective goods to free-ride on the advocacy work of others. Small groups, or groups pursuing selective goods that could only be enjoyed by their members, were generally immune to this. But larger groups pursuing goods that anyone could enjoy, such as access to firearms, must contend with this free-rider problem.[103] Since then, neopluralist scholars have tried to reconcile these two assumptions, emphasizing resource mobilization: that is, how groups amass resources despite the free-rider problem.[104] One way to study the potential success of a movement is to examine how it gathers both human and financial resources to fill its political war chest and influence policy.

Scholars from the United States have noted that pro-gun movements have a distinct advantage when it comes to grassroots resource mobilization, as gun owners are primed to be politically active and to donate money to protect their rights.[105]

Follow the Money

A major myth surrounding firearm advocacy in Canada is that it is primarily funded by business donations. When asked about the financial contributions of gun companies to their movements, most of the advocates I spoke with derided this assumption. "You know that copper wire was invented by two-gun dealers fighting over a penny, right? There is no money in the firearms industry in Canada; most of them [businesses] are barely surviving."[106]

The CCFR, for example, estimates that about 4 per cent of its funding comes from the industry, mostly in the form of $250 business memberships.[107] Given the small size of Canada's market, with only 2.2 million licensed gun owners spread over a massive territory, there is little incentive for American manufacturers to get involved in the fight. The state of California alone, for example, has twice as many gun owners as Canada.[108] When trying to fundraise from Canadian small businesses, advocacy groups often run into the free-rider problem.

> It is one of the axioms we work with that this is the only industry in the country where you have to go to them hat in hand and beg them to save themselves. I'm dead serious, you would not believe that this could be as dramatic as it is ... What you get from the industry is sometimes a donation in kind, where, for example, the distributor will allow you to buy a firearm at wholesale cost, so you can raffle it to your members. Okay, but in terms of like "hey, here's a cheque"? That's funny.[109]

De Groot echoed this message, noting that many gun shops are "disconnected from the debate," being located in rural and remote areas, and do not see the value in paying for industry representation. As a result, the organization often suffers from fundraising issues.[110]

But if gun manufacturers are not funding firearm advocacy in Canada, where does the money come from? Olson's concept of selective incentives offers the answer to this puzzle.

Selective Incentives (Club Memberships)

Like other social identities, leisure-based identities, when challenged, can serve as a rallying point for advocacy.[111] In fact, these movements have an inherent advantage, given their pre-established mobilization structure and their ability to offer selective incentives to members. In the case of Canadian firearms advocates, the most powerful selective incentives they have to offer are range memberships and insurance.

Gun ranges in Canada are required by law to carry at least $2 million in liability insurance.[112] Further, members of shooting ranges benefit from purchasing liability insurance as well. Pro-gun advocacy groups realized that offering insurance to individuals and clubs can be a way to boost their funding and memberships. As a result, groups offer liability insurance to both members and clubs as a selected incentive. This means that signing up for a range membership often comes with membership in a pro-gun advocacy organization or a provincial conservation group whether or not the individual is aware of it.

As a result, pro-gun organizations compete fiercely to win the patronage of gun clubs. Despite seeing eye-to-eye on most issues, a major point of contention for the provincial conservation groups has been that gun-owner groups, primarily made up of sports shooters, have been slowly taking over the club insurance business. Darrell Crabbe of the Saskatchewan Wildlife Federation, for example, noted that their group had about sixty ranges across the province that were "owned, controlled, and insured by us." However, Crabbe was concerned that at some of the ranges groups of sports shooters had become involved in the board of directors of the range and shifted their priorities towards the gun-owner groups.[113] Given that owners of restricted firearms in Canada need a range membership in order to own handguns, these sports shooters are incentivized to become range members, while hunters may only take their guns to the range once or twice a year to sight in their rifles for hunting season.

The issue of club membership also makes it harder for newer groups to enter the field. Despite being one of the most visible gun advocacy groups, the relatively young CCFR has the smallest membership of the big three, claiming about 35,000[114] members at the time of writing, compared with the NFA's claimed 72,000[115] and the CSSA's claimed 37,000.[116]

Network of Clubs

The network of gun clubs is valuable to the broader movement not just for selling memberships, but for spreading information and gathering donations. The CCFR's legal- challenge fund has been financed principally through donations from clubs and associations, as well as fundraisers run by gun stores. The CCFR has committed to thanking each club for its donation with a post on the organization's public Twitter page. This has made it possible to track donations. For example, between May 2021 and May 2022, the organization received $105,051 in donations from twenty-two clubs and four firearm retailers, specifically for their legal fund.

In addition to raising funds, these clubs and retailers also provide a space for gun-owner groups to advertise and to spread the word to gun owners about how to become more involved. Having this existing infrastructure of clubs and stores is a major grassroots advantage for the pro-gun movement.

Community Service

Advocacy groups enjoy support from the community because they offer services to the community. Groups I spoke with provide a variety of services for the communities they represent. Indigenous peoples in Canada possess special treaty rights, guaranteed by the constitution, to protect their traditional hunting practices. The Eeyou/Eenou (Cree) people in Northern Quebec are one such group. The James Bay and Northern Quebec Agreement (JBNQA) was signed in November of 1975 between the governments of Quebec and Canada on one hand, and the Eeyou/Eenou and Inuit peoples on the other.[117] The agreement protects the hunting rights of the Eeyou/Eenou people, and in 1978 the Cree Trappers Association (CTA) was created to help administer these rights, as well as work towards wildlife conservation in the area, so that the traditional hunting and trapping practices could be "passed on in a sustainable manner."[118]

With regard to firearms, the CTA helps deliver the Canadian Firearms Safety Course within Eeyou/Eenou communities eighteen to twenty-five times per year. The organization sees this as a way of protecting Indigenous cultural practices.

We try to certify as many people in the Cree communities because it's our duty, and the importance of teaching younger generations how to take care of guns out on the land and the safety protocols that need to be

transferred from an elder or from an instructor ... We still have people that
live off the land. The importance of having that gun ownership ... It means
a lot for our elders and the people, for our future generations to continue
practising the traditional way of life.[119]

Groups like the CTA also help these communities navigate the
bureaucracy related to gun ownership in Canada. A major concern is
the long-gun registry. While the federal registry no longer exists, Quebec maintains its own provincial registry. This has prompted resistance
in Indigenous communities, who, like settler gun owners, see it as an
unnecessary imposition with little connection to public safety. While
the CTA has encouraged its members to register their firearms and
offers services to help them navigate the process, they note that they
have received a lot of pushback, especially among those who rely on
firearms for subsistence hunting and fear that registration may be a step
towards firearm confiscation.[120]

Other groups provide services to their members as well. For example,
Clare noted that the NFA often helps gun owners who have run afoul of
Canada's complex maze of gun-control bureaucracy.[121]

Guns, Rights, and Culture

In this chapter, I have delved into the pro-gun movement, exploring the
groups and individuals that compose it and their motivations for advocacy. I have covered the resource-mobilization structure of the various
groups, as well as the tactics they use to influence policy.

The pro-gun advocacy coalition is a useful example to better understand how advocacy occurs in Canadian politics. By exploring a predominantly right-wing advocacy network, it also gives us an interesting
perspective into the difference that institutional structures make in
determining advocacy strategies. The courts have been a major resource
for the pro-gun movement in the United States.[122] Further, since the
1980s, well-resourced advocacy groups in Canada representing left-
wing causes, like gay and lesbian rights, abortion rights, and medical
assistance in dying, have achieved considerable success through Canada's legal system.[123] Despite this, the pro-gun groups we encountered
were reticent to use the legal system to fight their battles, knowing that
their odds were poor and that accessing the system was expensive.

The pro-gun advocates I spoke to, on the whole, were very different from their American counterparts. They spoke of the practical
realities of gun ownership, not of absolute rights or wars against tyrannical governments. Most of the groups supported gun regulation that

would be controversial south of the border. When they spoke of rights, it was about the right to fair treatment from the government, the right to have policy based on evidence rather than negative perceptions of the community, and the right to protect their culture and heritage. In other words, these groups were motivated by a very Canadian view of citizenship, rather than the discourses of armed citizenship so popular south of the border. This sentiment was encapsulated perfectly in my conversation with Matt DeMille of OFAH:

> What I'd like to see in firearms policy and in our gun laws is just some stability. And I think that's what firearms owners want. They just see this constant change, and the more that things are layered in, the less they understand about why it's being done, and they have trouble rationalizing it. They want to do the right thing, they want to be a part of the solution. They believe in public safety. A lot of them believe in having a system of firearms laws that, you know, guide what happens in Canada. But as things get tightened, and tightened, and tightened, they just tend to not be able to understand how those additional layers are, are actually helping.[124]

The pro-gun advocates I spoke with considered themselves to be fighting for the survival of their culture. For them, the increasing encroachment of policymakers on their serious leisure pursuit over the past fifty years is seen not as a policy conversation designed to advance public safety, but as a way to destroy the culture of gun ownership in Canada.[125]

7

The Hunters Become the Hunted – Bill C-21 and the Future

With no warning and no consultation, the Liberals have announced their plan to ban hunting rifles and shotguns. The hunters have become the hunted.
— Dane Lloyd, MP, Sturgeon River-Parkland, during question period discussions on C-21

When the Liberal government set out to ban what they labelled "assault-style" weapons, they unwittingly landed in a quagmire. Since 2015, the government had been careful to avoid putting forward policies that would risk mobilizing the hunting community, having seemingly learned the lessons of the long-gun registry. Gun policy is a useful wedge issue when hunters sit out the fight, but when mobilized, they can be a force to be reckoned with. The Liberals thus faced a choice. Identify "assault-style" firearms by their make and model rather than their mechanical function, leaving many hunters untouched but themselves open to scrutiny and gun industry work-arounds, or ban all semi-automatic firearms with detachable magazines and risk drawing hunters, including Indigenous hunters, into the fray.

Bill C-21 was first put forward by the minority Liberal government in 2021 and sold as a solution to rising handgun crime in large Canadian urban centres. It included measures like expanded red-flag laws, despite Canada already having a robust system for dealing with gun owners exhibiting troubling behaviour; a ban on airsoft replica firearms; and a freeze on handgun ownership. As the bill reached the Standing Committee on Public Safety and National Security (SECU), it seemed certain to pass with the support of the NDP and Bloc Québécois. For reasons that remain unclear at time of writing, the government decided that this was the time to resolve the "assault-style" paradox. Liberal committee member Paul Chiang proposed an amendment at the committee stage that would have added thousands of rifles to the prohibited list, including some single-shot rifles and bolt-action rifles targeted for their large calibre, and ban all semi-automatic firearms capable of accepting a removable magazine. For the Conservatives, this was the opportunity they had been waiting for. They published the news widely, and Canadian hunters awoke from their slumber.[1]

The move resulted in the first significant celebrity endorsement that Canadian gun owners had enjoyed in recent times. Montreal Canadiens goaltender Carey Price, an Indigenous British Columbian well-known in the city for his philanthropic work, posted a picture of himself online, waterfowl hunting with a semi-automatic shotgun, proclaiming his support for hunters and opposition to the bill. Price faced significant blowback for the timing of the post, which came only a few days before the anniversary of the Polytechnique Massacre, with few reporters managing to note the obvious: that Price was simply following the government's timing in introducing the amendment. The celebrity endorsement catapulted the issue into the news cycle.[2] Instead of backing down, Price defended himself, stating: "While I have no control over the timing of the amendment to Bill C-21 I stand by the opinions I've shared, I acknowledge that amplifying any conversation around this week may have upset some of those impacted most by the events here in 1989 and to them I apologize."

The next major blow to Bill C-21 came when the Assembly of First Nations (AFN) passed an emergency resolution at its annual conference condemning the amendment to the bill. Given the scope of the firearms banned, including the Soviet SKS often used by Indigenous hunters, the AFN expressed their concern that the ban would interfere with Indigenous treaty hunting rights, and harm subsistence hunters who relied on these firearms to put food on the table for their families and communities.[3]

A deluge of letters and emails descended on Parliament Hill. NDP MP Alistair McGregor, from British Columbia, complained in December 2022: "Some members of my caucus had not received one single piece of correspondence until this amendment dropped, and now it's making up half their correspondence."[4] This led to several high-profile defections from parties that the Liberals would need to pass the legislation. NDP leader Jagmeet Singh followed the AFN resolution by stating that the NDP could not support the bill as it stood. Charlie Angus, a rural NDP MP, called the government's handling of the amendment "one of the dumbest things I've ever seen."[5] Even Liberal MPs from rural areas started feeling nervous. MP Brendan Hanley openly called in the house for the bill to be "clarified," and said he did not feel the "rural voice" had been heard on the issue.[6]

The offending amendments were quietly withdrawn, and when the bill was reintroduced early in 2023, the government clarified that the new evergreen definition would only apply to future firearms, while a committee of experts would be assembled to examine those firearms still on the market and make a case-by-case determination.[7] Reassured that the government was not coming for their guns, hunters quieted down, and the bill was sent through the House of Commons and Senate, gaining royal assent in December of 2023.

The case of Bill C-21 ties together many of the central points this book has discussed. First, it highlights the special role that hunting plays in the imagination of the public. Bill C-21 in its original and then final form targeted collectors and sports shooters, leaving many hunters untouched. As a result, it had widespread public support. The bill will formalize the government's freeze on handgun sales, resulting in the slow but steady death of many of the communities of sports shooters I spoke with for this volume, with little public outcry. Without a way to attract new members, communities like Ava's Cowboy Action club will slowly fall apart. IPSC, the dynamic shooting sport so central to the life of people like Kevin and Bruce, will become extinct north of the border. By banning the sale, inheritance, or transfer of handguns, the bill will lead to the eventual destruction of historic collections like Claude's. These modest personal tragedies will go largely unnoticed outside of the community of gun owners. Given the spectre of American gun violence, most Canadians care little about what happens to these groups of enthusiasts.

But, as we have seen, hunting is a different story. Thanks to the work of hunter-conservationist groups over the past century, and the connection between hunting and Canada's Indigenous peoples, Canadian politicians attack hunters at their own peril. When the hunters become the hunted, political capital seems to disappear. Conservative politicians and pro-gun groups were quick to jump on this framing when the amendment was put forward, with Conservative leader Pierre Poilievre accusing Trudeau of going after "Grandpa Joe's hunting rifle."[8]

The debate also brought to the public conversation the ambiguity and complexity around definitions like "assault weapon" or "military-style." As we have seen, the term "assault-style" is more of a framing technique than a technical designation. Further, carving out a clear distinction between a "military-style" firearm and a hunting weapon is more difficult than politicians make it out to be. This was highlighted when, in an interview on CBC, journalist David Cochrane pressed then

Public Safety Minister Marco Mendocino on the fact that many rifles, like the Lee-Enfield and SKS, began their lives as military rifles before becoming popular hunting tools.[9]

The debate highlights the extent to which the fate of advocacy groups in the gun debate is tied to the winds of public opinion and the political opportunity structure. As we have seen, that structure heavily favours the pro-control coalition in Canada, making gun control initiatives that would prove too controversial to even raise in the United States non-issues in Canadian politics. But public goodwill is not boundless. Attempts to target firearms perceived by the public to be more appropriate for hunting still raise enough public ire to give politicians pause.

The debate highlights the role that rural-urban relations and Western alienation play in the Canadian gun debate. As we have seen throughout this book, firearms are seen by the public as rural tools, appropriate for hunters and farmers to own. The framing of Bill C-21 reflects this. During the early December 2022 debate on the bill, the Liberals were keen to stress that the legislation was not meant to target hunters, while Conservatives fought to frame the bill as an attack on "Grandpa Joe" and his hunting rifle. Further, much of the mutiny that the Liberal-NDP coalition faced came from rural MPs fearful of losing their seats thanks to angry hunters.

From the vantage point of the broader pro-gun movement, the pushback against Bill C-21 was a brief reprieve, rather than deliverance. Even with the offensive amendments removed from the bill, the freeze on handgun ownership and the existing 2020 prohibition of firearms like the AR-15 and Ruger Mini-14 will be politically challenging for any future party to reverse. The leisure communities we have met in these pages may die out or have to drastically adapt their competitions and gatherings.

Citizenship, Risk, and Regulation

Debates over citizenship are often debates about managing risk. In the twenty-first century, citizens have ceded much of the responsibility for managing risk to their government. They expect it to regulate which objects are too risky to allow ordinary people to own. This risk calculus is tied to utility. Risky activities that are broadly practised, or that enjoy widespread public support, are generally tolerated. Most Canadians own cars. The Canadian public accepts that cars, potentially dangerous objects, are useful enough that their risk is justified. Many Canadians drink alcohol. They accept alcohol, and the risks that accompany it, despite a significant social cost. Smoking, a practice that has been declining in the Global North given the success of public health campaigns aimed at stamping out the process, may soon turn the corner of the risk-utility calculus if other countries follow the lead of New Zealand, which briefly banned anyone born on or after 1 January 2009 from purchasing cigarettes.[10]

When the Canadian public is convinced of the value of firearms, generally as tools of hunting, it is broadly tolerant of their ownership. Sports shooting and collecting, poorly understood and publicized activities, elicit little public support.

Citizenship regimes are also important because they influence the goals that movements set out and the strategies they use to achieve those goals. As we have seen, the pro-gun coalition uses this language of citizenship to make its rights claims. Far from being absolutists, the gun owners and advocates that I spoke with sought fair treatment from their government. They saw themselves as highly regulated citizens who have worked hard to comply with a demanding, confusing, and often contradictory system of laws and rules, shaped as often by political calculations as by a genuine concern for public safety. Their activism is motivated by this sense of injustice.

An important lesson to be drawn from this book is that the Canadian government is missing an opportunity. Treating firearms issues as a political rather than policy issue, adopting a poorly fitting American framework for the gun debate, and using firearm policy to campaign rather than govern, misses an opportunity to create partnerships between regulator and regulated. The history of the conservation movement has shown that such relationships can be profitable for governments and help to ensure buy-in for the system. Conservation groups like those that we have met in this book, help provincial governments regulate the practice of hunting and preserve habitat and biodiversity. This partnership is a net win for hunters and the public.

Canadian gun owners are open to and supportive of regulations that they see as useful in limiting the negative externalities of their serious leisure pursuits. The community is highly organized and represented by an advocacy coalition with both grassroots ties and institutional connections. It is bound together by a network of clubs and groups across the country, as well as an entire industry. They care about public safety and have considerable expertise and incentives to contribute to building a better Canada. We should let them.

Appendix A – Survey of Gun Owners

Question: Political Activities of Canadian Gun Owners

In the past twelve months, how many of the following political activities have you taken part in related to firearm policy and gun rights? (select yes or no to all that apply)

A) Contacted a politician, government, or local government official.
B) Volunteered or worked for a political party or gun rights group.
C) Voted based on a candidate's firearm policy.
D) Donated money to a gun rights group.
E) Worn or displayed a sticker or logo from a gun rights group.
F) Joined a political party.
G) Joined a gun rights group.
H) Written or shared a firearm policy–related social media post, image, meme, or video (Twitter, Facebook, Instagram, Reddit, etc.).
I) Talked to friends and family members about firearm policy.
J) Signed a petition or e-petition.
K) Attended a public meeting.
L) Spoken out at a public meeting.
M) Taken part in a lawful demonstration.
N) Boycotted certain companies or products based on their stance on guns.
O) Written to a newspaper or online news service.
P) Other (please fill in).

Appendix B – Interview Questions

Note – interviews were semi-structured. Prompts were used; however, interviewees were encouraged to take the interview in any direction they liked.

Questions for Advocates

1. I want to understand more about your journey into the gun world. How long have you owned and used firearms? What got you into guns? How did you acquire your first firearm? What kind of firearm-related activities do you participate in?
2. How did you get involved in firearm advocacy? What made you want to get involved in the first place?
3. Tell me more about your organization. What is its mission? What are its main functions? What does it do?
4. Tell me more about your organization's history. When was it founded? How has it changed over the years?
5. What kind of tactics does your organization use for advocacy? Why?
6. How many members does your organization have? What do you think motivates or drives your members to be a part of your movement?
7. What do you think about Canada's current gun laws? What would you like to see changed? Why?
8. One of the tricky issues when talking about guns in Canada is the issue of self-defence. Canadians seem less comfortable talking about self-defence than Americans do. What role do you think self-defence plays in Canadian gun culture? Why do you think Canadians are so hesitant to talk about it?
9. When talking about guns in Canada, our neighbour to the south gets brought up a lot. What role do you think Canada's

relationship with, or Canadians' perspective on, the United States plays in the gun debate in Canada?

10. What do you think of the broader conversation on guns in Canada, or the way that guns or gun owners are presented in the media?

11. How does it feel to be a gun owner in 2021/22?

Now that the interview is over, is there any information that you want me to remove from the transcript or interview notes?

Gun Owner Interviews

Q1 – Do you identify as any of the following:
- A sports shooter
- A hunter
- A casual shooter/plinker
- A collector

Q2 – Next, I want to understand more about your journey into the gun world. How long have you owned and used firearms? What got you into guns? How did you acquire your first firearm?

Q3 – Are you a member of a pro-gun/gun rights organization (CCFR, NFA, CSSA, etc.)? Are you a member of a hunting organization (i.e. OFAH)? What made you join? Do you feel like your group is doing a good job?

Q4 – Do you participate in any formal political activities related to gun ownership, like volunteering, writing to elected officials, signing e-petitions, etc.?

Q5 – Do you engage in any informal political activities (talking to friends or family members about guns, engaging in debates online, etc.)?

Q6 – When you think about gun ownership, what kinds of things come to mind? These could be values, principles, stories, anything you like.

Q7 – What do you think about Canada's current gun laws? What would you like to see changed? Why?

Q8 – How does it feel to be a gun owner in 2021/22?

Q9 – What do you think of the broader conversation on guns in Canada, or the way that guns or gun owners are presented in the media?

Q10 – Can you share a memory with me that is especially meaningful to you?

Demographic Questions:

The following questions are meant to give my reader an idea of the kinds of people that I interviewed. These are commonly used in academic research in order to make sure that the people I interviewed are representative of the broader Canadian population (i.e. I did not just interview wealthy people). Once again all of this information is confidential. Remember you can choose not to answer any of the following questions – just say "pass."

1. What language do you speak most often at home?
   A. English
   B. French
   C. Spanish
2. In which province/territory do you currently reside?
3. What is your gender? (M/F/Other/Prefer not to state)
4. What is the highest level of formal education that you have completed?
5. How old are you?
6. With what ethnic/racial group do you identify?
7. Do you identify as a/an Indigenous/First Nations/Métis or Inuit person?
8. Would you describe yourself as living in an urban, suburban, or rural area?
9. What would you estimate is your annual income?

Now that the interview is over, is there any information that you want me to remove from the transcript or interview notes?

Notes

Acronyms & Key Terms

1 Josh Sugarmann, "Assault Weapons and Accesssories in America" (Washington, DC, 1988).
2 "Engagement Summary Report – Reducing Violent Crime: A Dialogue on Handguns and Assault-Style Firearms," 2019, www.publicsafety.gc.ca/cnt /rsrcs/pblctns/2019-rdcng-vlnt-crm-dlg/index-en.aspx.

Timeline of Contemporary Gun Control in Canada

1 R. Blake Brown, *Arming and Disarming: A History of Gun Control in Canada* (Toronto: University of Toronto Press, 2012).
2 Anthony Fleming, Dylan S. McLean, and Raymond Tatalovich, "Debating Gun Control in Canada and the United States," *World Affairs* 181, no. 4 (2018): 348–71, https://doi.org/10.1177/0043820018812609.
3 Russel Aurore Bouchard, *Armes à Feu Au Canada et Au Québec: La Vérité Derrière Le Faux Débat* (Chicoutimi: University of Quebec at Chicoutimi, 2017).
4 Brown, *Arming and Disarming*.
5 Gary A. Mauser and H. Taylor Buckner, "Canadian Attitudes Toward Gun Control: The Real Story" (Toronto, ON, 1997), www.researchgate.net /profile/Gary-Mauser/publication/237801446_Canadian_Attitudes _Toward_Gun_Control_The_Real_Story/links/00b4952aa155b2e6c3000000 /Canadian-Attitudes-Toward-Gun-Control-The-Real-Story.pdf.
6 Philip C. Stenning, "Long Gun Registration: A Poorly Aimed Longshot," *Canadian Journal of Criminology* 45 (2003): 479–88; "Gun Registry Cost Soars to $2 Billion," *CBC News*, 13 February 2004, www.cbc.ca/news/canada /gun-registry-cost-soars-to-2-billion-1.513990.
7 Fleming, McLean, and Tatalovich, "Debating Gun Control."

1. Introduction

1 Tim Stockwell and Matthew Young, "Canadian Substance Use Costs and Harms" (Victoria, BC, 2018), www.ccsa.ca/sites/default/files/2019-04/CSUCH-Canadian-Substance-Use-Costs-Harms-Report-2018-en.pdf.

2 Jessica Fitterer, "Alcohol-Attributable Crime in Britisth Columbia" (Victoria, BC, 2013), www.uvic.ca/research/centres/cisur/assets/docs/report-alcohol-attributable-crime.pdf.

3 "WHO Facts on Alcohol and Violence: Intimate Partner Violence and Alcohol" (Geneva, Switzerland, 2006), www.canada.ca/content/dam/phac-aspc/migration/phac-aspc/sfv-avf/sources/fem/fem-intin-alco/pdf/fem-whoms-alco-eng.pdf.

4 Stockwell and Young, "Canadian Substance Use."

5 Courtney Shea, "'Two Drinks a Week Is Practically Personal Prohibition': This Professor Is Taking Canada's New Alcohol Guidelines to Task," *Toronto Life*, 9 March 2023, https://torontolife.com/city/two-drinks-a-week-is-practically-personal-prohibition-this-professor-is-taking-canadas-new-alcohol-guidelines-to-task/.

6 David Yamane, "The Sociology of U.S. Gun Culture," *Sociology Compass* 11, no. 7 (2017): 1–10, https://doi.org/10.1111/soc4.12497.

7 Noah S. Schwartz, *On Target: Gun Culture, Storytelling, and the NRA* (Toronto: University of Toronto Press, 2022).

8 David Yamane, *Conceald Carry Revolution: Expanding the Right to Bear Arms in America* (Berkeley, CA: Anewpress, 2021).

9 For links to these pieces please see my website: www.noahschwartz.ca/media-outreach.

10 Virginia Braun and Victoria Clarke, "Using Thematic Analysis in Psychology," *Qualitative Research in Psychology* 3, no. 2 (2006): 77–101.

11 Gareth Terry et al., "Thematic Analysis," in *The SAGE Handbook of Qualitative Research Psychology*, edited by Carla Willig and Wendy Stainton Rogers (London: SAGE Publications, 2017), 17–35.

2. Leisure Culture, Citizenship, and Alienation

1 Seymour Martin Lipset, "Historical Traditions and National Characteristics: A Comparative Analysis of Canada and the United States," *Canadian Journal of Sociology/Cahiers Canadiens de Sociologie*, 1986, 113–55.

2 Mauser and Buckner, "Canadian Attitudes Toward Gun Control."

3 I would highly encourage those interested in a comprehensive history of gun laws in Canada to read R. Blake Brown's *Arming and Disarming: A History of Gun Control in Canada* (Toronto: University of Toronto Press, 2012).

4　There is often confusion in public discussions about the differences between semi-automatic and fully automatic firearms. A semi-automatic firearm fires one shot with each depression of the trigger. A fully automatic firearm fires either a three-round burst, or a continuous stream of fire, as long as the trigger is depressed.

5　The government is not required to provide public justification for placing certain firearms on the restricted list. Oftentimes, guns are placed in these categories based on cosmetic features or the notoriety of a particular firearm.

6　Brown, *Arming and Disarming*.

7　Interview with Jackson, 20 January 2022.

8　Interview with Karl, 17 January 2022.

9　Interview with Karl, 17 January 2022.

10　The use of the term "terrorist" here rather than "mass shooter" is deliberate. The FBI defines terrorism as the illegal use of force to "intimidate or coerce" a population or its government. That is to say, the victims of terror are not just those directly physically impacted by it. The shooter in Montreal, who left behind a frightening manifesto attempting to justify his actions, certainly sought to terrorize women beyond those that he injured and killed.

11　For ethical reasons, the name of the killer will not be repeated in this book.

12　Kristin Goss, *Disarmed: The Missing Movement for Gun Control in America* (Princeton, NJ: Princeton University Press, 2006).

13　Fleming, McLean, and Tatalovich, "Debating Gun Control."

14　Melinda Meng, "Bloody Blockades: The Legacy of the Oka Crisis," *Harvard International Review*, June 2020, https://hir.harvard.edu/bloody -blockades-the-legacy-of-the-oka-crisis/.

15　Brown, *Arming and Disarming*.

16　Mauser and Buckner, "Canadian Attitudes Toward Gun Control."

17　Bouchard, *Armes à Feu Au Canada et Au Québec*.

18　Brown, *Arming and Disarming*.

19　Patrick J. Charles, "The Black Panthers, NRA, Ronald Reagan, Armed Extremists, and the Second Amendment," Duke Center for Firearms Law, 2020, https://sites.law.duke.edu/secondthoughts/2020/04/08/the -black-panthers-nra-ronald-reagan-armed-extremists-and-the-second -amendment/.

20　John Dixon, "A Gang That Couldn't Shoot Straight," *The Globe & Mail*, 8 January 2003, www.theglobeandmail.com/opinion/a-gang-that-couldnt -shoot-straight/article748138/.

21　Interview with Sheldon Clare, National Firearms Association, 19 January 2022.

22 Brown, *Arming and Disarming*.

23 Stenning, "Long Gun Registration."

24 Stenning; "Gun Registry Cost Soars."

25 "Quebec Court Orders Feds to Turn over Gun Registry Data," *CTV News Montreal*, 10 September 2012, https://montreal.ctvnews.ca/quebec -court-orders-feds-to-turn-over-gun-registry-data-1.949649.

26 Lorne Gunter, "The New Backdoor Long-Gun Registry," *Toronto Sun*, 29 December 2015, https://torontosun.com/2015/12/29/the-new -backdoor-long-gun-registry.

27 "New Zealand: Rate of All Gun Deaths per 100,000 People," University of Sydney School of Public Health, 2022, www.gunpolicy.org/firearms /compareyears/128/rate_of_all_gun_deaths_per_100_000_people.

28 Kurt Bayer, "Christchurch Mosque Shooter Should Never Have Been Granted Firearms Licence, Sources Say," *New Zealand Herald*, 51 June 2020, www.nzherald.co.nz/nz/christchurch-mosque-shooter -should-never-have-been-granted-firearms-licence-sources-say /LW66KNA56IWIIH6TRFLH7BUL3A/.

29 Kathleen Harris, "Liberals Promise to Prohibit Semi-Automatic Assault Rifles, Allow Cities to Ban Handguns," *CBC News*, 20 September 2019, www.cbc.ca/news/politics/liberal-gun-control-trudeau-2019-1.5290950.

30 Matt DeMille, "What Firearms Are Reasonable and Proportionate for Hunting in Canada," 2021.

31 Noah S. Schwartz, "Aiming for Success: Toward an Evidence-Based Evaluation Framework for Gun Control Policies," *World Affairs* 185, no. 3 (2022): 442–70, https://doi.org/10.1177/00438200221107412.

32 Brian Lilley, "LILLEY: After Two Years, Liberals Still Trying to Design Gun Buyback Program," *Toronto Sun*, 2022, https://torontosun.com /opinion/columnists/lilley-after-two-years-liberals-still-trying-to -design-gun-buyback-program.

33 Hayley Cooper, "Eighty-Two Per Cent of Handguns in Toronto Come from the U.S.: Saunders," *Newstalk 1010*, 20 December 2019, www .iheartradio.ca/newstalk-1010/news/eighty-two-per-cent-of-handguns -in-toronto-come-from-the-u-s-saunders-1.10361296; "As Gun Violence Rises in Canada, Weapons from the U.S. Complicate Gun Control Efforts," *NPR*, 9 July 2022, www.npr.org/2022/07/09/1108967278 /canada-gun-control-us-guns-trafficking; Brian Passifiume, "Guns Used in Crimes Are Coming from U.S., Not Legal Gun Owners: Police Chiefs," *National Post*, 8 February 2022, https://nationalpost.com /news/politics/guns-used-in-crimes-are-coming-from-u-s-not-legal -gun-owners-police-chiefs.

34 "The Political Exploitation of a Tragedy," *Toronto Sun*, 6 June 2022, https://torontosun.com/opinion/editorials/editorial-the-political -exploitation-of-a-tragedy; Jamil Jivani, "Canadian Politicians Import

American Culture Wars to Exploit Tragedy," *National Post*, 26 May 2022, https://nationalpost.com/opinion/jamil-jivani-canadian-politicians -import-american-culture-wars-to-exploit-tragedy.

35 Haley Ryan, "High-Ranking Mountie Insists Lucki Pressed Him about Releasing Gun Details after N.S. Shooting," *CBC News*, 16 August 2022, www.cbc.ca/news/politics/nova-scotia-massacre-lucki-campbell -guns-1.6552322.

36 Miriam Smith, *Group Politics and Social Movements in Canada* (North York, ON: University of Toronto Press, 2014).

37 Mancur Olson, *The Logic of Collective Action* (Cambridge, MA: Harvard University Press, 1965).

38 Lisa Young and Joanna Everitt, *Advocacy Groups* (Vancounver: University of British Columbia Press, 2004).

39 Dominique Clément, *Canada's Rights Revolution: Social Movements and Social Change, 1937–82* (Vancouver: University of British Columbia Press, 2009).

40 Brenda O'Neill, "Continuity and Change in the Contemporary Canadian Feminist Movement," *Canadian Journal of Political Science* 50, no. 2 (2017): 443–59, https://doi.org/10.1017/S0008423917000087.

41 Robert C. Paehlke, "Climate Change Mitigation, Adaptation, and Development," *Environmental Politics* 23, no. 1 (2014): 179–84, https:// doi.org/https://doi.org/10.1080/09644016.2014.878090; Debra J. Salazar and Donald K. Alper, "Reconciling Environmentalism and the Left: Perspectives on Democracy and Social Justice in British Columbia's Enviromental Movement," *Canadian Journal of Political Science* 35, no. 3 (2002): 527–66, https://doi.org/10.1017/S0008423902778347.

42 Smith, *Gr. Polit. Soc. Movements Canada*; Miriam Smith, "Social Movements and Equality Seeking: The Case of Gay Liberation in Canada," *Canadian Journal of Political Science* 31, no. 2 (1998): 285–309.

43 Michael Orsini and Miriam Smith, "Social Movements, Knowledge and Public Policy: The Case of Autism Activism in Canada and the US," *Critical Policy Studies* 4, no. 2 (2010): 38–57.

44 Paul Saurette and Shane Gunster, "Canada's Conservative Ideological Infrastructure: Brewing a Cup of Cappuccino Conservatism," in *Tax Is Not a Four Letter Word*, edited by Alex Himelfarb and Himelfarb Jordan (Waterloo, ON: Wilfred Laurier University Press, 2013), 227–66.

45 Trevor W. Harrison, "Populist and Conservative Christian Evangelical Movements: A Comparison of Canada and the United States," in *Group Politics and Social Movements in Canada*, edited by Miriam Smith (Toronto: Broadview Press, 2008), 203–24.

46 Paul Saurette and Kelly Gordon, *The Changing Voice of the Anti-Abortion Movement: The Rise of "pro-Woman" Rhetoric in Canada and the United States* (Toronto: University of Toronto Press, 2016); Paul Saurette and

Kelly Gordon, "Arguing Abortion: The New Anti-Abortion Discourse in Canada," *Canadian Journal of Political Science* 46, no. 1 (2013): 157–85.

47 Robert Alan Dahl, *Who Governs?: Democracy and Power in an American City*, vol. 4 (New Haven, CT: Yale University Press, 1961); Andrew S McFarland, "Neopluralism," in *Annual Review of Political Science*, vol. 10 (PALO ALTO: ANNUAL REVIEWS, 2007), 45–66, https://doi .org/10.1146/annurev.polisci.10.072005.152119.

48 John D. McCarthy and Mayer N. Zald, "Resource Mobilization and Social Movements: A Partial Theory," *American Journal of Sociology* 82, no. 6 (1977): 1212–41.

49 David Camfield, "Re-Orienting Class Analysis: Working Classes as Historical Formations," *Science & Society* 68, no. 4 (2005): 421–46.

50 Alexandra Dobrowolsky, "The Women's Movement in Fulx: Feminism and Framing, Passion, and Politics," in *Group Politics and Social Movements in Canada*, edited by Miriam Smith (Peterborough, ON: Broadview Press, 2008).

51 John Meisel, "Political Culture and the Politics of Culture," *Canadian Journal of Political Science1* 7, no. 4 (1974): 601–15.

52 Meisel, 604.

53 Robert A. Stebbins, "Serious Leisure: A Conceptual Statement," *Sociological Perspectives* 25, no. 2 (1982): 251–72, https://doi.org /10.2307/1388726.

54 Stebbins, "Serious Lesiure," 251.

55 Robert A. Stebbins, *Between Work & Leisure: The Common Ground of Two Separate Worlds* (New Brunswick, NJ: Transaction Publishers, 2004).

56 Stebbins, "Serious Leisure," 257.

57 Stebbins, "Serious Leisure."

58 Dair L. Gillespie, Ann Leffler, and Elinor Lerner, "If It Weren't for My Hobby, I'd Have a Life: Dog Sports, Serious Leisure, and Boundary Negotiations," *Leisure Studies* 21, nos. 3–4 (2002): 285–304, https://doi.org /10.1080/0261436022000030632.

59 Junhyoung Kim et al., "Predicting Personal Growth and Happiness by Using Serious Leisure Model," *Social Indicators Research* 122, no. 1 (2015): 147–57, https://doi.org/10.1007/s11205-014-0680-0.

60 Eva (Hui Ping) Cheng, Robert Stebbins, and Jan Packer, "Serious Leisure among Older Gardeners in Australia," *Leisure Studies* 36, no. 4 (2017): 505–18, https://doi.org/10.1080/02614367.2016.1188137.

61 R. Misra and M. McKean, "College Students' Academic Stress and Its Relation to Their Anxiety, Time Management, and Leisure Satisfaction," *American Journal of Health Studies* 16, no. 1 (2000): 41–51.

62 Karen Gallant, Susan Arai, and Bryan Smale, "Serious Leisure as an Avenue for Nurturing Community," *Leisure Sciences* 35, no. 4 (2013):

320–36, https://doi.org/10.1080/01490400.2013.797324; Gerard Kyle and Gary Chick, "The Social Nature of Leisure Involvement," *Journal of Leisure Research* 34, no. 4 (2002): 426–48.

63 Carroll A. Brown, Francis A. McGuire, and Judith Voelkl, "The Link between Successful Aging and Serious Leisure," *International Journal of Aging and Human Development* 66, no. 1 (2008): 73–95, https://doi.org /10.2190/AG.66.1.d.

64 Susan Hutchinson and Galit Nimrod, "Leisure as a Resource for Successful Aging by Older Adults with Chronic Health Conditions," *International Journal of Aging and Human Development* 74, no. 1 (2012): 41–65, https://doi.org/10.2190/AG.74.1.c.

65 Masoumeh Bagheri-Nesami, Forough Rafii, and Seyede Fatemeh H Oskouie, "Coping Strategies of Iranian Elderly Women: A Qualitative Study," *Educational Gerontology* 36, no. 7 (2010): 573–91, https://doi .org/10.1080/03601270903324438.

66 Hyunmin Tim Yang, Junhyoung Kim, and Jinmoo Heo, "Serious Leisure Profiles and Well-Being of Older Korean Adults," *Leisure Studies* 38, no. 1 (2019): 88–97, https://doi.org/10.1080/02614367.2018.1499797.

67 A.D. Olmsted, "Gun Ownership as Serious Leisure," in *The Gun Culture & Its Enemies*, edited by William R. Tonso (Bellevue, WA: Merril Press, 1990), 61–76; Douglas W. Murray et al., "Serious Leisure: The Sport of Target Shooting and Leisure Satisfaction," *Sport in Society* 19, no. 7 (2016): 891–905, https://doi.org/10.1080/17430437.2015.1067780; David Spencer Martin et al., "Target Shooting as a Serious Leisure Pursuit – an Exploratory Study of the Motivations Driving Participant Engagement," *World Leisure Journal* 56, no. 3 (2014): 204–19, https://doi .org/https://doi.org/10.1080/04419057.2013.836560; Jon Littlefield and Julie L. Ozanne, "Socialization into Consumer Culture: Hunters Learning to Be Men," *Consumption Markets and Culture* 14, no. 4 (2011): 333–60, https://doi.org/10.1080/10253866.2011.604494; Christi Hubbs, "Just for Fun: Talk and Tactical Shooting in Southern Saskatchewan," *Journal of Undergraduate Ethnography* 7, no. 2 (2017): 19–33.

68 Martin et al., "Target Shooting"; Murray et al., "Serious Leisure."

69 Littlefield and Ozanne, "Socialization," 347.

70 Littlefield and Ozanne, "Socialization," 355.

71 Hubbs, "Just for Fun."

72 Jennifer Carlson, *Citizen-Protectors: The Everyday Politics of Guns in An Age of Decline* (Oxfofrd: Oxford University Press, 2015); Abigail A. Kohn, *Shooters: Myths and Realities of America's Gun Cultures* (Oxford: Oxford University Press, 2004); Schwartz, *On Target*.

73 *America as a Gun Culture* (Rockville, MD: American Heritage Publishing Company, 1970).

74 Schwartz, *On Target*.

75 Jennifer Carlson, "Revisiting the Weberian Presumption: Gun Militarism, Gun Populism, and the Racial Politics of Legitimate Violence in Policing," *American Journal of Sociology* 125, no. 3 (2019): 633–82, https://doi.org/https://doi.org/10.1086/707609; Carlson, *Citizen-Protectors*.

76 Noah S. Schwartz, "Guns in the North: Assessing the Impact of Social Identity on Firearms Advocacy in Canada," *Politics & Policy* 49, no. 3 (2021): 795–818, https://doi.org/10.1111/polp.12412.

77 "Maintaining the Trail: Collective Action in a Serious-Leisure Community," *Journal of Contemporary Ethnography* 42, no. 6 (2013): 643, https://doi.org/10.1177/0891241613483560.

78 Rosenbaum, "Maintaining the Trail: Collective Action in a Serious-Leisure Community."

79 Scott David Setchfield, "Leisure Consumption and Political Action in a State Motorcycle Rights Organization" (Indiana University, 2019), https://search.proquest.com/openview/74301185a179d26779c205e3c2e2a07b/1?pq-origsite=gscholar&cbl=18750&diss=y.

80 Rebecca Schild, "Fostering Environmental Citizenship: The Motivations and Outcomes of Civic Recreation," *Journal of Environmental Planning and Management* 61, nos. 5–6 (2018): 924–49, https://doi.org/10.1080/09640568.2017.1350144.

81 "Standing Out While Fitting In: Serious Leisure Identities and Aligning Actions among Skydivers and Gun Collectors," *Journal of Contemporary Ethnography* 39, no. 1 (2010): 34–59, https://doi.org/10.1177/0891241609343291.

82 Olson, *The Logic of Collective Action*; Mancur Olson, "The Logic of Collective Action: Public Goods and the Theory of Groups" (Cambridge, MA: Harvard University Press, 1971).

83 Young and Everitt, *Advocacy Groups*.

84 Miriam Smith, "Theories of Group and Movement Organization," in *Group Politics and Social Movements in Canada*, edited by Miriam Smith (Peterborough, ON: Broadview Press, 2008); McFarland, "Neopluralism."

85 Michael Mintrom and Phillipa Norman, "Policy Entrepreneurship and Policy Change," *Policy Studies Journal* 37, no. 4 (2009): 649–67; McFarland, "Neopluralism."

86 McFarland, "Neopluralism."

87 A. Paul Pross, *Group Politics and Public Policy* (Toronto: Oxford University Press, 1992).

88 Karen Zivi, *Making Rights Claims: A Practice of Democratic Citizenship* (Oxford: Oxford University Press, 2011); Neil Stammers, *Human Rights and Social Movements* (London: Pluto Press, 2009); Miriam Catherine Smith, *Lesbian and Gay Rights in Canada: Social Movements and Equality-Seeking, 1971–1995* (Toronto: University of Toronto Press, 1999).

89 Will Kymlicka and W.J. Norman, *Citizenship in Diverse Societies LK – Https://Concordiauniversity.on.Worldcat.Org/Oclc/42580193, TA – TT –* (Oxford; SE – xiii 444 pages; 24 cm: Oxford University Press, 2000), www.myilibrary.com?id=194387; Will Kymlicka, *Finding Our Way: Rethinking Ethnocultural Relations in Canada LK – Https://Concordiauniversity.on.Worldcat.Org/Oclc/38916912, TA – TT –* (Toronto; SE – viii, 220 pages; 23 cm: Oxford University Press, 1998), http://catdir .loc.gov/catdir/enhancements/fy0638/98197715-t.html; Megan Gaucher, "Monogamous Canadian Citizenship, Constructing Foreignness and the Limits of Harm Discourse," *Canadian Journal of Political Science* 49, no. 3 (2016): 519–38, https://doi.org/10.1017 /S0008423916000810; Miriam Smith, "Diversity and Canadian Political Development," *Canadian Journal of Political Science* 42, no. 4 (2009): 831–54, https://doi.org/10.1017/S0008423909990692.

90 Jane Jenson, "Fated to Live In Interesting Times: Canada's Changing Citizenship Regime," *Canadian Journal of Political Science* 30, no. 4 (1997): 628.

91 Jenson, "Fated to Live In Interesting Times."

92 Jenson, "Fated to Live in Interesting Times"; Alexandra Dobrowolsky and Jane Jenson, "Shifting Representations of Citizenship: Canadian Politics of 'Women' and 'Children,'" *Social Politics* 11, no. 2 (2004): 154–80.

93 Jenson, "Fated to Live In Interesting Times."

94 Tracey Raney and Loleen Berdahl, "Birds of a Feather? Citizenship Norms, Group Identity, and Political Participation in Western Canada," *Canadian Journal of Political Science* 42, no. 1 (2009): 187–209, https://doi .org/10.1017/S0008423909090076.

95 Dobrowolsky and Jenson, "Shifting Representations of Citizenship."

96 Jenson, "Fated to Live In Interesting Times."

97 Jenson, "Fated to Live in Interesting Times."

98 Lipset, "Historical Traditions."

99 Loleen Berdahl, "The Persistence of Western Alienation," *Institute for Research on Public Policy*, 2021, 1–10.

100 Jenson, "Fated to Live In Interesting Times."

101 Brown, *Arming and Disarming*.

102 Brown, *Arming and Disarming*.

103 Quoted in Stephen P. Hallbrook, *That Every Man Be Armed: The Evolution of a Constitutional Right* (Albuquerque: University of New Mexico Press, 2013), 45.

104 Patrick J. Charles, *Armed in America: A History of Gun Rights from Colonial Militias to Concealed Carry* (Amherst, NY: Prometheus, 2018).

105 Mark V. Tushnet, *Out of Range: Why the Constitution Can't End the Battle Over Guns* (Oxford: Oxford University Press, 2007), 18.

106 Charles, *Armed in America*, 47.

107 R. Blake Brown, "Firearm 'Rights' in Canada: Law and History in the Debates," *Canadian Journal of Law and Society* 32, no. 1 (2017): 97–116, https://doi.org/doi:10.1017/cls.2017.5.

108 Brown, *Arming and Disarming*, 47.

109 W.T. Stanbury and Allan Smithies, "A Brief History of Gun Control in Canada," *The Hill Times*, 10 March 2003, https://cssa-cila.org/a-brief -history-of-gun-control-in-canada-1867-to-1945/.

110 Brown, *Arming and Disarming*.

111 *R. v. Hasselwander* (1993), https://scc-csc.lexum.com/scc-csc/scc-csc/en /item/1007/index.do; Brown, "Firearm 'Rights' in Canada."

112 Interview with Allison De Groot, CSAAA, 4 November 2021.

113 Maureen Gail Reed and John Parkins, *Social Transformation in Rural Canada: Community, Cultures, and Collective Action* (Vancouver: University of British Columbia Press, 2013).

114 Katherine J. Cramer, *The Politics of Resentment: Rural Consciousness in Wisconsin and the Rise of Scott Walker* (Chicago: University of Chicago Press, 2016).

115 Clark Banack, "Ethnography and Political Opinion: Identity, Alienation and Anti-Establishmentarianism in Rural Alberta," *Canadian Journal of Political Science* 54, no. 1 (2021): 1–22, https://doi.org/10.1017 /S0008423920000694.

116 Cramer, *The Politics of Resentment*.

117 Reed and Parkins, *Social Transformation in Rural Canada*.

118 Rogers Epp, "The Political De-Skilling of Rural Communities. in *Writing Off the Rural West*, edited by Roger Epp and Dave Whitson (Edmonton: University of Alberta Press, 2001), 301–24.

119 Cramer, *The Politics of Resentment*.

120 Bill Reimer, "Rural-Urban Interdependence: Understanding Our Common Interest," in *Social Transformation in Rural Canada*, edited by Maureen Gail Reed and John Parkins (Vancouver: University of British Columbia Press, 2013), 91–109.

121 Cramer, *The Politics of Resentment*.

122 Banack, "Ethnography and Political Opinion: Identity, Alienation and Anti-Establishmentarianism in Rural Alberta."

123 David A. Armstrong, Jack Lucas, and Zack Taylor, "The Urban-Rural Divide in Canadian Federal Elections, 1896–2019," *Canadian Journal of Political Science* 55, no. 1 (2022): 84–106, https://doi.org/DOI: 10.1017 /S0008423921000792.

124 Banack, "Ethnography and Political Opinion."

125 Banack, "Ethnography and Political Opinion."

126 Berdahl, "The Persistence of Western Alienation."

127 Roger Gibbins, *Prairie Politics & Society: Regionalism in Decline* (Toronto: Butterworth & Co, 1980).

128 Gibbins, *Prairie Politics & Society*.

129 Berdahl, "The Persistence of Western Alienation."

130 Roger Gibbins and Loleen Berdahl, *Western Visions, Western Futures: Perspectives on the West in Canada*, 2nd ed. (Peterborough, ON: Broadview Press, 2003).

131 Berdahl, "The Persistence of Western Alienation," 1.

132 Berdahl, "The Persistence of Western Alienation," 2.

3. Canadian Gun Culture

1 Robert Sopuck, "Hunting with Dad," in *The Culture of Hunting in Canada*, edited by Jean L. Manore and Dale Miner (Vancouver: University of British Columbia Press, 2006), 21–4.

2 Richard Hoftstadter, "America As a Gun Culture," *American Heritage*, 1970, www.americanheritage.com/america-gun-culture; Yamane, "The Sociology of U.S. Gun Culture."

3 Schwartz, "Guns in the North."

4 Yamane, "The Sociology of U.S. Gun Culture"; Jennifer Carlson, "Gun Studies and the Politics of Evidence," *Annual Review of Law and Social Science* 16 (2020): 183–202, 10.1146/annurev-lawsocsci-020620 -%0A111332.

5 Yamane, "The Sociology of U.S. Gun Culture," 1.

6 Brown, *Arming and Disarming*.

7 Brown, *Arming and Disarming*.

8 Andrew J. Kilsby, *The Riflemen: A History of the National Rifle Association of Australia (1888–1988)* (Belmont, QLD: National Rifle Association of Australia, n.d.), https://nraa.com.au/wp-content/uploads/2020/02 /The-Riflemen-A-History-of-the-NRA-of-Australia-1888-1988.pdf.

9 "History of NRANZ," National Rifle Association of New Zealand, 2021, www.nranz.com/organisation/history-of-nranz/.

10 Yamane, "The Sociology of U.S. Gun Culture."

11 Carlson, "Gun Studies and the Politics of Evidence."

12 In most American states, citizens in good legal standing can receive a permit to carry a concealed handgun. This practice is referred to simply as "concealed carry." There is no Canadian equivalent.

13 Paul M. Barrett, *Glock: The Rise of America's Gun* (New York: Broadway Books, 2013).

14 David Yamane, Sebastian L. Ivory, and Paul Yamane, "The Rise of Self-Defense in Gun Advertising," *Gun Studies*, 2019, 9–27, https://doi .org/10.4324/9781315696485-2; David Yamane, *Concealed Carry Revolution: Expanding the Right to Bear Arms in America* (Berkeley, CA: Anewpress, 2021).

15 Yamane, "The Sociology of U.S. Gun Culture."

16 Yamane, Ivory, and Yamane, "The Rise of Self-Defense in Gun Advertising."

17 Yamane, *Conceald Carry Revolution*.

18 Robert J. Spitzer, "The Politics of Gun Control" (London, Boulder, CO: Paradigm Publishers, 2015).

19 Yamane, *Concealed Carry Revolution*.

20 Barrett, *Glock: The Rise of America's Gun*.

21 David Yamane, Jesse DeDeyne, and Alonso O.A. Mendez, "Who Are the Liberal Gun Owners?," *Sociological Inquiry* 91, no. 2 (2020): 483–98, https://doi.org/10.1111/soin.12406.

22 "One in Five American Households Purchased a Gun During the Pandemic" (Chicago, 2022), www.norc.org/NewsEventsPublications /PressReleases/Pages/one-in-five-american-households-purchased-a -gun-during-the-pandemic.aspx.

23 Matthew Simonson et al., "The COVID States Project: Report #37 Gun Purchases During the COVID-19 Pandemic," 2021, https://news.northeastern.edu/wp-content/uploads/2021/02 /COVID19-CONSORTIUM-REPORT-37-GUNS-Feb-2021.pdf# _ga=2.256279432.22422079.1633455371-777786272.1633455371.

24 Aaron Smith, "Black Americans Have Been Buying More Guns During the Pandemic," *Forbes*, 9 April 2021, www.forbes.com/sites /aaronsmith/2021/04/09/black-americans-have-been-buying-more -guns-during-the-pandemic/?sh=27fd05d5281e.

25 Alyssa J. Perry and Shereen M. Meraji, "Black And Up in Arms," *NPR Code Switch*, 16 December 2020, www.npr.org/sections /codeswitch/2020/12/09/944615029/black-and-up-in-arms.

26 Dylan S. McLean, "Gun Talk Online: Canadian Tools, American Values," *Social Science Quarterly* 99, no. 3 (2018): 977–92, https://doi.org/10.1111 /ssqu.12476.

27 The Canadian Firearms Act classifies firearms into three categories. Most long guns in Canada are classified as non-restricted firearms, though some (like the AR-15) were classified before 1 May 2020 as restricted firearms. There is no objective qualification for this division, given the fact that many guns that function in the same manner as the AR-15 are listed as non-restricted firearms. As mentioned, restricted firearms are made up of handguns and certain long guns.

28 Daniel Leblanc, "As Handgun Crimes Go Up, Liberals and Conservatives Disagree on Remedy," *The Globe & Mail*, 25 November 2018, www .theglobeandmail.com/politics/article-as-handgun-crimes-go-up-liberals -and-conservatives-disagree-on-remedy/.

29 Kim Parker et al., "America's Complex Relationship with Guns," 2017, www.pewsocialtrends.org/2017/06/22/guns-and-daily-life-identity -experiences-activities-and-involvement/.

30 Parker et al., "America's Complex Relationship with Guns."

31 Ashifa Kassam, "'Why Does Anyone Need a Gun?': Toronto Shooting Prompts Calls for Handgun Ban," *The Guardian*, 25 July 2018, www .theguardian.com/world/2018/jul/25/toronto-shooting-handgun-ban -canada.

32 "The Economic Footprint of Angling, Hunting, Trapping and Sport Shooting in Canada," 2020, https://www.conferenceboard.ca/in-fact /angling-hunting-trapping-and-sport-shooting/.

33 "Economic Footprint."

34 "Economic Footprint."

35 Brenda Lucki, "2019 Commissionter of Firearms Report" (Ottawa, ON, 2020), www.rcmp-grc.gc.ca/en/firearms/2019-commissioner-firearms -report#a3-5.

36 Interview with Alison De Groot – Canadian Sporting Arms and Ammunition Association, 4 November 2021.

37 While hunting with a handgun is illegal in Canada, many US jurisdictions allow handgun hunting. Hunting with a handgun was practised in Canada before the 1970s.

38 David Yamane, "What's Next? Understanding and Misunderstanding America's Gun Culture," in *Understanding America's Gun Culture*, edited by C. Hovey and L. Fisher (Lanham, MD: Lexington Books, 2018).

39 Interview with Aaron, 28 February 2022.

40 Interview with Paul, 17 January 2022.

41 Bush is a term often used to describe wilderness in Canada.

42 Interview with Rick, 22 April 2022.

43 Interview with Flora, 17 February 2022.

44 Interview with Debbie, 31 January 2022.

45 Interview with Colleen, 5 February 2022.

46 Decoys are generally wooden or plastic replicas of geese or ducks used to lure the animals to land in a particular spot where the hunters wait concealed in a blind, a camouflaged hut or tent.

47 Interview with Teagan, 3 March 2022.

48 Interview with Debbie, 31 January 2022.

49 Interview with Roderick, 27 January 2022.

50 Interview with Kane, 14 April 2022.

51 Interview with Mireille, 14 April 2022.

52 Cabela's is a popular big-box outdoors store that sells hunting and shooting equipment.

53 Interview with Bruce, 13 January 2022.

54 Interview with Zhi, 14 April 2022.

55 Interview with Mani, 24 February 2022.

56 Interview with Nicole, 28 February 2022.

57 Interview with Pierre, 14 April 2022.

58 Interview with Enzo, 2 February 2022.

59 Interview with Allison, 21 April 2022.

60 Interview with Annie, 17 February 2022.

61 Interview with Jack, 3 February 2022.

62 Interview with Emily Brown, 10 February 2022. Emily expressed her willingness to participate using her real name.

63 Interview with Matthew, 3 February 2022.

64 Interview with Matt DeMille, OFAH, 3 June 2022.

65 Interview with Matt DeMille, OFAH, 3 June 2022.

66 Roy Rosenzweig and David Thelen, *The Presence of the Past – Popular Uses of History in American Life* (New York: Columbia University Press, 1998).

67 Gerald Friesen, Del Muise, and David Northrup, "Variations on the Theme of Remembering: A National Survey of How Canadians Use the Past," *Journal of the Canadian Historical Association* 20, no. 1 (2009): 221–48, https://doi.org/10.7202/039788ar.

68 Interview with Matt DeMille, OFAH, 3 June 2022.

69 Interview with Donal, 31 January 2022.

70 Interview with Steffan, 9 February 2022.

71 Interview with Wes, 24 January 2022.

72 Interview with Wes, 24 January 2022.

73 "Plains of Abraham Re-Enactment Cancelled," *CTV News*, 2009, www .ctvnews.ca/plains-of-abraham-re-enactment-cancelled-1.371078.

74 Interview with Jack, 3 February 2022.

75 "Regulations Prescribing Certain Firearms and Other Weapons, Components and Parts of Weapons, Accessories, Cartridge Magazines, Ammunition and Projectiles as Prohibited or Restricted (SOR/98-462)" (2020), https://laws-lois.justice.gc.ca/eng/regulations/sor-98-462 /page-2.html.

76 Bill Blair (@BillBlair). "There is misinformation circulating online surrounding the types of guns that were prohibited in Canada on May 1st . . ." 22 May 2020. https://twitter.com/billblair /status/1263964392992972811.

77 Interview with Claude, 27 January 2022.

78 It should be noted that at the time of writing there is no plan to confiscate handguns from existing owners.

79 Interview with Bruce, 13 January 2022.

80 Interview with Steffan, 9 February 2022.

81 John J. Shea and Matthew L. Sisk, "Complex Projectile Technology and Human Dispersal," *PaleoAnthropology*, 2010, 100–22, https://doi .org/10.4207/PA.2010.ART36.

82 For a deeper exploration of the relationship between human development and projectile weaponry, see The Liberal Gun Owners Lens: The Human-Weapon Relationship: https://lgolens.com/anthropillar/.

83 Interview with Caleb, 14 February 2022.
84 Interview with Caleb, 14 February 2022.
85 Interview with Bruce, 13 January 2022
86 Brown, *Arming and Disarming*.
87 Interview with Hugh, 21 April 2022.
88 Interview with Hugh, 21 April 2022.
89 Here the participant references the women who served as Soviet sharpshooters during the Second World War.
90 Interview with Wes, 24 January 2022.
91 Interview with Annie, 17 February 2022.
92 Interview with Tracey Wilson, CCFR, 21 October 2021.
93 Actual figure for Canada is 62 per cent of women. Butler, Signa. "1 in 3 girls drops out of sports by late teens, study finds." *CBC Sports*, 11 June 2020, www.cbc.ca/sports/youth-sports-teenagers-female-male-participation-1.5607509.
94 Interview with Emily Brown, 10 February 2022.
95 Terrence D Hill et al., "Sexual Dysfunction and Gun Ownership in America: When Hard Data Meet a Limp Theory," *American Journal of Men's Health* 15, no. 5 (2021): 15579883211044342.
96 Interview with Talia, 24 February 2022.
97 Interview with Dirk, 21 March 2022.
98 Interview with Debbie, 31 January 2022.
99 Interview with Dawson, 14 February 2022.
100 Interview with Aaron, 28 February 2022.
101 Interview with Ava, 20 January 2022.
102 Interview with Kevin, 24 January 2022.
103 Interview with Kevin, 24 January 2022.
104 Interview with Tammy, 17 February 2022.
105 Interview with Tammy, 17 February 2022.
106 Interview with Steffan, 9 February 2022.
107 Statscan, "Linguistic Characteristics of Canadians" (Ottawa, 2018), https://www12.statcan.gc.ca/census-recensement/2011/as-sa/98-314-x/98-314-x2011001-eng.cfm.
108 Canadian Firearm Licences are called PALs or RPALs, the latter indicating that the licence holder has completed the additional steps to be able to purchase restricted firearms, like handguns or some semi-automatic rifles.
109 Rachel Gilmore, "Few Canadian Women Own Guns, but Are Twice as Likely to Be Attacked with One: Analysis," CTV News, 2019, www.ctvnews.ca/politics/few-canadian-women-own-guns-but-are-twice-as-likely-to-be-attacked-with-one-analysis-1.4374216.
110 Statistics Canada, "Census Profile, 2016 Census," Government of Canada, 2016, https://www12.statcan.gc.ca/census-recensement/2016

/dp-pd/prof/details/page.cfm?Lang=E&Geo1=PR&Code1=01&Geo2=P
R&Code2=01&Data=Count&SearchText=Canada&SearchType=Begins&S
earchPR=01&B1=Ethnic+origin&TABID=1.

111   Noah S. Schwartz, "Called to Arms: The NRA, the Gun Culture &
      Women," *Critical Policy Studies*, 3 December 2019, 1–16, https://doi.org
      /10.1080/19460171.2019.1697892.

112   Gilmore, "Few Canadian Women Own Guns."

113   Yamane, DeDeyne, and Mendez, "Who Are the Liberal Gun Owners?"

114   Young and Everitt, *Advocacy Groups*.

115   Brown, *Arming and Disarming*.

116   Yamane, DeDeyne, and Mendez, "Who Are the Liberal Gun Owners?"

117   "Courses: Possession and Aquisition License (PAL)," Firearms Safety
      Education Service of Ontario, 2022, https://fseso.org/courses/.

118   "Changes to Service Fees," Royal Canadian Mounted Police, 2022, www
      .rcmp-grc.gc.ca/en/firearms/changes-service-fees.

119   Chief Firearm Office of Ontario, "Shooting Club Policy" (2014), http://
      rrgc.ca/wp-content/uploads/2014/03/Shooting-Club-Policy-Chief
      -Firearms-Office-Ontario.pdf.

120   Data was collected using Google Maps. Two gun clubs were chosen
      from each province, with the exception of PEI, for which no data was
      available. One gun club was selected from an urban area and one
      from a rural area. One gun range was chosen from each territory. The
      total sample was twenty gun ranges in Canada, out of a total 1,245.
      Membership fees ranged from a low of $35 per year to a high of $475.
      When clubs had multiple memberships (for example, some clubs offer
      VIP memberships with special benefits), the standard membership was
      chosen. Costs tended to be higher in urban areas in central and western
      Canada, while being cheaper in rural areas and the Maritimes.

121   For example, the Ruger 10/22 is one of the most commonly owned
      firearms, as it is a relatively inexpensive rifle that uses a widely available
      and affordable cartridge. Cabela's/Bass Pro Shop, a large big-box firearm
      retailer operating across North America, sells the base model 10/22 for
      $489.99 CAD ($491 USD) in Canada, but for $363.41 CAD ($289.99 USD)
      in the United States.

122   "TTC-Bylaw," Toronto Transit Commission, 2022, www.ttc.ca/by-law
      -no-1.

123   Steve 1954- Bruce and Steven. T A – T T – Yearley, "The Sage Dictionary
      of Sociology LK – Https://Concordiauniversity.on.Worldcat.Org
      /Oclc/290532493" (London: SAGE, 2006), http://site.ebrary.com
      /id/10218157.

124   "Application for a Possession And Acquisition License Under the
      Firearms Act" (Ottawa, ON: Royal Canadian Mounted Police, 2022),

www.rcmp-grc.gc.ca/wam/media/4535/original/76d55b8e6f1e9345ba5
927e46aae9252.pdf.

125 Interview with Rick, 22 April 2022.

126 "Interview with Anonymous Source within Alberta CFO's Office, January 26" (Ottawa, ON, 2022).

127 "Interview with Anonymous Source within Alberta CFO's Office, January 26."

128 "Interview with Anonymous Source within Alberta CFO's Office, January 26."

129 Alexandra Middlewood et al., *Intersectionality in Action: Gun Ownership and Women's Political Participation, Social Science Quarterly*, vol. 100 (London, New York: Routledge, 2019), https://doi.org/10.1111 /ssqu.12697; Carlson, *Citizen-Protectors*; Jennifer D. Carlson, "From Gun Politics to Self-Defense Politics: A Feminist Critique of the Great Gun Debate," *Violence Against Women* 20, no. 3 (2014): 1–9, https://doi .org/10.1177/1077801214526045; Kristin A. Goss, "The Socialization of Conflict and Its Limits: Gender and Gun Politics in America," *Social Science Quarterly* 98, no. 2 (2017): 455–70, https://doi.org/10.1111 /ssqu.12419; Mary Zeiss Stange and Carol K. Oyster, *Gun Women: Firearms and Feminism in Contemporary America* (New York: New York University Press, 2000); Scott Melzer, *Gun Crusaders: The NRA's Culture War* (New York: New York University Press, 2009); Kohn, *Shooters: Myths and Realities of America's Gun Cultures.*

130 Interview with Allison, 21 April 2022.

131 Interview with Allison, 21 April 2022.

132 Interview with Allison, 21 April 2022.

133 Interview with Allison. April 21, 2022.

134 Stebbins, "Serious Leisure," 1982.

135 Interview with Aaron, 28 February 2022.

136 Interview with Claude, 27 January 2022.

137 Interview with Annie, 17 February 2022.

138 Interview with Harrison, 10 February 2022.

139 Interview with Lindsay, 14 March 2022.

140 Interview with Matt DeMille, OFAH, 3 June 2022.

4. The Canadian Pro-Gun Movement

1 John L. Campbell, "Where Do We Stand? Common Mechanisms in Organizations and Social Movements Research," in *Social Movements and Organization Theory*, edited by Gerald F. Davis (Cambridge: Cambridge University Press, 2005), 41–68; Sidney Tarrow, *Power in Movement* (Cambridge: Cambridge University Press, 2022).

2   Daniel Beland, *How Ideas and Institutions Shape the Politics of Public Policy* (Cambridge: Cambridge University Press, 2019).

3   Elizabeth Borland, "Cultural Opportunities and Tactical Choice in the Argentine and Chilean Reproductive Rights Movements," *Mobilization: An International Quarterly* 9, no. 3 (2004): 327–39; Barbara Sutton and Elizabeth Borland, "Framing Abortion Rights in Argentina's Encuentros Nacionales de Mujeres," *Feminist Studies* 39, no. 1 (2013): 194–234.

4   Fleming, McLean, and Tatalovich, "Debating Gun Control."

5   Miriam Smith, "Identity and Opportunity: The Lesbian and Gay Rights Movement," in *Group Politics and Social Movements in Canada*, edited by Miriam Smith (Toronto: Broadview Press, 2008), 181–202.

6   *Carter v. Canada (Attorney General)* (2015).

7   Fleming, McLean, and Tatalovich, "Debating Gun Control."

8   Joyce Lee Malcolm, *To Keep and Bear Arms: The Origins of an Anglo-American Right* (Cambridge, MA: Harvard University Press, 1996); Stephen P. Halbrook, *That Every Man Be Armed: The Evolution of a Constitutional Right*, Rev. and u (Albuquerque: University of New Mexico Press, 2013); Spitzer, "The Politics of Gun Control"; Charles, *Armed in America*.

9   *R. v. Hasselwander*.

10 "Bruce Montague Firearms Case Won't Be Heard by Supreme Court of Canada," *CBC News*, 21 November 2014, www.cbc.ca/news/canada /thunder-bay/bruce-montague-firearms-case-won-t-be-heard-by -supreme-court-of-canada-1.2844859.

11 Hallbrook, *That Every Man Be Armed*.

12 William Weir, *A Well Regulated Milita: The Battle Over Gun Control* (New Haven, CT: Archon Books, 1997).

13 Hallbrook, *That Every Man Be Armed*.

14 Weir, *A Well Regulated Milita*.

15 Hallbrook, *That Every Man Be Armed*; Weir, *A Well Regulated Milita*.

16 Quoted in Hallbrook, *That Every Man Be Armed: The Evolution of a Constitutional Right*.

17 Charles, *Armed in America*, 68–9.

18 Hallbrook, *That Every Man Be Armed*.

19 Malcolm, *To Keep and Bear Arms*.

20 Hallbrook, *That Every Man Be Armed*, 44–5.

21 Quoted in Halbrook, *That Every Man Be Armed*, 47.

22 Charles, *Armed in America*.

23 David B. Kopel, Paul Gallant, and Joanne D. Eisen, "The Human Right to Self-Defense," *Brigham Young University Journal of Public Law* 22, no. 1 (2007): 43–178; David B. Kopel, "The Universal Right to Self-Defense and the Auxiliary Right to Defensive Arms," in *The Second Amendment and*

Gun Control: Freedom, Fear, and the American Constitution, edited by Kevin Yuill and Joe Street (London: Routledge, 2018), 139–54.

24 For a comprehensive treatment of this topic, see: Brown, "Firearm 'Rights' in Canada."

25 *R. v. Hasselwander*; Attorney General, *Hudson v. Canada* (2007); ONCA, *R. v. Montague* (2010).

26 General, *Hudson v. Canada*, SKQB.

27 ONCA, *R. v. Montague*, 141.

28 Charles, *Armed in America*; Tushnet, *Out of Range*; Halbrook, *That Every Man Be Armed*; Jennifer Tucker, "Introduction," in *A Right to Bear Arms? The Contested Role of History in the Contemporary Debate on the Second Amendment*, edited by Jennifer Tucker, Barton C. Hacker, and Margaret Vining (Washington, DC: Smithsonian Scholarly Press, 2019).

29 Antonin Scalia, *District of Columbia et al. v. Heller* (2008).

30 Samuel Alito, *McDonald v. City of Chicago* (2010).

31 Clarence Thomas, *New York State Rifle & Pistol Association Inc. et al. v. Bruen, Superintendent of New York State Police, et al.* (2022).

32 Yamane, *Concealed Carry Revolution*.

33 Alexander Alvaro, "Why Property Rights Were Excluded from the Canadian Charter of Rights and Freedoms," *Canadian Journal of Political Science/Revue Canadienne de Science Politique* 24, no. 2 (1991): 309–29.

34 Bryan Passifiume, "Federal Court Strikes down Challenge to 2020 Ban on 'Assault' Firearms," *The National Post*, 30 October 2023, https://nationalpost.com/news/politics/federal-court-strikes-down-gun-ban-challenge.

35 Rifat Darina Kamal and Charles Burton, "Policy Gridlock versus Policy Shift in Gun Politics: A Comparative Veto Player Analysis of Gun Control Policies in the United States and Canada," *World Affairs* 181, no. 4 (2018): 317–47.

36 Kamal and Burton, "Policy Gridlock"; B. Timothy Heinmiller and Matthew A. Hennigar, *Aiming to Explain: Theories of Policy Change and Canadian Gun Control* (Toronto: University of Toronto Press, 2022).

37 Parker et al., "America's Complex Relationship with Guns."

38 "Firearms, Accidental Deaths, Suicide and Violent Crime: An Updated Review of the Literature with Special Reference to the Canadian Situation," Department of Justice, 2022, www.justice.gc.ca/eng/rp-pr/csj-sjc/jsp-sjp/wd98_4-dt98_4/p2.html.

39 Heinmiller and Hennigar, *Aiming to Explain: Theories of Policy Change and Canadian Gun Control*.

40 Alexandra T. Middlewood, "A Silver Bullet: Gun Ownership and Political Participation in Rural America," *Great Plains Research* 31, no. 2 (2021): 159–71.

41 Middlewood, "A Silver Bullet," 161.
42 Matthew J. Lacombe, *Firepower: How the NRA Turned Gun Owners Into a Political Force* (Princeton, NJ: Princeton University Press, 2021); Schwartz, *On Target*.
43 Interview with Tracey Wilson, CCFR, 21 October 2021.
44 Lacombe, *Firepower*.
45 Interview with Sheldon Clare, NFA, 19 January 2022.
46 John Ibbitson, "Erin O'Toole Pivots on Gun Policy in Increasingly Tight Election Race," *The Globe & Mail*, 5 September 2021, www.theglobeandmail.com/politics/article-erin-otoole-pivots-on-gun-policy-in-increasingly-tight-election-race/.
47 Interview with Tony Bernardo, CSSA, 4 November 2022.
48 "Alberta Won't Participate in Federal Efforts to Seize Prohibited Weapons, Shandro Says," *CBC News*, 26 September 2022, www.cbc.ca/news/canada/calgary/alberta-guns-federal-legislation-1.6596683.
49 Brown, "Firearm 'Rights' in Canada"; Heinmiller and Hennigar, *Aiming to Explain*.
50 Supreme Court of Canada, Reference re Firearms Act (Can.) (2000).
51 Dylan S. McLean and Jason Sorens, "The Changing Ideological Politics of U.S. State Firearms Regulation," *Politics & Policy* 47, no. 4 (2019): 638–72, https://doi.org/10.1111/polp.12321; Mark Gius, "The Impact of State and Federal Assault Weapons Bans on Public Mass Shootings," *Applied Economics Letters* 22, no. 4 (2015): 281–4.
52 Gary Reich and Jay Barth, "Planting in Fertile Soil: The National Rifle Association and State Firearms Legislation," *Social Science Quarterly* 98, no. 2 (2017): 485–99.
53 Yamane, *Conceald Carry Revolution: Expanding the Right to Bear Arms in America*.
54 Tom W. Smith, "The 75% Solution: An Analysis of the Structure of Attitudes on Gun Control, 1959–1977," *Journal of Criminal Law and Criminology* 71, no. 3 (1980): 316, https://doi.org/10.2307/1142702; Howard Schuman and Stanley Presser, "The Attitude-Action Connection and the Issue of Gun Control," *The Annals of the American Academy of Political and Social Science* 455, no. 1 (1981): 40–7, https://doi.org/10.1177/000271628145500105; Middlewood et al., *Intersectionality in Action*.
55 Goss, *Disarmed*; Phillip J. Cook and Kristin A. Goss, *The Gun Debate: What Everyone Needs to Know* (Oxford: Oxford University Press, 2014).
56 Brown, *Arming and Disarming*.
57 Meng, "Bloody Blockades: The Legacy of the Oka Crisis."
58 Heinmiller and Hennigar, *Aiming to Explain: Theories of Policy Change and Canadian Gun Control*.

59 "SOR/98–205 Aboriginal Peoples of Canada Adaptations Regulations (Firearms)" (1998), https://laws-lois.justice.gc.ca/eng/regulations /SOR-98-205/page-1.html.

60 Tristin Hopper, "Why First Nations Hate Gun Control, Love Housing Programs," *National Post*, 2021, https://nationalpost.com/news /politics/election-2021/election-insights-why-first-nations-hate-gun -control-love-housing-programs.

61 "Meeting 45 – Bill C-21" (2022), https://parlvu.parl.gc.ca/Harmony/en /PowerBrowser/PowerBrowserV2/20221103/-1/37980?Embedded=true &globalstreamId=20&viewMode=3.

62 Tonya Perron, "Brief to the Senate Committee on National Security, Defence and Veterans Affairs," 2023.

63 Interview with Jack, 3 February 2022.

64 "Canadians Say Gun Violence Rising; Prefer National Policy over Provincial Regulations," Angus Reid Institute, 2022, https://angusreid .org/canada-gun-control-handgun-ban-buyback/.

65 Fleming, McLean, and Tatalovich, "Debating Gun Control"; Timothy F. Hartnagel, "Gun Control in Alberta: Explaining Public Attitudes Concerning Legislative Change," *Canadian Journal of Criminology* 44, no. 4 (2002): 403–24.

66 Schwartz, "Aiming for Success."

67 Smith, "The 75% Solution"; Gary Kleck, Marc Gertz, and Jason Bratton, "Why Do People Support Gun Control?: Alternative Explanations of Support for Handgun Bans," *Journal of Criminal Justice* 37, no. 5 (2009): 496–504; Robin M. Wolpert and James G. Gimpel, "Self-Interest, Symbolic Politics, and Public Attitudes toward Gun Control," *Political Behavior* 20, no. 3 (1998): 241–62; Goss, "The Socialization of Conflict"; Alexandra Filindra and Noah Kaplan, "Testing Theories of Gun Policy Preferences Among Blacks, Latinos, and Whites in America," *Social Science Quarterly* 98, no. 2 (2017): 413–28, https://doi.org/10.1111/ssqu.12418; Steven V. Miller, "What Americans Think About Gun Control: Evidence from the General Social Survey, 1972–2016," *Social Science Quarterly* 100, no. 1 (2019): 272–88.

68 Lucki, "2019 Commissionter of Firearms Report."

69 Mauser and Buckner, "Canadian Attitudes Toward Gun Control: The Real Story."

70 Jenson, "Fated to Live In Interesting Times: Canada's Changing Citizenship Regime."

71 John Valentine, "Cultural Nationalism, Anti-Americanism, and the Federal Defense of the Canadian Football League," *American Review of Canadian Studies* 49, no. 3 (2019): 376–93.

72 Corwin R. Kruse, "The Movement and the Media: Framing the Debate Over Animal Experimentation," *Political Communication* 18, no. 1

(1 January 2001): 67–87, https://doi.org/10.1080/10584600150217668; Kenneth T. Andrews and Michael Biggs, "The Dynamics of Protest Diffusion: Movement Organizations, Social Networks, and News Media in the 1960 Sit-Ins," *American Sociological Review* 71, no. 5 (2006): 752–77; Miriam Catherine Smith, *A Civil Society?: Collective Actors in Canadian Political Life*, Second (Toronto [Ontario]: University of Toronto Press, 2018).

73 Shanto Iyengar, "Framing Responsibility for Political Issues: The Case of Poverty," *Political Behavior* 12, no. 1 (1990): 19–40, https://doi.org/10.1007/BF00992330; Kelly Blidook, "Media, Public Opinion and Health Care in Canada: How the Media Affect 'The Way Things Are,'" *Canadian Journal of Political Science* 41, no. 2 (2008): 355–74, https://doi.org/DOI: 10.1017/S0008423908080426.

74 See chapter 5.

75 Douglas Downs, "Representing Gun Owners: Frame Identification as Social Reponsibility in News Media Discourse," *Written Communication* 19, no. 1 (2002): 44–75.

76 Karen Callaghan Schnell Frauke, "Assessing the Democratic Debate: How the News Media Frame Elite Policy Discourse," *Political Communication* 18, no. 2 (1 April 2001): 183–213, https://doi.org/10.1080/105846001750322970.

77 Mickey Djuric, "Federal Public Safety Minister Says Proposed Gun Reforms Not Meant to Target Farmers," *Toronto Star*, 2 June 2022, www.thestar.com/politics/2022/06/02/federal-public-safety-minister-says-proposed-gun-reforms-not-meant-to-target-farmers.html.

78 Interview with Lindsay, 3 March 2022.

79 Interview with Pierre, 14 April 2022.

80 Interview with Robert, 14 February 2022.

81 Interview with Lindsay, 14 March 2022.

82 Interview with Solomon, 20 January 2022.

83 Interview with Allison, 21 April 2022.

84 Interview with Mikael, 7 February 2022.

85 While this is untrue, as activities like natural resource extraction and farming also provide funding to rural areas, it does not discount the fact that hunting is a significant source of tourism revenue for rural communities.

86 Interview with Darrell Crabbe, 9 March 2022.

87 This was an interesting nod to Professor David Yamane, a sociologist of American gun culture, who has popularized this phrase using networks like the Liberal Gun Owners group on Facebook, of which Pierre is a member.

88 Interview with Pierre, 14 April 2022.

89 Interview with Annie, 17 February 2022.
90 Armstrong, Lucas, and Taylor, "The Urban-Rural Divide."
91 Interview with Jack, 3 February 2022.
92 Interview with Donal, 31 January 2022.
93 Interview with Floyd, 10 February 2022.
94 Interview with Harrison, 10 February 2022.
95 Interview with Robert, 14 February 2022.
96 Interview with Teddy, 13 January 2022.
97 Jennifer Carlson and Jessica Cobb, "From Play to Peril: A Historical Examination of Media Coverage of Accidental Shootings Involving Children*," *Social Science Quarterly* 98, no. 2 (2017): 397–412, https://doi.org/10.1111/ssqu.12416; F. Carson Mencken and Paul Froese, "Gun Culture in Action," *Social Problems* 66, no. 1 (2019): 3–27, https://doi.org/10.1093/socpro/spx040; Ronald Burns and Charles Crawford, "School Shootings, the Media, and Public Fear: Ingredients for a Moral Panic," *Crime, Law and Social Change* 32, no. 2 (1999): 147–68; H. Jaymi Elsass et al., "Moral Panic, Fear of Crime, and School Shootings: Does Location Matter?," *Sociological Inquiry* 91, no. 2 (2021): 426–54; Jaclyn Schildkraut, H. Jaymi Elsass, and Mark C. Stafford, "Could It Happen Here? Moral Panic, School Shootings, and Fear of Crime Among College Students," *Crime, Law and Social Change* 63, no. 1 (2015): 91–110; Erich Goode and Nachman Ben-Yehuda, "Moral Panic," in *The Routledge Handbook of Deviant Behavior* (Routledge, 2012), 46–52.
98 Interview with Emily, 10 February 2022.
99 Brown, *Arming and Disarming.*
100 Interview with Zhi, 14 April 2022.
101 Interview with Karl, 17 January 2022.
102 Interview with Rowan, 13 January 2022.
103 Rosh Hashanah is the Jewish New Year.
104 Interview with Ben, 20 January 2022.
105 Interview with Amos, 10 February 2022.
106 Interview with Nicole, 28 February 2022.
107 Interview with Glen, 28 February 2022.
108 Middlewood, "A Silver Bullet."
109 "Trudeau: 'You Don't Need an AR-15 to Bring Down a Deer,'" *BBC News*, 1 May 2020, www.bbc.com/news/av/world-us-canada-52510137.
110 Logan Stein, "'I'll Do Whatever It Takes': Canada's Minister of Public Safety Talks Gun Bill in Regina," *650 CKOM*, 2 June 2022, www.ckom.com/2022/06/02/ill-do-whatever-it-takes-canadas-minister-of-public-safety-talks-gun-bill-in-regina/.
111 Brown, *Arming and Disarming.*

112 Shane P. Mahoney and John J. Jackson III, "Enshrining Hunting as a Foundation for Conservation – the North American Model," *International Journal of Environmental Studies* 70, no. 3 (2013): 448–59.

113 Mahoney and Jackson III, "Enshrining Hunting," 449.

114 Mahoney and Jackson III, "Enshrining Hunting," 449.

115 John F. Reiger, *American Sportsmen and the Origins of Conservation*, 3rd ed. (Corvallis: Oregon State University Press, 2001).

116 Mahoney and Jackson III, "Enshrining Hunting."

117 Reiger, *American Sportsmen*; James R. Heffelfinger, Valerius Geist, and William Wishart, "The Role of Hunting in North American Wildlife Conservation," *International Journal of Environmental Studies* 70, no. 3 (2013): 399–413.

118 Tina Loo, "Making a Modern Wilderness: Conserving Wildlife in Twentieth-Century Canada," *Canadian Historical Review* 82, no. 1 (2001): 91–121.

119 Mahoney and Jackson III, "Enshrining Hunting," 451.

120 Mahoney and Jackson III, "Enshrining Hunting," 452.

121 Mateen A. Hessami et al., "Indigenizing the North American Model of Wildlife Conservation," *Facets* 6, no. 1 (2021): 1285–306.

122 Mahoney and Jackson III, "Enshrining Hunting."

123 Jessica Love-Nichols, "'Tied to the Land': Climate Change Activism Among U.S. Hunters and Fishers," *Frontiers in Communication* 5, no. 1 (2020): 1–14, https://doi.org/10.3389/fcomm.2020.00001.

124 Reiger, *American Sportsmen*; Mahoney and Jackson III, "Enshrining Hunting."

125 Mahoney and Jackson III, "Enshrining Hunting," 455.

126 Reiger, *American Sportsmen*.

127 Mahoney and Jackson III, "Enshrining Hunting," 458.

128 Heffelfinger, Geist, and Wishart, "The Role of Hunting."

129 Interview with Alain Cossette, FQCP, 12 May 2022.

130 Interview with Darrell Crabbe, SWF, 9 March 2022.

131 Caren Cooper et al., "Are Wildlife Recreationists Conservationists? Linking Hunting, Birdwatching, and Pro-environmental Behavior," *The Journal of Wildlife Management* 79, no. 3 (2015): 446–57.

132 Heffelfinger, Geist, and Wishart, "The Role of Hunting," 410.

133 Heffelfinger, Geist, and Wishart, "The Role of Hunting," 406.

134 Mahoney and Jackson III, "Enshrining Hunting," 453.

135 Heffelfinger, Geist, and Wishart, "The Role of Hunting."

136 Love-Nichols, "'Tied to the Land.'"

137 Interview with Matt DeMille, OFAH, 3 June 2022.

138 Hessami et al., "Indigenizing the North American Model of Wildlife Conservation."

139 Hessami et al., "Indigenizing the North American Model of Wildlife Conservation."
140 Interview with Darrell Crabbe, SWF, 9 March 2022.
141 Mark Damian et al., "Americans' Attitudes Toward Hunting, Fishing, Sport Shooting, and Trapping" (Harrisonburg, VA, 2019), www.fishwildlife.org/application/files/7715/5733/7920/NSSF_2019_Attitudes_Survey_Report.pdf.
142 Mario Canseco, "Most Canadians Oppose Trophy Hunting, Fur Farming and Rodeos," Researchco, 2022, https://researchco.ca/2022/04/08/animals-canada-2/.
143 Nanos Research, "Considerable Majority of Canadians Agree or Somewhat Agree That Fish and Wildlife Conservation Should Be a Priority in Canada," October 2017. Slide deck provided by Matt DeMille, Ontario Federation of Anglers and Hunters (OFAH), 14 November 2022.

5. From Pastime to Politics

1 Interview with Caleb, 14 February 2022.
2 While the term "safety" can have dual meanings in the context of firearm ownership, that is, firearms as tools of ensuring safety as well as the need to handle firearms safety, looking at the context within which the comments were provided it seems that most participants leaned towards the latter meaning.
3 McLean, "Gun Talk Online."
4 Brown, *Arming and Disarming*.
5 For example, Trudeau has used the term "thoughts and prayers" in both his policy statements (https://liberal.ca/our-platform/gun-control/) and speeches (www.macleans.ca/news/canada/justin-trudeau-announces-federal-ban-on-military-grade-assault-weapons-in-canada-full-transcript/) when discussing his intention to ban "assault-style" firearms. This phrase is commonly derided in American progressive circles as empty rhetoric used by Republican politicians responding to mass shootings that are a result of a lack of policy action on gun control. It makes little sense in the Canadian context, where major mass shootings like the École Polytechnique massacre were followed by major overhauls of existing firearm legislation.
6 This is based on my personal experience having taken the Canadian Firearms Safety Course, Canadian Restricted Firearms Safety Course, and Ontario Hunter Education course in the spring/summer of 2018.
7 Actual quote reads: "The totalitarian states can do great things but there is one thing they cannot do: they cannot give the factory-worker a rifle and tell him to take it home and keep it in his bedroom. That rifle hanging

on the wall of the working class flat or labourer's cottage is the symbol of democracy. It is our job to see that it stays there." Quoted from "Don't Let Colonel Blimp Ruin the Home Guard," *Evening Standard*, London, 8 January 1941.

8 Interview with Steffan, 9 February 2022.
9 Interview with Robert, 14 February 2022.
10 Interview with Mani, 24 February 2022.
11 Interview with Stanley, 22 April 2022.
12 Interview with Sheldon Clare, National Firearms Association, 19 January 2022.
13 Interview with Rod, 20 January 2022.
14 Interview with Donal, 31 January 2022.
15 FBI, "FBI Uniform Crime Report: Expanded Homicide Data Table 8," 2019, https://ucr.fbi.gov/crime-in-the.u.s/2019/crime-in-the.u.s.-2019/tables /expanded-homicide-data-table-8.xls.
16 Sugarmann, "Assault Weapons"; Barrett, *Glock*.
17 Interview with Roger, 28 February 2022.
18 Interview with Ava, 20 January 2022.
19 Interview with Matthew, 3 February 2022.
20 Interview with Bruce, 13 January 2022.
21 Interview with Rowan, 13 January 2022.
22 Interview with Joe, 27 January 2022.
23 CCFR/CCDAF. Twitter Post. 10 April 2020. 4:01 a.m. https://twitter.com /CCFR_CCDAF/status/1380838250982555650?ref_src=twsrc%5Etfw%7Ct wcamp%5Etweetembed%7Ctwterm%5E1380838250982555650%7Ctwgr%5 E70a4c35f18f62a802018e551f7eeae861adec4bd%7Ctwcon%5Es1 _&ref_url=https%3A%2F%2Ffirearmrights.ca%2Fblair-calls-ccfr-members -violent-extremists%2F.
24 Interview with Claude, 27 January 2022.
25 Interview with Enzo, 2 February 2022.
26 Interview with Matthew, 3 February 2022.
27 Interview with Jackson, 20 January 2022.
28 Schwartz, "Aiming for Success."
29 Interview with Debbie, 31 January 2022.
30 The RCMP does not make public the number of firearm licencees responsible for committing homicides in a given year, though it is likely higher than 1 per cent. Estimates conducted by scholars like Mauser, however, demonstrate that licensed gun owners are less likely to commit homicide than the average Canadian. See Gary Mauser, "Ten Myths About Firearms and Violence in Canada," *Journal on Firearms & Public Policy* 23 (2011): 76.
31 Interview with Talia, 24 February 2022.

32 Interview with Harrison, 10 February 2022.

33 Interview with Mani, 24 February 2022.

34 Interview with Jerry, 27 January 2022.

35 Interview with Robert, 14 February 2022.

36 Interview with Nikolasz, 3 February 2022.

37 Interview with Adrian, 20 January 2022.

38 Interview with Allison, 21 April 2022.

39 Interview with Mireille, 14 April 2022.

40 *Canadian Coalition for Firearm Rights et al. v. Attorney General.* Cross -Examination of Murray Smith (2020).

41 Interview with Emily Brown, 10 February 2022.

42 Interview with Warren, 13 January 2022.

43 Interview with Hugh, 21 April 2022.

44 Bobby Hristova, "Renowned Gunsmith Killed in Toronto Police Raid. Family, Experts Want to Know Why," *CBC News*, 18 November 2021, www.cbc.ca/news/canada/hamilton/rodger-kotanko-police -shooting-1.6252238.

45 Canadian Press, "Gunsmith's Family Launches Lawsuit Against Toronto Police over Shooting Death," *Global News*, 18 January 2022, https:// globalnews.ca/news/8519619/kotanko-lawsuit-toronto-police-death/.

46 Interview with Claude, 27 January 2022.

47 In order to be able to validate their story, Chris and Lindsay both agreed to be named in the book.

48 Interview with Chris Levesque, 10 March 2022.

49 "The National 2003–06–30 (Segment 004)," *The National – CBC Television* (Toronto: Canadian Broadcasting Corporation, 30 June 2003), https:// lib-ezproxy.concordia.ca/login?qurl=https%3A%2F%2Fwww .proquest.com%2Fother-sources%2Fnational-2003-06-30-segment -004%2Fdocview%2F190714839%2Fse-2%3Faccountid%3D10246.

50 Eric Goodwin could not be contacted for verification.

51 The Canadian Firearms Centre is located in Miramachi, NB.

52 Interview with Chris Levesque, 10 March 2022.

53 Stenning, "Long Gun Registration."

54 Gordon L. Campbell, "R. v. Levesque" (2009), www.canlii.org/en/pe /pesctd/doc/2009/2009pesc12/2009pesc12.html?searchUrlHash=AAA AAQASSXNsYW5kIEd1bnMgJiBHZWFyAAAAAAE&resultIndex=28; David H. Jenkins, "R. v. Levesque" (2010), www.canlii.org/en/pe /pescad/doc/2010/2010peca21/2010peca21.html?searchUrlHash=AAAA AQASSXNsYW5kIEd1bnMgJiBHZWFyAAAAAAE&resultIndex=9; Gordon L. Campbell, "R. v. Levesque" (2007), www.canlii.org/en/pe/pesctd /doc/2007/2007pesctd19/2007pesctd19.html?searchUrlHash=AAAAA QASSXNsYW5kIEd1bnMgJiBHZWFyAAAAAAE&resultIndex=1; M.M.

Murphy, "R. v. Christopher Roland Levesque" (2009), www
.canlii.org/en/pe/pescad/doc/2009/2009peca22/2009peca22.html?search
UrlHash=AAAAAQAOUi4gdi4gTGV2ZXNxdWUAAAAAAQ&resultInd
ex=4#document.

55 Murphy, "R. v. Christopher Roland Levesque."
56 Campbell, "R. v. Levesque," 2009; Campbell, "R. v. Levesque," 2007.
57 Murphy, "R. v. Christopher Roland Levesque"; Jenkins, "R. v. Levesque."
58 Campbell, "R. v. Levesque," 2007.
59 Natalia Goodwin, "Former RCMP Officer Sentenced to 3 Years in Prison
   for Weapons-Related Charges," *CBC News*, 26 May 2016, www.cbc.ca
   /news/canada/prince-edward-island/pei-rcmp-gillis-1.4132705.
60 Interview with Chris Levesque, 10 March 2022.
61 Interview with Chris Levesque, 10 March 2022.
62 Interview with Lindsay Levesque, 14 March 2022.
63 Interview with Warren, 13 January 2022.
64 Trapshooting is an Olympic shotgun sport that involves shooting clay
   pigeons that are launched from a covered bunker called a trap.
65 Interview with Annie, 17 February 2022.
66 Mark R. Joslyn, *The Gun Gap: The Influence of Gun Ownership on Political
   Behavior and Attitudes* (Oxford: Oxford University Press, 2020).
67 Joslyn, *The Gun Gap*, 51.
68 Joslyn, *The Gun Gap*, 64.
69 Middlewood et al., *Intersectionality in Action*.
70 Middlewood, "A Silver Bullet."
71 Schwartz, "Guns in the North."
72 Schwartz, "Called to Arms."
73 Interview with Annie, 17 February 2022.
74 Interview with Mani, 24 February 2022.
75 Interview with Dawson, 14 February 2022.
76 Interview with Rick, 22 April 2022.
77 Smith, "Black Americans Have Been Buying More Guns."
78 Interview with Lowell, 27 January 2022.
79 Interview with Francis, 24 February 2022.
80 Interview with Donal, 31 January 2022.
81 Interview with Zhi, 14 April 2022.
82 Interview with Archie, 24 February 2022.
83 Interview with Emily Brown, 10 February 2022.
84 Interview with Leo, 3 May 2022.
85 Interview with Caleb, 14 February 2022.
86 Interview with Rod, 20 January 2022.
87 Interview with Lowell, 27 January 2022.

6. Formal Pro-Gun Advocacy

1 Interview with Christine Generoux, 13 January 2022.
2 Interview with Sheldon Clare, former NFA president, 19 January 2022.
3 Interview with Jamie Elliott, CCFR president, 23 November 2021.
4 Interview with Jamie Elliott, 23 November 2021.
5 Interview with Rod Giltaca, 28 October 2021
6 Interview with Tony Bernardo, CSSA, 4 October 2021.
7 Interview with Alison De Groot, CSAAA, 4 November 2021.
8 Alice Sowry, "Reconciling the Clash: A Comparison of the Australian and Canadian Legal Approaches to Burdening Indigenous Hunting Rights," *Public Interest Law Journal of New Zealand* 154, no. 2 (2015): 154–64; David Natcher et al., "Conservation and Indigenous Subsistence Hunting in the Peace River Region of Canada," *Human Ecology* 49, no. 2 (2021): 109–20, https://doi.org/10.1007/s10745-020-00210-z.
9 Interview with Thomas Stevens, Cree Trappers Association, 3 March 2022.
10 Thomas W. Hughes and Karen Lee, "The Role of Recreational Hunting in the Recovery and Conservation of the Wild Turkey (Meleagris Gallopavo Spp.) in North America," *Environmental Studies Monographs* 72, no. 5 (2015): 797–809, https://doi.org/10.1080/00207233.2015.1022998.
11 Puzzling refers to when advocacy groups work collaboratively with governments to create better policies.
12 Interview with Matt DeMille, OFAH, 3 June 2022.
13 Interview with Matt DeMille, OFAH, 3 June 2022; Interview with Alain Cossette, FQCP, 12 May 2022; Interview with Darrell Crabbe, SWF, 9 March 2022.
14 Interview with Alain Cossette, FQCP, 12 May 2022.
15 Olson, *The Logic of Collective Action*.
16 Norman Frohlich, Joe A. Oppenheimer, and Oran R. Young, *Political Leadership and Collective Goods* (Princeton, NJ: Princeton University Press, 1971); John Chamberlin, "Provision of Collective Goods as a Function of Group Size," *The American Political Science Review* 68, no. 2 (1974): 707–16; McFarland, "Neopluralism."
17 Mintrom and Norman, "Policy Entrepreneurship and Policy Change."
18 John W. Kingdon, "Agendas, Alternatives, and Public Policies" (Boston: Little, Brown, 1984); Nicole Herweg, Nikolaos Zahariadis, and Reimut Zolnhofer, "The Multiple Streams Framework: Foundations, Refinements, and Empirical Applications," in *Theories of the Policy Process*, edited by Christopher M. Weible and Paul A. Sabatier, 4th ed. (New York: Westview Press, 2018), 17–55.

19 Christopher M. Weible and Karin Ingold, "The Advocacy Coalition Framework," in *Theories of the Policy Process 2*, edited by Christopher M. Weible and Paul A. Sabatier, 4th ed. (Westview Press, 2018), 449–67.

20 Mintrom and Norman, "Policy Entrepreneurship."

21 Interview with Sheldon Clare, former NFA president, 19 January 2022.

22 Interview with Sheldon Clare, 19 January 2022.

23 Interview with Christine Generoux, 13 January 2022.

24 Interview with Christine Generoux, 13 January 2022.

25 Interview with Jamie Elliott, CCFR president, 23 November 2021.

26 Interview with Rod Giltaca, 28 October 2021.

27 Interview with Rod Giltaca, 28 October 2021.

28 Florian Weiler and Matthias Brändli, "Inside Versus Outside Lobbying: How the Institutional Framework Shapes the Lobbying Behaviour of Interest Groups," *European Journal of Political Research* 54, no. 4 (2015): 745–66; Young and Everitt, *Advocacy Groups*.

29 Jan Beyers, "Voice and Access: Political Practices of European Interest Associations," *European Union Politics* 5, no. 2 (2004): 211–40; Anne Binderkrantz, "Interest Group Strategies: Navigating between Privileged Access and Strategies of Pressure," *Political Studies* 53, no. 4 (2005): 694–715; Marcel Hanegraaff, Jan A.N. Beyers, and Iskander De Bruycker, "Balancing Inside and Outside Lobbying: The Political Strategies of Lobbyists at Global Diplomatic Conferences," *European Journal of Political Research* 55, no. 3 (2016): 568–88; Ken Kollman, "Outside Lobbying," in *Outside Lobbying* (Princeton, NJ: Princeton University Press, 2021).

30 Young and Everitt, *Advocacy Groups*.

31 Interview with Tracey Wilson, CCFR, 21 October 2021.

32 Interview with Tony Bernardo, CSSA, 4 November 2021.

33 Interview with Tony Bernardo, CSSA, 4 November 2021.

34 Interview with Tony Bernardo, CSSA, 4 November 2021.

35 Interview with Sheldon Clare, NFA, 19 January 2022.

36 Interview with Sheldon Clare, 26 January 2022.

37 Interview with Tracey Wilson, CCFR, 21 October 2021.

38 Interview with Tracey Wilson, CCFR, 21 October 2021.

39 Interview with Alison De Groot, CSAAA, 4 November 2021.

40 Interview with Alison De Groot, CSAAA, 4 November 2021.

41 Interview with Alison De Groot, CSAAA, 4 November 2021.

42 Interview with Tony Bernardo, CSSA, 4 November 2021.

43 Interview with Tony Bernardo, CSSA, 4 November 2021.

44 Interview with Allison De Groot, CSAAA, 4 November 2021.

45 Interview with Sheldon Clare, 19 January 2022.

46 *Quebec (Attorney General) v. Canada (Attorney General)* (2015).

47 Interview with Alain Cossette, FQCP, 12 May 2022.

48 Interview with Tony Bernardo, CSSA, 4 November 2021.

49 Interview with Sheldon Clare, NFA, 19 January 2022.

50 Interview with Rod Giltaca, CCFR, 18 October 2021.

51 Interview with Jamie Elliott, CCFR president, 23 November 2021.

52 Interview with Tracey Wilson, CCFR, 21 October 2021.

53 Interview with Tracey Wilson, CCFR, 21 October 2021.

54 Interview with Jamie Elliott, CCFR, 23 November 2021.

55 Canadian Coalition for Firearm Rights, "Ban the AR 15: It's Just Common Sense." *YouTube* video. 02:20. 11 August 2017. www.youtube.com /watch?v=KZ3o7Fr6yV4

56 *Vice*, "How to Buy a Gun in Canada: Armed and Reasonable." *YouTube* video. 22:09. 14 December 2016. www.youtube.com /watch?v=q9El7gEvJWU&t=76s

57 Brown, *Arming and Disarming*.

58 Interview with Tracey Wilson, 21 October 2021.

59 Interview with Tracey Wilson, 21 October 2021.

60 Interview with Jamie Elliott, 23 November 2021.

61 Interview with Allison, 21 April 2022.

62 Interview with Jamie Elliott, 23 November 2021.

63 The author attended the march and witnessed events for himself.

64 The Canadian Press, "Pro-Gun Marchers Speak Out on Federal Government's Assault-Style Weapons Ban," *CBC News*, 2020, www.cbc .ca/news/politics/gun-marchers-assault-weapons-ban-1.5722051.

65 Interview with Alain Cossette, FQCP, 12 May 2022.

66 Interview with Matt DeMille, OFAH, 3 June 2022.

67 Elmer Eric Schattschneider, *The Semisovereign People : A Realist's View of Democracy in America* (New York: Holt, Rinehart and Winston, 1960).

68 Interview with Tracey Wilson, 21 October 2021.

69 Nadine Yousif, "'A Pandemic of Grief': StatCan's First-Ever Data on Black Victims of Homicide Prompts Calls for Targeted Trauma Services," *Toronto Star*, 17 November 2020, www.thestar.com/news /gta/2020/11/16/a-pandemic-of-grief-statcans-first-ever-data-on-black -victims-of-homicide-prompts-calls-for-targeted-trauma-services.html; Department of Justice, "Indigenous Overrepresentation in the Criminal Justice System" (Ottawa, ON, 2019), www.justice.gc.ca/eng/rp-pr/jr /jf-pf/2019/may01.html.

70 Interview with Evelyn Fox, 17 March 2022.

71 Interview with Tracey Wilson, 21 October 2022.

72 Full report available here: www.children.gov.on.ca/htdocs/English /professionals/oyap/roots/index.aspx

73 Interview with Evelyn Fox, 17 March 2022.

74 Interview with Evelyn Fox, 17 March 2022.

75 Interview with Evelyn Fox, 17 March 2022.
76 Interview with Evelyn Fox, 17 March 2022.
77 Canadian Coalition for Firearm Rights, "The Government Can Take My Property? You Bet it Can." *YouTube* video. 02:01. 21 July 2020. www .youtube.com/watch?v=UIiwpgcl1uU&t=1s
78 Alvaro, "Why Property Rights Were Excluded."
79 Interview with Matt DeMille, 3 June 2022.
80 Young and Everitt, *Advocacy Groups*.
81 Smith, "Identity and Opportunity."
82 Brown, "Firearm 'Rights' in Canada."
83 *R. v. Hasselwander*.
84 Interview with Sheldon Clare, 26 January 2022.
85 Mark Nielsen, "Local Gun Shop Owner Taking Legal Action Against Firearms Ban," *Prince George Citizen*, 24 September 2020, www .princegeorgecitizen.com/local-news/local-gun-shop-owner-taking -legal-action-against-firearms-ban-3741440.
86 Tim Naumetz, "Western Gun Groups Lead Fundraising in Legal Fight Against Firearm Ban," *IPolitics*, 2020, https://ipolitics.ca/2020/08/22 /western-gun-groups-lead-fundraising-in-legal-fight-against-firearm -ban/.
87 Passifiume, "Federal Court Strikes Down Challenge."
88 The most recent addition to the pro-control coalition is Doctors for Protection from Guns, established in 2019 by trauma-care physicians in Toronto, most notably Dr. Najma Ahmed. Arguing that even one firearm injury or death in Canada is too many, the group lobbies for stricter gun control and makes frequent media appearances.
89 True North Wire, "Gun Rights Group Challenges Gun Control Activist to Debate for Charity," *True North*, 20 December 2019, https://tnc .news/2019/12/20/gun-rights-group-challenges-gun-control-activist-to -debate-for-charity/.
90 Rod Giltaca, "CCFR Radio – Ep. 116. Firearm Registration Is Back! Tracey Wilson in Studio, MCC Presentation & More," *Youtube* (Canada, 2022), www.youtube.com/watch?v=tcnPB2NrzaI.
91 Interview with Christine Generoux, 21 January 2022.
92 Eric Montpetit, "Are Interest Groups Useful or Harmful? Take Two," in *Canadian Politics*, edited by James Bickerton and Alain G. Gagnon (Toronto: University of Toronto Press, 2014).
93 "Reloading" one's own ammunition refers to the process of home -producing ammunition from various components. A modern cartridge contains a projectile (a bullet), a propellant (gunpowder), a primer (a small disc struck by the gun's hammer or firing pin that ignites the gunpowder), and a casing (the shell that holds these components

together). Purchasing these components separately can make shooting more economical, an important consideration given that a single round of hunting ammunition often costs as much as a Starbucks coffee. Reloading also allows hunters and sports shooters to "customize" their cartridges by using varying amounts of powder. For example, cowboy action shooters often fire at steel targets. To minimize the risk of an accident from ricochet, they use rounds with a milder powder charge.

94 Muzzle-loading firearms, like muskets, are an antiquated form of firearm that load from the far end of the gun's barrel (the muzzle) rather than the rear end closest to the shooter (the breech). These firearms generally use black powder, or a black-powder substitute, rather than modern smokeless gunpowder. The components – the projectile, propellant, primer, and casing – come separately, not in convenient cartridges. They are generally much slower to load, and more difficult to use, than modern firearms. Because black powder is highly corrosive, these firearms involve a much greater level of cleaning and care. Further, black powder can be dangerous to store in large quantities. So why would anyone own a muzzle-loading firearm? For those who shoot reproductions of traditional muzzle-loading firearms, they feel a connection to the past or enjoy a slower and more challenging target-shooting experience. For those who use modern "inline" muzzleloaders, which more closely resemble modern hunting rifles, and often have a scope fitted to them, it is all about hunting restrictions. Because muzzle-loading firearms are harder to use and require more skill, many provinces and U.S. states have longer hunting seasons for muzzleloaders. Further, more densely populated hunting zones may not allow the use of modern rifles for hunting, given the danger of bullets travelling beyond their intended targets. Hunters in these areas must choose among shotguns, bows, or muzzleloaders.

95 Interview with Sheldon Clare, NFA, 26 January 2022.

96 Interview with Alison De Groot, CSAAA, 4 November 2021.

97 Canadian Border Service Agency.

98 Interview with Alison De Groot, 4 November 2021.

99 Interview with Matt DeMille, OFAH, 3 June 2022.

100 Brown, *Arming and Disarming*.

101 Interview with Alain Cossette, FQCP, 12 May 2022.

102 Dahl, *Who Governs?*; Robert A. Dahl, "A Critique of the Ruling Elite Model," *American Political Science Review* 52 (1958): 463–9.

103 Olson, *The Logic of Collective Action*.

104 McFarland, "Neopluralism"; Miriam Smith, "Introduction: Theories of Group Movement Organizing," in *Group Politics and Social Movements in Canada*, edited by Miriam Smith (Toronto: Broadview Press, 2008), 15–34.

105 Schuman and Presser, "The Attitude-Action Connection"; Middlewood et al., *Intersectionality in Action*; Joslyn, *The Gun Gap*; Reich and Barth, "Planting in Fertile Soil: The National Rifle Association and State Firearms Legislation."
106 Interview with Tony Bernardo, CSSA, 4 November 2021.
107 Interview with Tracey Wilson, CCFR, 21 October 2021.
108 "Firearm Ownership in California" (Davis, CA, 2018), https://health .ucdavis.edu/vprp/UCFC/Fact_Sheets/CSaWSBrief_InjPrev_Kravitz -Wirtz.pdf.
109 Interview with Tony Bernardo, CSSA, 4 November 2021.
110 Interview with Alison De Groot, CSAAA, 4 November 2021.
111 Matthew J. Lacombe, "The Political Weaponization of Gun Owners: The National Rifle Association's Cultivation, Dissemination, and Use of a Group Social Identity," *The Journal of Politics* 81, no. 4 (2019): 1342–56, https://doi.org/https://doi.org/10.1086/704329.
112 "Shooting Clubs and Shooting Ranges Regulations" (1998), https://laws -lois.justice.gc.ca/eng/regulations/sor-98-212/FullText.html.
113 Interview with Darrell Crabbe, Saskatchewan Wildlife Federation, 9 March 2022.
114 Interview with Rod Giltaca, CCFR, 28 October 2021.
115 Interview with Sheldon Clare, NFA, 19 January 2022.
116 Interview with Tony Bernardo, CSSA, 4 November 2021.
117 "The James Bay and Northern Quebec Agreement and the Northeastern Quebec Agreement – Annual Reports 2008–2009 / 2009–2010" (Ottawa, 2014), www.rcaanc-cirnac.gc.ca/eng/1407867973532/1542984538197.
118 Interview with Thomas Stevens, CTA, 3 March 2022.
119 Interview with Thomas Stevens, CTA, 3 March 2022.
120 Interview with Thomas Stevens, CTA, 3 March 2022.
121 Interview with Sheldon Clare, NFA, 26 January 2022.
122 Spitzer, "The Politics of Gun Control."
123 Young and Everitt, *Advocacy Groups*; Smith, "Identity and Opportunity."
124 Interview with Matt DeMille, OFAH, 3 June 2022.
125 Interview with Sheldon Clare, 19 January 2022.

7. The Hunters Become the Hunted: Bill C-21 and the Future

 1 Evan Dyer, "How Bill C-21 Turned from Banning Handguns to Hunting Guns," *CBC News*, 5 December 2022, www.cbc.ca/news/politics/bill-c21 -sporting-guns-1.6673730.
 2 Aaron D'Andrea, "Trudeau Says Firearms Bill Doesn't Target Hunters as Carey Price, Critics Attack Reforms," *Global News*, 6 December 2022, https://globalnews.ca/news/9328630/justin-trudeau-carey-price-gun -control/.

3 Ka'nhenhsí:io Deer, "AFN Passes Emergency Resolution to Oppose Federal Gun Control Legislation," *CBC News*, 8 December 2022, www.cbc.ca /news/indigenous/afn-resolution-gun-control-legislation-1.6679444.

4 Matthew Horwood, "Bill C-21 to Be Delayed Until After Christmas Break," *The Western Standard*, 14 December 2022, www.westernstandard.news /news/bill-c-21-to-be-delayed-until-after-christmas-break/article _b6c1bdac-7bb7-11ed-9a8a-07f3748e880b.html.

5 Campbell Clark, "It Took a Lot for the Liberals to Screw Up a Gun Bill This Badly," *The Globe & Mail*, 14 December 2022, www.theglobeandmail.com /politics/article-it-took-a-lot-for-the-liberals-to-screw-up-a-gun-bill-this -badly/.

6 "'This Type of a Ban Will Affect the Hunters': Yukon Leaders Say Federal Gun Bill Worrisome," *CBC News*, 7 December 2022, www.cbc.ca/news /canada/north/yukon-hunters-federal-bill-c-21-amendments-1.6676806.

7 Rachel Aiello, "Liberal Gun Control Legislation Passes House of Commons," *CTV News*, 18 May 2023, www.ctvnews.ca/politics/liberal -gun-control-legislation-passes-house-of-commons-1.6404572.

8 "House of Commons Hansard #138 of the 44th Parliament, 1st Session" (2022), https://openparliament.ca/debates/2022/11/30/pierre -poilievre-8/.

9 *CBC News*, "Bill C-21 That Would Ban Some Hunting Rifles, Shotguns Gets Pushback" (Canada: Canadian Broadcasting Corporation, 2022), www .youtube.com/watch?v=xVucO7BQNTs.

10 Tess McClure, "New Zealand Passes World-First Tobacco Law to Ban Smoking for Next Generation," *The Guardian*, 13 December 2022, www .theguardian.com/world/2022/dec/13/new-zealand-passes-world-first -tobacco-law-to-ban-smoking-by-2025.

References

Aiello, Rachel. "Liberal Gun Control Legislation Passes House of Commons." *CTV News*, May 18, 2023. www.ctvnews.ca/politics/liberal-gun-control -legislation-passes-house-of-commons-1.6404572.

"Alberta Won't Participate in Federal Efforts to Seize Prohibited Weapons, Shandro Says." *CBC News*, September 26, 2022. www.cbc.ca/news /canada/calgary/alberta-guns-federal-legislation-1.6596683.

Alito, Samuel. McDonald v. City of Chicago (2010).

Alvaro, Alexander. "Why Property Rights Were Excluded from the Canadian Charter of Rights and Freedoms." *Canadian Journal of Political Science /Revue Canadienne de Science Politique* 24, no. 2 (1991): 309–29. https:// doi.org/10.1017/s0008423900005102

Anderson, Leon, and Jimmy D. Taylor. "Standing Out While Fitting In: Serious Leisure Identities and Aligning Actions among Skydivers and Gun Collectors." *Journal of Contemporary Ethnography* 39, no. 1 (2010): 34–59. https://doi.org/10.1177/0891241609343291

Andrews, Kenneth T., and Michael Biggs. "The Dynamics of Protest Diffusion: Movement Organizations, Social Networks, and News Media in the 1960 Sit-Ins." *American Sociological Review* 71, no. 5 (2006): 752–77. https:// doi.org/10.1177/000312240607100503

"Application for a Possession Adn Acquisition License Under the Firearms Act." Ottawa, ON: Royal Canadian Mounted Police, 2022. www.rcmp -grc.gc.ca/wam/media/4535/original/76d55b8e6f1e9345ba5927e46a ae9252.pdf.

Armstrong, David A, Jack Lucas, and Zack Taylor. "The Urban-Rural Divide in Canadian Federal Elections, 1896–2019." *Canadian Journal of Political Science* 55, no. 1 (2022): 84–106. https://doi.org/10.1017 /s0008423921000792

"As Gun Violence Rises in Canada, Weapons from the U.S. Complicate Gun Control Efforts." *NPR*, July 9, 2022. www.npr.org/2022/07/09/1108967278 /canada-gun-control-us-guns-trafficking.

Bagheri-Nesami, Masoumeh, Forough Rafii, and Seyede Fatemeh H Oskouie. "Coping Strategies of Iranian Elderly Women: A Qualitative Study." *Educational Gerontology* 36, no. 7 (2010): 573–91. https://doi.org /10.1080/03601270903324438

Banack, Clark. "Ethnography and Political Opinion: Identity, Alienation and Anti-Establishmentarianism in Rural Alberta." *Canadian Journal of Political Science* 54, no. 1 (2021): 1–22. https://doi.org/10.1017/s0008423920000694

Barrett, Paul M. *Glock: The Rise of America's Gun*. New York City, NY: Broadway Books, 2013.

Bayer, Kurt. "Christchurch Mosque Shooter Should Never Have Been Granted Firearms Licence, Sources Say." *New Zealand Herald*. June 15, 2020. www .nzherald.co.nz/nz/christchurch-mosque-shooter-should-never-have -been-granted-firearms-licence-sources-say/ LW66KNA56IWIIH6TRFLH7BUL3A/.

Beland, Daniel. *How Ideas and Institutions Shape the Politics of Public Policy*. Cambridge, UK: Cambridge University Press, 2019.

Berdahl, Loleen. "The Persistence of Western Alienation." Institute for Research on Public Policy, 2021, 1–10. https://doi.org/10.34266 /jnks.2021.7.1.

Beyers, Jan. "Voice and Access: Political Practices of European Interest Associations." *European Union Politics* 5, no. 2 (2004): 211–40. https:// doi.org/10.1177/1465116504042442

Binderkrantz, Anne. "Interest Group Strategies: Navigating between Privileged Access and Strategies of Pressure." *Political Studies* 53, no. 4 (2005): 694–715. https://doi.org/10.1111/j.1467-9248.2005.00552.x

Blidook, Kelly. "Media, Public Opinion and Health Care in Canada: How the Media Affect 'The Way Things Are.'" *Canadian Journal of Political Science* 41, no. 2 (2008): 355–74. https://doi.org/10.1017/s0008423908080426

Borland, Elizabeth. "Cultural Opportunities and Tactical Choice in the Argentine and Chilean Reproductive Rights Movements." *Mobilization: An International Quarterly* 9, no. 3 (2004): 327–39. https://doi.org/10.17813 /maiq.9.3.h21v5383812780j5

Bouchard, Russel Aurore. *Armes à Feu Au Canada et Au Québec: La Vérité Derrière Le Faux Débat*. Chicoutimi: University of Quebec at Chicoutimi, 2017.

Braun, Virginia, and Victoria Clarke. "Using Thematic Analysis in Psychology." *Qualitative Research in Psychology* 3, no. 2 (2006): 77–101. https://doi.org/10.1191/1478088706qp063oa

Brown, Carroll A., Francis A. McGuire, and Judith Voelkl. "The Link between Successful Aging and Serious Leisure." *International Journal of Aging and Human Development* 66, no. 1 (2008): 73–95. https://doi.org/10.2190 /ag.66.1.d

Brown, R. Blake. *Arming and Disarming: A History of Gun Control in Canada.* Toronto: University of Toronto Press, 2012.

– "Firearm 'Rights' in Canada: Law and History in the Debates." *Canadian Journal of Law and Society* 32, no. 1 (2017): 97–116. https://doi.org/10.1017/cls.2017.5

"Bruce Montague Firearms Case Won't Be Heard by Supreme Court of Canada." *CBC News.* November 21, 2014. www.cbc.ca/news/canada /thunder-bay/bruce-montague-firearms-case-won-t-be-heard-by -supreme-court-of-canada-1.2844859.

Bruce, Steve 1954-, and Steven. T A – T T – Yearley. "The Sage Dictionary of Sociology LK – Https://Concordiauniversity.on.Worldcat.Org /Oclc/290532493." London; SAGE, 2006. http://site.ebrary.com /id/10218157.

Burns, Ronald, and Charles Crawford. "School Shootings, the Media, and Public Fear: Ingredientsfor a Moral Panic." *Crime, Law and Social Change* 32, no. 2 (1999): 147–68. https://doi.org/10.1023/a:1008338323953

Camfield, David. "Re-Orienting Class Analysis: Working Classes as Historical Formations." *Science & Society* 68, no. 4 (2005): 421–46. https://doi.org /10.1521/siso.68.4.421.52058

Campbell, Gordon L. "R. v. Levesque." 2007. www.canlii.org/en/pe/pesctd /doc/2007/2007pesctd19/2007pesctd19.html?searchUrlHash=AAAAAQA SSXNsYW5kIEd1bnMgJiBHZWFyAAAAAAE&resultIndex=1.

– "R. v. Levesque." 2009. www.canlii.org/en/pe/pesctd/doc/2009/2009pesc12 /2009pesc12.html?searchUrlHash=AAAAAQASSXNsYW5kIEd1bnMgJiBHZ WFyAAAAAAE&resultIndex=28.

Campbell, John L. "Where Do We Stand? Common Mechanisms in Organizations and Social Movements Research." In *Social Movements and Organization Theory.*, edited by Gerald F. Davis, 41–68. Cambridge, UK: Cambridge University Press, 2005.

Canada, Statistics. "Census Profile, 2016 Census." Government of Canada, 2016. https://www12.statcan.gc.ca/census-recensement/2016/dp-pd /prof/details/page.cfm?Lang=E&Geo1=PR&Code1=01&Geo2=PR&Code2 =01&Data=Count&SearchText=Canada&SearchType=Begins&SearchPR=01 &B1=Ethnic+origin&TABID=1.

Canadian Coalition for Firearm Rights et al v. Attorney General. Cross -Examination of Murray Smith. (2020).

"Canadians Say Gun Violence Rising; Prefer National Policy over Provincial Regulations." Angus Reid Institute, 2022. https://angusreid.org/canada -gun-control-handgun-ban-buyback/.

Canseco, Mario. "Most Canadians Oppose Trophy Hunting, Fur Farming and Rodeos." Researchco, 2022. https://researchco.ca/2022/04/08/animals -canada-2/.

Carlson, Jennifer. *Citizen-Protectors: The Everyday Politics of Guns in An Age of Decline*. Oxfofrd: Oxford UP, 2015.

– "Gun Studies and the Politics of Evidence." *Annual Review of Law and Social Science*. 16 (2020): 183–202. 10.1146/annurev-lawsocsci-020620-%0A111332.

– "Revisiting the Weberian Presumption: Gun Militarism, Gun Populism, and the Racial Politics of Legitimate Violence in Policing." *American Journal of Sociology* 125, no. 3 (2019): 633–82. https://doi.org/https://doi.org/10.1086/707609.

Carlson, Jennifer D. "From Gun Politics to Self-Defense Politics: A Feminist Critique of the Great Gun Debate." *Violence Against Women* 20, no. 3 (2014): 1–9. https://doi.org/10.1177/1077801214526045

Carlson, Jennifer, and Jessica Cobb. "From Play to Peril: A Historical Examination of Media Coverage of Accidental Shootings Involving Children*." *Social Science Quarterly* 98, no. 2 (2017): 397–412. https://doi.org/10.1111/ssqu.12416

Carson Mencken, F., and Paul Froese. "Gun Culture in Action." *Social Problems* 66, no. 1 (2019): 3–27. https://doi.org/10.1093/socpro/spx040

Carter v. Canada (Attorney General) (2015).

Chamberlin, John. "Provision of Collective Goods as a Function of Group Size." *The American Political Science Review* 68, no. 2 (1974): 707–16. https://doi.org/10.1017/s0003055400117496

"Changes to Service Fees." Royal Canadian Mounted Police, 2022. www.rcmp-grc.gc.ca/en/firearms/changes-service-fees.

Charles, Patrick J. *Armed in America: A History of Gun Rights from Colonial Militias to Concealed Carry*. Amherst, NY: Prometheus, 2018.

– "The Black Panthers, NRA, Ronald Reagan, Armed Extremists, and the Second Amendment." Duke Center for Firearms Law, 2020. https://sites.law.duke.edu/secondthoughts/2020/04/08/the-black-panthers-nra-ronald-reagan-armed-extremists-and-the-second-amendment/.

Cheng, Eva (Hui Ping), Robert Stebbins, and Jan Packer. "Serious Leisure among Older Gardeners in Australia." *Leisure Studies* 36, no. 4 (2017): 505–18. https://doi.org/10.1080/02614367.2016.1188137

Clark, Campbell. "It Took a Lot for the Liberals to Screw up a Gun Bill This Badly." *The Globe and Mail*. December 14, 2022. www.theglobeandmail.com/politics/article-it-took-a-lot-for-the-liberals-to-screw-up-a-gun-bill-this-badly/.

Clément, Dominique. *Canada's Rights Revolution: Social Movements and Social Change, 1937–82*. Vancouver: UBC Press, 2009.

Cook, Phillip J., and Kristin A. Goss. *The Gun Debate: What Everyone Needs to Know*. Oxford, UK: Oxford UP, 2014.

Cooper, Caren, Lincoln Larson, Ashley Dayer, Richard Stedman, and Daniel Decker. "Are Wildlife Recreationists Conservationists? Linking Hunting, Birdwatching, and Pro-environmental Behavior." *The Journal of Wildlife Management* 79, no. 3 (2015): 446–57. https://doi.org/10.1002/jwmg.855

Cooper, Hayley. "Eighty-Two Per Cent of Handguns in Toronto Come from the U.S.: Saunders." *Newstalk 1010*. December 20, 2019. www.iheartradio.ca/newstalk-1010/news/eighty-two-per-cent-of-handguns-in-toronto-come-from-the-u-s-saunders-1.10361296.

"Courses: Possession and Aquisition License (PAL)." Firearms Safety Education Service of Ontario, 2022. https://fseso.org/courses/.

Cramer, Katherine J. *The Politics of Resentment: Rural Consciousness in Wisconsin and the Rise of Scott Walker*. Chicago, IL: University of Chicago Press, 2016.

Dahl, Robert A. "A Critique of the Ruling Elite Model." *American Political Science Review* 52 (1958): 463–69. https://doi.org/10.2307/1952327

Dahl, Robert Alan. *Who Governs?: Democracy and Power in an American City*. Vol. 4. New Haven, CT: Yale University Press, 1961.

D'Andrea, Aaron. "Trudeau Says Firearms Bill Doesn't Target Hunters as Carey Price, Critics Attack Reforms." *Global News*, December 6, 2022. https://globalnews.ca/news/9328630/justin-trudeau-carey-price-gun-control/.

Deer, Ka'nhenhsi:io. "AFN Passes Emergency Resolution to Oppose Federal Gun Control Legislation." *CBC News*, December 8, 2022. www.cbc.ca/news/indigenous/afn-resolution-gun-control-legislation-1.6679444.

DeMille, Matt. "What Firearms Are Reasonable and Proportionate for Hunting in Canada.," 2021.

Department of Justice. "Indigenous Overrepresentation in the Criminal Justice System." Ottawa, ON, 2019. www.justice.gc.ca/eng/rp-pr/jr/jf-pf/2019/may01.html.

Dixon, John. "A Gang That Couldn't Shoot Straight." *The Globe & Mail*. January 8, 2003. www.theglobeandmail.com/opinion/a-gang-that-couldnt-shoot-straight/article748138/.

Djuric, Mickey. "Federal Public Safety Minister Says Proposed Gun Reforms Not Meant to Target Farmers." *Toronto Star*. June 2, 2022. www.thestar.com/politics/2022/06/02/federal-public-safety-minister-says-proposed-gun-reforms-not-meant-to-target-farmers.html.

Dobrowolsky, Alexandra. "The Women's Movement in Fulx: Feminism and Framing, Passion, and Politics." In *Group Politics and Social Movements in Canada*, edited by Miriam Smith. Peterborough, ON: Broadview Press, 2008.

Dobrowolsky, Alexandra, and Jane Jenson. "Shifting Representations of Citizenship: Canadian Politics of 'Women' and 'Children'." *Social Politics* 11, no. 2 (2004): 154–80. https://doi.org/10.1093/sp/jxh031

Downs, Douglas. "Representing Gun Owners: Frame Identification as Social Reponsibility in News Media Discourse." *Written Communication* 19, no. 1 (2002): 44–75. https://doi.org/10.1177/074108830201900103

Duda, Mark Damian et al. "Americans' Attitudes Toward Hunting, Fishing, Sport Shooting, and Trapping." Harrisonburg, VA, 2019. www.fishwildlife.org/application/files/7715/5733/7920/NSSF_2019_Attitudes_Survey_Report.pdf.

Dyer, Evan. "How Bill C-21 Turned from Banning Handguns to Hunting Guns." *CBC News*, December 5, 2022. www.cbc.ca/news/politics/bill-c21-sporting-guns-1.6673730.

"The Economic Footprint of Angling, Hunting, Trapping and Sport Shooting in Canada.," 2020. www.conferenceboard.ca/research/angling-hunting-trapping-and-sport-shooting#:~:text=In 2018%2C Canadians spent %2418.9,%246.1 billion in government revenues.

Elsass, H Jaymi, Jaclyn Schildkraut, Ross Haenfler, Brian V Klocke, Eric Madfis, and Glenn W Muschert. "Moral Panic, Fear of Crime, and School Shootings: Does Location Matter?" *Sociological Inquiry* 91, no. 2 (2021): 426–54. https://doi.org/10.1111/soin.12407

"Engagement Summary Report – Reducing Violent Crime: A Dialogue on Handguns and Assault-Style Firearms.," 2019. www.publicsafety.gc.ca/cnt/rsrcs/pblctns/2019-rdcng-vlnt-crm-dlg/index-en.aspx.

Epp, Rogers. "The Political De-Skilling of Rural Communities." In *Writing Off the Rural West*, edited by Roger Epp and Dave Whitson, 301–324. Edmonton, AB: University of Alberta Press, 2001.

FBI. "FBI Uniform Crime Report: Expanded Homicide Data Table 8.," 2019. https://ucr.fbi.gov/crime-in-the.u.s/2019/crime-in-the.u.s.-2019/tables/expanded-homicide-data-table-8.xls.

Filindra, Alexandra, and Noah Kaplan. "Testing Theories of Gun Policy Preferences Among Blacks, Latinos, and Whites in America." *Social Science Quarterly* 98, no. 2 (2017): 413–28. https://doi.org/10.1111/ssqu.12418

"Firearm Ownership in California." Davis, CA, 2018. https://health.ucdavis.edu/vprp/UCFC/Fact_Sheets/CSaWSBrief_InjPrev_Kravitz-Wirtz.pdf.

"Firearms, Accidental Deaths, Suicide and Violent Crime: An Updated Review of the Literature with Special Reference to the Canadian Situation." Department of Justice, 2022. www.justice.gc.ca/eng/rp-pr/csj-sjc/jsp-sjp/wd98_4-dt98_4/p2.html.

Fitterer, Jessica. "Alcohol-Attributable Crime in Britisth Columbia." Victoria, BC, 2013. www.uvic.ca/research/centres/cisur/assets/docs/report-alcohol-attributable-crime.pdf.

Fleming, Anthony, Dylan S. McLean, and Raymond Tatalovich. "Debating Gun Control in Canada and the United States." *World Affairs* 181, no. 4 (2018): 348–371. https://doi.org/10.1177/0043820018812609

Friesen, Gerald, Del Muise, and David Northrup. "Variations on the Theme of Remembering: A National Survey of How Canadians Use the Past." *Journal of the Canadian Historical Association* 20, no. 1 (2009): 221–48. https://doi.org/10.7202/039788ar

Frohlich, Norman, Joe A. Oppenheimer, and Oran R. Young. *Political Leadership and Collective Goods*. Princeton, N.J: Princeton University Press, 1971.

Gallant, Karen, Susan Arai, and Bryan Smale. "Serious Leisure as an Avenue for Nurturing Community." *Leisure Sciences* 35, no. 4 (2013): 320–36. https://doi.org/10.1080/01490400.2013.797324

Gaucher, Megan. "Monogamous Canadian Citizenship, Constructing Foreignness and the Limits of Harm Discourse." *Canadian Journal of Political Science* 49, no. 3 (2016): 519–38. https://doi.org/10.1017/s0008423916000810

General, Attorney. Hudson v Canada (2007).

Gibbins, Roger. *Prairie Politics & Society: Regionalism in Decline*. Toronto, ON: Buttersworth & Co, 1980.

Gibbins, Roger, and Loleen Berdahl. *Western Visions, Western Futures: Perspectives on the West in Canada*. 2nd ed. Peterborough, ON: Broadview Press, 2003.

Gillespie, Dair L, Ann Leffler, and Elinor Lerner. "If It Weren't for My Hobby, I'd Have a Life: Dog Sports, Serious Leisure, and Boundary Negotiations." *Leisure Studies* 21, no. 3–4 (2002): 285–304. https://doi.org/10.1080/0261436022000030632

Giltaca, Rod. "CCFR Radio – Ep. 116. Firearm Registration Is Back! Tracey Wilson in Studio, MCC Presentation & More." *Youtube*. Canada, 2022. www.youtube.com/watch?v=tcnPB2NrzaI.

Gimore, Rachel. "Fe Canadian Women Own Guns, but Are Twice as Likely to Be Attacked with One: Analysis." CTV News, 2019. www.ctvnews.ca/politics/few-canadian-women-own-guns-but-are-twice-as-likely-to-be-attacked-with-one-analysis-1.4374216.

Gius, Mark. "The Impact of State and Federal Assault Weapons Bans on Public Mass Shootings." *Applied Economics Letters* 22, no. 4 (2015): 281–84. https://doi.org/10.1080/13504851.2014.939367

Goode, Erich, and Nachman Ben-Yehuda. "Moral Panic." In *The Routledge Handbook of Deviant Behavior*, 46–52. Routledge, 2012. https://doi.org/10.4324/9780203880548.ch6

Goodwin, Natalia. "Former RCMP Officer Sentenced to 3 Years in Prison for Weapons-Related Charges." *CBC News*. May 26, 2016. www.cbc.ca/news/canada/prince-edward-island/pei-rcmp-gillis-1.4132705.

Goss, Kristin. *Disarmed: The Missing Movement for Gun Control in America*. Princeton, N.J: Princeton University Press, 2006.

Goss, Kristin A. "The Socialization of Conflict and Its Limits: Gender and Gun Politics in America." *Social Science Quarterly* 98, no. 2 (2017): 455–70. https://doi.org/10.1111/ssqu.12419

"Gun Registry Cost Soars to $2 Billion." *CBC News*, February 13, 2004. www .cbc.ca/news/canada/gun-registry-cost-soars-to-2-billion-1.513990.

Gunter, Lorne. "The New Backdoor Long-Gun Registry." *Toronto Sun*. December 29, 2015. https://torontosun.com/2015/12/29/the-new -backdoor-long-gun-registry.

Halbrook, Stephen P. *That Every Man Be Armed: The Evolution of a Constitutional Right*. Rev. and u. Albuquerque, NM: University of New Mexico Press, 2013.

Hanegraaff, Marcel, Jan A N Beyers, and Iskander De Bruycker. "Balancing inside and Outside Lobbying: The Political Strategies of Lobbyists at Global Diplomatic Conferences." *European Journal of Political Research* 55, no. 3 (2016): 568–88. https://doi.org/10.1111/1475-6765.12145

Harris, Kathleen. "Liberals Promise to Prohibit Semi-Automatic Assault Rifles, Allow Cities to Ban Handguns." *CBC News*, September 20, 2019. www.cbc .ca/news/politics/liberal-gun-control-trudeau-2019-1.5290950.

Harrison, Trevor W. "Populist and Conservative Christian Evangelical Movements: A Comparison of Canada and the United States." In *Group Politics and Social Movements in Canada*, edited by Miriam Smith, 203–24. Toronto: Broadview Press, 2008.

Hartnagel, Timothy F. "Gun Control in Alberta: Explaining Public Attitudes Concerning Legislative Change." *Canadian Journal of Criminology* 44, no. 4 (2002): 403–24. https://doi.org/10.3138/cjcrim.44.4.403

Heffelfinger, James R, Valerius Geist, and William Wishart. "The Role of Hunting in North American Wildlife Conservation." *International Journal of Environmental Studies* 70, no. 3 (2013): 399–413. https://doi.org/10.1080/002 07233.2013.800383

Heinmiller, B. Timothy, and Matthew A. Hennigar. *Aiming to Explain: Theories of Policy Change and Canadian Gun Control*. Toronto, ON: University of Toronto Press, 2022.

Herweg, Nicole, Nikolaos Zahariadis, and Reimut Zolnhofer. "The Multiple Streams Framework: Foundations, Refinements, and Empirical Applications." In *Theories of Hte Policy Process*, edited by Christopher M Weible and Paul A Sabatier, 4th ed., 17–55. New York City: Westview Press, 2018.

Hessami, Mateen A, Ella Bowles, Jesse N Popp, and Adam T Ford. "Indigenizing the North American Model of Wildlife Conservation." *Facets* 6, no. 1 (2021): 1285–1306. https://doi.org/10.1139/facets -2020-0088

Hill, Terrence D, Benjamin Dowd-Arrow, Christopher G Ellison, Ginny Garcia-Alexander, John P Bartkowski, and Amy M Burdette. "Sexual Dysfunction and Gun Ownership in America: When Hard Data Meet a Limp Theory." *American Journal of Men's Health* 15, no. 5 (2021): https://doi.org/10.1177/15579883211044342

"History of NRANZ." National Rifle Association of New Zealand, 2021. www.nranz.com/organisation/history-of-nranz/.

Hofstadter, Richard. *America as a Gun Culture.* American Heritage Publishing Company., 1970.

Hoftstadter, Richard. "America As a Gun Culture." *American Heritage*, 1970. www.americanheritage.com/america-gun-culture.

Hopper, Tristin. "Why First Nations Hate Gun Control, Love Housing Programs." *National Post*, 2021. https://nationalpost.com/news/politics/election-2021/election-insights-why-first-nations-hate-gun-control-love-housing-programs.

Horwood, Matthew. "Bill C-21 to Be Delayed until after Christmas Break." *The Western Standard*, December 14, 2022. www.westernstandard.news/news/bill-c-21-to-be-delayed-until-after-christmas-break/article_b6c1bdac-7bb7-11ed-9a8a-07f3748e880b.html.

"House of Commons Hansard #138 of the 44th Parliament, 1st Session." 2022. https://openparliament.ca/debates/2022/11/30/pierre-poilievre-8/.

Hristova, Bobby. "Renowned Gunsmith Killed in Toronto Police Raid. Family, Experts Want to Know Why." *CBC News*. November 18, 2021. www.cbc.ca/news/canada/hamilton/rodger-kotanko-police-shooting-1.6252238.

Hubbs, Christi. "Just for Fun: Talk and Tactical Shooting in Southern Saskatchewan." *Journal of Undergraduate Ethnography* 7, no. 2 (2017): 19–33. https://doi.org/10.15273/jue.v7i2.8415

Hughes, Thomas W., and Karen Lee. "The Role of Recreational Hunting in the Recovery and Conservation of the Wild Turkey (Meleagris Gallopavo Spp.) in North America." *Environmental Studies Monographs* 72, no. 5 (2015): 797–809. https://doi.org/10.1080/00207233.2015.1022998

Hutchinson, Susan, and Galit Nimrod. "Leisure as a Resource for Successful Aging by Older Adults with Chronic Health Conditions." *International Journal of Aging and Human Development* 74, no. 1 (2012): 41–65. https://doi.org/10.2190/ag.74.1.c

Ibbitson, John. "Erin O'Toole Pivots on Gun Policy in Increasingly Tight Election Race." *The Globe and Mail*. September 5, 2021. www.theglobeandmail.com/politics/article-erin-otoole-pivots-on-gun-policy-in-increasingly-tight-election-race/.

"Interview with Anonymous Source within Alberta CFO's Office, January 26." Ottawa, ON, 2022.

Iyengar, Shanto. "Framing Responsibility for Political Issues: The Case of Poverty." *Political Behavior* 12, no. 1 (1990): 19–40. https://doi.org/10.1007/bf00992330

"The James Bay and Northern Quebec Agreement and the Northeastern Quebec Agreement – Annual Reports 2008–2009 / 2009–2010." Ottawa, 2014. www.rcaanc-cirnac.gc.ca/eng/1407867973532/1542984538197.

Jenkins, David H. "R. v. Levesque." 2010. www.canlii.org/en/pe/pescad/doc/2010/2010peca21/2010peca21.html?searchUrlHash=AAAAAQASSXNsYW5kIEd1bnMgJiBHZWFyAAAAAAE&resultIndex=9.

Jenson, Jane. "Fated to Live In Interesting Times: Canada's Changing Citizenship Regime." *Canadian Journal of Political Science* 30, no. 4 (1997): 627–44. https://doi.org/10.1017/s0008423900016450

Jivani, Jamil. "Canadian Politicians Import American Culture Wars to Exploit Tragedy." *National Post*. May 26, 2022. https://nationalpost.com/opinion/jamil-jivani-canadian-politicians-import-american-culture-wars-to-exploit-tragedy.

Joslyn, Mark R. *The Gun Gap: The Influence of Gun Ownership on Political Behavior and Attitudes*. Oxford, UK: Oxford University Press, 2020. https://doi.org/10.1093/oso/9780190064822.001.001.

Kamal, Rifat Darina, and Charles Burton. "Policy Gridlock versus Policy Shift in Gun Politics: A Comparative Veto Player Analysis of Gun Control Policies in the United States and Canada." *World Affairs* 181, no. 4 (2018): 317–47. https://doi.org/10.1177/0043820018814356

Kassam, Ashifa. "'Why Does Anyone Need a Gun?': Toronton Shooting Promps Calls for Handgun Ban." *The Guardian*. July 25, 2018. www.theguardian.com/world/2018/jul/25/toronto-shooting-handgun-ban-canada.

Kilsby, Andrew J. The Riflemen: A History of the National Rifle Association of Australia (1888–1988). Belmont, QLD: National Rifle Association of Australia, n.d. https://nraa.com.au/wp-content/uploads/2020/02/The-Riflemen-A-History-of-the-NRA-of-Australia-1888-1988.pdf.

Kim, Junhyoung, Jinmoo Heo, In Heok Lee, and Jun Kim. "Predicting Personal Growth and Happiness by Using Serious Leisure Model." *Social Indicators Research* 122, no. 1 (2015): 147–57. https://doi.org/10.1007/s11205-014-0680-0

Kingdon, John W. "Agendas, Alternatives, and Public Policies." Boston: Little, Brown, 1984.

Kleck, Gary, Marc Gertz, and Jason Bratton. "Why Do People Support Gun Control?: Alternative Explanations of Support for Handgun Bans." *Journal of Criminal Justice* 37, no. 5 (2009): 496–504. https://doi.org/10.1016/j.jcrimjus.2009.07.010

Kohn, Abigail A. *Shooters: Myths and Realities of America's Gun Cultures*. Oxford: Oxford UP, 2004.

Kollman, Ken. "Outside Lobbying." In *Outside Lobbying*. Princeton University Press, 2021.

Kopel, David B. "The Universal Right to Self-Defense and the Auxiliary Right to Defensive Arms." In *The Second Amendment and Gun Control: Freedom, Fear, and the American Constitution.*, edited by Kevin Yuill and Joe Street, 139–54. London: Routledge, 2018.

Kopel, David B., Paul Gallant, and Joanne D. Eisen. "The Human Right to Self-Defense." *Brigham Young University Journal of Public Law* 22, no. 1 (2007): 43–178. https://doi.org/10.1093/acprof:oso/9780190655020.003.0003

Kruse, Corwin R. "The Movement and the Media: Framing the Debate Over Animal Experimentation." *Political Communication* 18, no. 1 (January 1, 2001): 67–87. https://doi.org/10.1080/10584600150217668

Kyle, Gerard, and Gary Chick. "The Social Nature of Leisure Involvement." *Journal of Leisure Research* 34, no. 4 (2002): 426–48. https://doi.org/10.1080/00222216.2002.11949980

Kymlicka, Will. *Finding Our Way: Rethinking Ethnocultural Relations in Canada LK – Https://Concordiauniversity.on.Worldcat.Org/Oclc/38916912. TA – TT -.* Toronto; SE – viii, 220 pages; 23 cm: Oxford University Press, 1998. http://catdir.loc.gov/catdir/enhancements/fy0638/98197715-t.html.

Kymlicka, Will., and W J Norman. *Citizenship in Diverse Societies LK – Https://Concordiauniversity.on.Worldcat.Org/Oclc/42580193. TA – TT -.* Oxford; SE – xiii 444 pages; 24 cm: Oxford University Press, 2000. www.myilibrary.com?id=194387.

Lacombe, Matthew J. *Firepower: How the NRA Turned Gun Owners Into a Political Force.* Princeton, N.J: Princeton University Press, 2021.

– "The Political Weaponization of Gun Owners: The National Rifle Association's Cultivation, Dissemination, and Use of a Group Social Identity." *The Journal of Politics* 81, no. 4 (2019): 1342–56. https://doi.org/10.1086/704329

Leblanc, Daniel. "As Handgun Crimes Go up, Liberals and Conservatives Disagree on Remedy." *The Globe and Mail*, November 25, 2018. www.theglobeandmail.com/politics/article-as-handgun-crimes-go-up-liberals-and-conservatives-disagree-on-remedy/.

Lilley, Brian. "LILLEY: After Two Years, Liberals Still Trying to Design Gun Buyback Program." *Toronto Sun.* 2022. https://torontosun.com/opinion/columnists/lilley-after-two-years-liberals-still-trying-to-design-gun-buyback-program.

Lipset, Seymour Martin. "Historical Traditions and National Characteristics: A Comparative Analysis of Canada and the United States." *Canadian Journal of Sociology/Cahiers Canadiens de Sociologie*, 1986, 113–55. https://doi.org/10.2307/3340795

Littlefield, Jon, and Julie L. Ozanne. "Socialization into Consumer Culture: Hunters Learning to Be Men." *Consumption Markets and Culture* 14, no. 4 (2011): 333–60. https://doi.org/10.1080/10253866.2011.604494

Loo, Tina. "Making a Modern Wilderness: Conserving Wildlife in Twentieth-Century Canada." *Canadian Historical Review* 82, no. 1 (2001): 91–121. https://doi.org/10.3138/chr.82.1.91

Love-Nichols, Jessica. "'Tied to the Land': Climate Change Activism Among U.S. Hunters and Fishers." *Frontiers in Communication* 5, no. 1 (2020): 1–14. https://doi.org/10.3389/fcomm.2020.00001

Lucki, Brenda. "2019 Commissionter of Firearms Report." Ottawa, ON, 2020. www.rcmp-grc.gc.ca/en/firearms/2019-commissioner-firearms-report#a3-5.

Mahoney, Shane P, and John J Jackson III. "Enshrining Hunting as a Foundation for Conservation – the North American Model." *International Journal of Environmental Studies* 70, no. 3 (2013): 448–59. https://doi.org/10.1080/00207233.2013.801178

Malcolm, Joyce Lee. *To Keep and Bear Arms: The Origins of an Anglo-American Right.* Cambridge, Mass: Harvard University Press, 1996.

Martin, David Spencer, Douglas Murray, Martin A. O'Neill, Martin MacCarthy, and Jason Gogue. "Target Shooting as a Serious Leisure Pursuit – an Exploratory Study of the Motivations Driving Participant Engagement." *World Leisure Journal* 56, no. 3 (2014): 204–19. https://doi.org/10.1080/04419057.2013.836560

Mauser, Gary A., and H. Taylor Buckner. "Canadian Attitudes Toward Gun Control: The Real Story." Toronto, ON, 1997. www.researchgate.net/profile/Gary-Mauser/publication/237801446_Canadian_Attitudes_Toward_Gun_Control_The_Real_Story/links/00b4952aa155b2e6c3000000/Canadian-Attitudes-Toward-Gun-Control-The-Real-Story.pdf.

McCarthy, John D., and Mayer N. Zald. "Resource Mobilization and Social Movements: A Partial Theory." *American Journal of Sociology* 82, no. 6 (1977): 1212–41. https://doi.org/10.1086/226464

McClure, Tess. "New Zealand Passes World-First Tobacco Law to Ban Smoking for next Generation." *The Guardian*, December 13, 2022. www.theguardian.com/world/2022/dec/13/new-zealand-passes-world-first-tobacco-law-to-ban-smoking-by-2025.

McFarland, Andrew S. "Neopluralism." In *Annual Review of Political Science*, 10:45–66. PALO ALTO: ANNUAL REVIEWS, 2007. https://doi.org/10.1146/annurev.polisci.10.072005.152119

McLean, Dylan S. "Gun Talk Online: Canadian Tools, American Values." *Social Science Quarterly* 99, no. 3 (2018): 977–92. https://doi.org/10.1111/ssqu.12476

McLean, Dylan S., and Jason Sorens. "The Changing Ideological Politics of U.S. State Firearms Regulation." *Politics & Policy* 47, no. 4 (2019): 638–72. https://doi.org/10.1111/polp.12321

"Meeting 45 – Bill C-21." 2022. https://parlvu.parl.gc.ca/Harmony/en /PowerBrowser/PowerBrowserV2/20221103/-1/37980?Embedded=true &globalstreamId=20&viewMode=3.

Meisel, John. "Political Culture and the Politics of Culture." *Canadian Journal of Political Science1* 7, no. 4 (1974): 601–15. https://doi.org/10.1017 /s0008423900048538

Melzer, Scott. *Gun Crusaders: The NRA's Culture War*. New York City: New York University Press, 2009.

Meng, Melinda. "Bloody Blockades: The Legacy of the Oka Crisis." *Harvard International Review*, June 2020. https://hir.harvard.edu/bloody-blockades -the-legacy-of-the-oka-crisis/.

Middlewood, Alexandra T. "A Silver Bullet: Gun Ownership and Political Participation in Rural America." *Great Plains Research* 31, no. 2 (2021): 159–71. https://doi.org/10.1353/gpr.2021.0022

Middlewood, Alexandra, Mark R Joslyn, Donald P Haider-Markel, and Sharon Macdonald. Intersectionality in Action: Gun Ownership and Women's Political Participation. *Social Science Quarterly*. Vol. 100. London; New York; Routledge, 2019. https://doi.org/10.1111/ssqu.12697

Miller, Steven V. "What Americans Think about Gun Control: Evidence from the General Social Survey, 1972–2016." *Social Science Quarterly* 100, no. 1 (2019): 272–88. https://doi.org/10.1111/ssqu.12555

Mintrom, Michael, and Phillipa Norman. "Policy Entrepreneurship and Policy Change." *Policy Studies Journal* 37, no. 4 (2009): 649–67. https:// doi.org/10.1111/j.1541-0072.2009.00329.x

Misra, R., and M. McKean. "College Students' Academic Stress and Its Relation to Their Anxiety, Time Management, and Leisure Satisfaction." *American Journal of Health Studies*. 16, no. 1 (2000): 41–51. https://doi.org /10.1037/1072-5245.11.2.132

Montpetit, Eric. "Are Interest Groups Useful or Harmful? Take Two." In *Canadian Politics*, edited by James Bickerton and Alain G. Gagnon. Toronto: University of Toronto Press, 2014.

Murphy, M.M. "R. v. Christopher Roland Levesque." 2009. www.canlii.org /en/pe/pescad/doc/2009/2009peca22/2009peca22.html?searchUrlHash =AAAAAQAOUi4gdi4gTGV2ZXNxdWUAAAAAAQ&resultIndex=4 #document.

Murray, Douglas W., David Martin, Martin O'Neill, and T. Jason Gouge. "Serious Leisure: The Sport of Target Shooting and Leisure Satisfaction." *Sport in Society* 19, no. 7 (2016): 891–905. https://doi.org/10.1080/17430437 .2015.1067780

Natcher, David, Shawn Ingram, Ana-Maria Bogdan, and Abigael Rice. "Conservation and Indigenous Subsistence Hunting in the Peace River Region of Canada." *Human Ecology* 49, no. 2 (2021): 109–20. https://doi.org/10.1007/s10745-020-00210-z

"The National 2003–06–30 (Segment 004)." *The National – CBC Television*. Toronto: Canadian Broadcasting Corporation, June 30, 2003. https://lib-ezproxy.concordia.ca/login?qurl=https%3A%2F%2Fwww.proquest.com%2Fother-sources%2Fnational-2003-06-30-segment-004%2Fdocview%2F190714839%2Fse-2%3Faccountid%3D10246.

Naumetz, Tim. "Western Gun Groups Lead Fundraising in Legal Fight against Firearm Ban." *IPolitics*, 2020. https://ipolitics.ca/2020/08/22/western-gun-groups-lead-fundraising-in-legal-fight-against-firearm-ban/.

"New Zealand: Rate of All Gun Deaths per 100,000 People." University of Sydney School of Public Health, 2022. www.gunpolicy.org/firearms/compareyears/128/rate_of_all_gun_deaths_per_100_000_people.

News, CBC. "Bill C-21 That Would Ban Some Hunting Rifles, Shotguns Gets Pushback." Canada: Canadian Broadcasting Corporation, 2022. www.youtube.com/watch?v=xVucO7BQNTs.

Nielsen, Mark. "Local Gun Shop Owner Taking Legal Action against Firearms Ban." *Prince George Citizen*. September 24, 2020. www.princegeorgecitizen.com/local-news/local-gun-shop-owner-taking-legal-action-against-firearms-ban-3741440.

Olmsted, A.D. "Gun Ownership as Serious Leisure." In *The Gun Culture & Its Enemies*, edited by William R. Tonso, 61–76. Bellevue, WA: Merril Press, 1990.

Olson, Mancur. *The Logic of Collective Action*. Boston, MA: Harvard University Press, 1965.

– "The Logic of Collective Action: Public Goods and the Theory of Groups." Cambridge, Mass: Harvard University Press, 1971.

ONCA *R v Montague* (2010).

"One in Five American Households Purchased a Gun During the Pandemic." Chicago, IL, 2022. www.norc.org/NewsEventsPublications/PressReleases/Pages/one-in-five-american-households-purchased-a-gun-during-the-pandemic.aspx.

O'Neill, Brenda. "Continuity and Change in the Contemporary Canadian Feminist Movement." *Canadian Journal of Political Science* 50, no. 2 (2017): 443–59. https://doi.org/10.1017/s0008423917000087

Ontario, Chief Firearm Office of. Shooting Club Policy (2014). http://rrgc.ca/wp-content/uploads/2014/03/Shooting-Club-Policy-Chief-Firearms-Office-Ontario.pdf.

Orsini, Michael, and Miriam Smith. "Social Movements, Knowledge and Public Policy: The Case of Autism Activism in Canada and the US." *Critical Policy Studies* 4, no. 2 (2010): 38–57. https://doi.org/10.1080/19460171003714989

Paehlke, Robert C. "Climate Change Mitigation, Adaptation, and Development." *Environmental Politics* 23, no. 1 (2014): 179–84. https://doi.org/10.1080/09644016.2014.878090

Parker, Kim, Juliana M. Horowitz, Ruth Igielnik, Baxter J. Oliphant, and Anna Brown. "America's Complex Relationship with Guns," 2017. www.pewsocialtrends.org/2017/06/22/guns-and-daily-life-identity-experiences-activities-and-involvement/.

Passifiume, Brian. "Guns Used in Crimes Are Coming from U.S., Not Legal Gun Owners: Police Chiefs." *National Post*. February 8, 2022. https://nationalpost.com/news/politics/guns-used-in-crimes-are-coming-from-u-s-not-legal-gun-owners-police-chiefs.

Passifiume, Bryan. "Federal Court Strikes down Challenge to 2020 Ban on 'assault' Firearms." *The National Post*, October 30, 2023. https://nationalpost.com/news/politics/federal-court-strikes-down-gun-ban-challenge.

Perron, Tonya. "Brief to the Senate Committee on National Security, Defence and Veterans Affairs.," 2023.

Perry, Alyssa J., and Shereen M. Meraji. "Black And Up in Arms." *NPR Code Switch*, December 16, 2020. www.npr.org/sections/codeswitch/2020/12/09/944615029/black-and-up-in-arms.

"Plains of Abraham Re-Enactment Cancelled." *CTV News*. 2009. www.ctvnews.ca/plains-of-abraham-re-enactment-cancelled-1.371078.

"The Political Exploitation of a Tragedy." *Toronto Sun*. June 6, 2022. https://torontosun.com/opinion/editorials/editorial-the-political-exploitation-of-a-tragedy.

Press, Canadian. "Gunsmith's Family Launches Lawsuit against Toronto Police over Shooting Death." *Global News*, January 18, 2022. https://globalnews.ca/news/8519619/kotanko-lawsuit-toronto-police-death/.

– "Pro-Gun Marchers Speak out on Federal Government's Assault-Style Weapons Ban." *CBC News*, 2020. www.cbc.ca/news/politics/gun-marchers-assault-weapons-ban-1.5722051.

Pross, A. Paul. *Group Politics and Public Policy*. Toronto, ON: Oxford University Press, 1992.

Quebec (Attorney General) v. Canada (Attorney General) (2015).

"Quebec Court Orders Feds to Turn over Gun Registry Data." *CTV News Montreal*. September 10, 2012. https://montreal.ctvnews.ca/quebec-court-orders-feds-to-turn-over-gun-registry-data-1.949649.

"R. v. Hasselwander." 1993. https://scc-csc.lexum.com/scc-csc/scc-csc/en/item/1007/index.do.

Raney, Tracey, and Loleen Berdahl. "Birds of a Feather? Citizenship Norms, Group Identity, and Political Participation in Western Canada."

Canadian Journal of Political Science 42, no. 1 (2009): 187–209. https://doi.org/10.1017/s0008423909090076

Reed, Maureen Gail, and John Parkins. *Social Transformation in Rural Canada: Community, Cultures, and Collective Action.* Vancouver, BC: UBC Press, 2013.

Regulations Prescribing Certain Firearms and Other Weapons, Components and Parts of Weapons, Accessories, Cartridge Magazines, Ammunition and Projectiles as Prohibited or Restricted (SOR/98–462). (2020). https://laws-lois.justice.gc.ca/eng/regulations/sor-98-462/page-2.html.

Reich, Gary, and Jay Barth. "Planting in Fertile Soil: The National Rifle Association and State Firearms Legislation." *Social Science Quarterly* 98, no. 2 (2017): 485–99. https://doi.org/10.1111/ssqu.12423

Reiger, John F. *American Sportsmen and the Origins of Conservation.* 3rd ed. Corvallis, OR: Oregon State University Press, 2001.

Reimer, Bill. "Rura-Urban Interdependence: Understanding Our Common Interest." In *Social Transformation in Rural Canada.*, edited by Maureen Gail Reed and John Parkins, 91–109. Vancouver, BC: UBC Press, 2013.

Rosenbaum, Michael S. "Maintaining the Trail: Collective Action in a Serious -Leisure Community." *Journal of Contemporary Ethnography* 42, no. 6 (2013): 639–67. https://doi.org/10.1177/0891241613483560

Rosenzweig, Roy, and David Thelen. *The Presence of the Past – Popular Uses of History in American Life.* New York: Columbia University Press, 1998.

Ryan, Haley. "High-Ranking Mountie Insists Lucki Pressed Him about Releasing Gun Details after N.S. Shooting." *CBC News*, August 16, 2022. www.cbc.ca/news/politics/nova-scotia-massacre-lucki-campbell -guns-1.6552322.

Salazar, Debra J., and Donald K. Alper. "Reconciling Environmentalism and the Left: Perspectives on Democracy and Social Justice in British Columbia's Enviromental Movement." *Canadian Journal of Political Science* 35, no. 3 (2002): 527–66. https://doi.org/10.1017/s0008423902778347

Saurette, Paul, and Kelly Gordon. "Arguing Abortion. The New Anti-Abortion Discourse in Canada." *Canadian Journal of Political Science* 46, no. 1 (2013): 157–85. https://doi.org/10.1017/s0008423913000176

– *The Changing Voice of the Anti-Abortion Movement: The Rise of "pro -Woman" Rhetoric in Canada and the United States.* Toronto: University of Toronto Press, 2016.

Saurette, Paul, and Shane Gunster. "Canada's Conservative Ideological Infrastructure: Brewing a Cup of Cappuccino Conservatism." In *Tax Is Not a Four Letter Word*, edited by Alex Himelfarb and Himelfarb Jordan, 227–66. Waterloo, ON: Wilfred Laurier University Press, 2013.

Scalia, Antonin. District of Columbia et al. v. Heller (2008).

Schattschneider, Elmer Eric. *The Semisovereign People: A Realist's View of Democracy in America.* New York, NY: Holt, Rinehart and Winston, 1960.

Schild, Rebecca. "Fostering Environmental Citizenship: The Motivations and Outcomes of Civic Recreation." *Journal of Environmental Planning and Management* 61, no. 5–6 (2018): 924–49. https://doi.org/10.1080/09640568 .2017.1350144

Schildkraut, Jaclyn, H Jaymi Elsass, and Mark C Stafford. "Could It Happen Here? Moral Panic, School Shootings, and Fear of Crime among College Students." *Crime, Law and Social Change* 63, no. 1 (2015): 91–110. https://doi .org/10.1007/s10611-015-9552-z

Schnell Frauke, Karen Callaghan. "Assessing the Democratic Debate: How the News Media Frame Elite Policy Discourse." *Political Communication* 18, no. 2 (April 1, 2001): 183–213. https://doi.org/10.1080/105846001750322970

Schuman, Howard, and Stanley Presser. "The Attitude-Action Connection and the Issue of Gun Control." *The Annals of the American Academy of Political and Social Science* 455, no. 1 (1981): 40–47. https://doi.org /10.1177/000271628145500105

Schwartz, Noah S. "Aiming for Success: Toward an Evidence-Based Evaluation Framework for Gun Control Policies." *World Affairs* 185, no. 3 (2022): 442–70. https://doi.org/10.1177/00438200221107412

– "Called to Arms: The NRA, the Gun Culture & Women." *Critical Policy Studies*, December 3, 2019, 1–16. https://doi.org/10.1080/19460171.2019.16 97892

– "Guns in the North: Assessing the Impact of Social Identity on Firearms Advocacy in Canada." *Politics & Policy* 49, no. 3 (2021): 795–818. https:// doi.org/10.1111/polp.12412

– *On Target: Gun Culture, Storytelling, and the NRA.* Toronto, ON: University of Toronto Press, 2022.

Setchfield, Scott David. "Leisure Consumption and Political Action in a State Motorcycle Rights Organization." Indiana University, 2019. https://search .proquest.com/openview/74301185a179d26779c205e3c2e2a07b/1?pq-origsi te=gscholar&cbl=18750&diss=y.

Shea, Courtney. "'Two Drinks a Week Is Practically Personal Prohibition': This Professor Is Taking Canada's New Alcohol Guidelines to Task." *Toronto Life.* March 9, 2023. https://torontolife.com/city/two-drinks-a-week-is -practically-personal-prohibition-this-professor-is-taking-canadas-new -alcohol-guidelines-to-task/.

Shea, John J., and Matthew L. Sisk. "Complex Projectile Technology and Human Dispersal." *PaleoAnthropology*, 2010, 100–122. https://doi.org /10.4207/pa.2010.art36

Shooting Clubs and Shooting Ranges Regulations. (1998). https://laws-lois .justice.gc.ca/eng/regulations/sor-98-212/FullText.html.

Simonson, Matthew, David Lazer, Roy H. Perlis, Uday Tandon, Matthew A. Baum, Jon Green, Adina Gitomer, et al. "The COVID States Project: Report

#37 Gun Purchases During the COVID-19 Pandemic.," 2021. https://news. northeastern.edu/wp-content/uploads/2021/02/COVID19 -CONSORTIUM-REPORT-37-GUNS-Feb-2021.pdf# _ga=2.256279432.22422079.1633455371-777786272.1633455371.

Smith, Aaron. "Black Americans Have Been Buying More Guns During The Pandemic." *Forbes*, April 9, 2021. www.forbes.com/sites /aaronsmith/2021/04/09/black-americans-have-been-buying-more -guns-during-the-pandemic/?sh=27fd05d5281e.

Smith, Miriam. "Diversity and Canadian Political Development." *Canadian Journal of Political Science* 42, no. 4 (2009): 831–54. https://doi.org/10.1017 /s0008423909990692

– *Group Politics and Social Movements in Canada*. North York, ON: University of Toronto Press, 2014.

– "Identity and Opportunity: The Lesbian and Gay Rights Movement." In *Group Politics and Social Movements in Canada*, edited by Miriam Smith, 181–202. Toronto: Broadview Press, 2008.

– "Introduction: Theories of Group Movement Organizing." In *Group Politics and Social Movements in Canada*, edited by Miriam Smith, 15–34. Toronto: Broadview Press, 2008.

– "Social Movements and Equality Seeking: The Case of Gay Liberation in Canada." *Canadian Journal of Political Science* 31, no. 2 (1998): 285–309. https://doi.org/10.1017/s0008423900019806

– "Theories of Group and Movement Organization." In *Group Politics and Social Movements in Canada.*, edited by Miriam Smith. Peterborough, ON: Broadview Press, 2008.

Smith, Miriam Catherine. *A Civil Society?: Collective Actors in Canadian Political Life*. Second. Toronto [Ontario]: University of Toronto Press, 2018.

– *Lesbian and Gay Rights in Canada: Social Movements and Equality-Seeking, 1971–1995*. University of Toronto Press, 1999.

Smith, Tom W. "The 75% Solution: An Analysis of the Structure of Attitudes on Gun Control, 1959–1977." *Journal of Criminal Law and Criminology* 71, no. 3 (1980): 316. https://doi.org/10.2307/1142702

Sopuck, Robert. "Hunting with Dad." In *The Culture of Hunting in Canada*, edited by Jean L. Manore and Dale Miner, 21–24. Vancouver, BC: UBC Press, 2006.

SOR/98–205 Aboriginal Peoples of Canada Adaptations Regulations (Firearms) (1998). https://laws-lois.justice.gc.ca/eng/regulations/SOR -98-205/page-1.html.

Sowry, Alice. "Reconciling the Clash: A Comparison of the Australian and Canadian Legal Approaches to Burdening Indigenous Hunting Rights." *Public Interest Law Journal of New Zealand*. 154, no. 2 (2015): 154–64.

Spitzer, Robert J. "The Politics of Gun Control." London;Boulder; Paradigm Publishers, 2015.

Stammers, Neil. *Human Rights and Social Movements*. JSTOR, 2009.

Stanbury, W.T., and Allan Smithies. "A Brief History of Gun Control in Canada." *The Hill Times*, March 10, 2003. https://cssa-cila.org/a-brief -history-of-gun-control-in-canada-1867-to-1945/.

Stange, Mary Zeiss, and Carol K Oyster. *Gun Women: Firearms and Feminism in Contemporary America*. New York: New York University Press, 2000.

Statscan. "Linguistic Characteristics of Canadians." Ottawa, 2018. https:// www12.statcan.gc.ca/census-recensement/2011/as-sa/98-314-x /98-314-x2011001-eng.cfm.

Stebbins, Robert A. *Between Work & Leisure: The Common Ground of Two Separate Worlds*. New Brunswick, N.J: Transaction Publishers, 2004.

– "Serious Leisure: A Conceptual Statement." *The Pacific Sociological Review* 25, no. 2 (1982): 251–72. https://doi.org/10.2307/1388726

– "Serious Leisure: A Conceptual Statement." *Sociological Perspectives* 25, no. 2 (1982): 251–72. https://doi.org/10.2307/1388726

Stein, Logan. "'I'Ll Do Whatever It Takes': Canada's Minister of Public Safety Talks Gun Bill in Regina." *650 CKOM*. June 2, 2022. www.ckom .com/2022/06/02/ill-do-whatever-it-takes-canadas-minister-of-public -safety-talks-gun-bill-in-regina/.

Stenning, Philip C. "Long Gun Registration: A Poorly Aimed Longshot." *Canadian Journal of Criminology* 45 (2003): 479–88. https://doi.org/10.3138 /cjccj.45.4.480

Stockwell, Tim, and Matthew Young. "Canadian Substance Use Costs and Harms." Victoria, BC, 2018. www.ccsa.ca/sites/default/files/2019-04 /CSUCH-Canadian-Substance-Use-Costs-Harms-Report-2018-en.pdf.

Sugarmann, Josh. "Assault Weapons and Accesssories in America." Washington, D.C, 1988.

Supreme Court of Canada. Reference re Firearms Act (Can.) (2000).

Sutton, Barbara, and Elizabeth Borland. "Framing Abortion Rights in Argentina's Encuentros Nacionales de Mujeres." *Feminist Studies* 39, no. 1 (2013): 194–234. https://doi.org/10.1353/fem.2013.0016

Tarrow, Sidney. *Power in Movement*. Cambridge university press, 2022.

Terry, Gareth, Nikki Hayfield, Victoria Clarke, and Virginia Braun. "Thematic Analysis." In *The SAGE Handbook of Qualitative Research Psychology*, edited by Carla Willig and Wendy Stainton Rogers, 17–35. London, UK: SAGE Publications, 2017.

"'This Type of a Ban Will Affect the Hunters': Yukon Leaders Say Federal Gun Bill Worrisome." *CBC News*, December 7, 2022. www.cbc.ca/news /canada/north/yukon-hunters-federal-bill-c-21-amendments-1.6676806.

Thomas, Clarence. New York State RIfle & Pistol Association Inc. et al. v. Bruen, Superintendent of New York State Police, et al. (2022).

"Trudeau: 'You Don't Need an AR-15 to Bring down a Deer.'" *BBC News*, May 1, 2020. www.bbc.com/news/av/world-us-canada-52510137.

"TTC-Bylaw." Toronto Transit Commission, 2022. www.ttc.ca/by-law-no-1.

Tucker, Jennifer. "Introduction." In *A Right to Bear Arms? The Contested Role of History in the Contemporary Debate on the Second Amendment.*, edited by Jennifer Tucker, Barton C. Hacker, and Margaret Vining. Washington, DC: Smithsonian Scholarly Press, 2019.

Tushnet, Mark V. *Out of Range: Why the Constitution Can't End the Battle Over Guns.* Oxford, UK: Oxford UP, 2007.

Valentine, John. "Cultural Nationalism, Anti-Americanism, and the Federal Defense of the Canadian Football League." *American Review of Canadian Studies* 49, no. 3 (2019): 376–93. https://doi.org/10.1080/02722011.2019.166 0454

Weible, Christopher M., and Karin Ingold. "The Advocacy Coalition Framework." In *Theories of the Policy Process2*, edited by Christopher M. Weible and Paul A Sabatier, 4th Editio., 449–67. Westview Press, 2018.

Weiler, Florian, and Matthias Brändli. "Inside versus Outside Lobbying: How the Institutional Framework Shapes the Lobbying Behaviour of Interest Groups." *European Journal of Political Research* 54, no. 4 (2015): 745–66. https://doi.org/10.1111/1475-6765.12106

Weir, William. *A Well Regulated Milita: The Battle Over Gun Control.* North Haven, CT: Archon Books, 1997.

"WHO Facts on Alcohol and Violence: Intimate Partner Violence and Alcohol." Geneva, Switzerland, 2006. www.canada.ca/content/dam /phac-aspc/migration/phac-aspc/sfv-avf/sources/fem/fem-intin-alco /pdf/fem-whoms-alco-eng.pdf.

Wire, True North. "Gun Rights Group Challenges Gun Control Activist to Debate for Charity." *Truth North*, December 20, 2019. https://tnc .news/2019/12/20/gun-rights-group-challenges-gun-control-activist-to -debate-for-charity/.

Wolpert, Robin M, and James G Gimpel. "Self-Interest, Symbolic Politics, and Public Attitudes toward Gun Control." *Political Behavior* 20, no. 3 (1998): 241–62. https://doi.org/10.1023/a:1024814624070

Yamane, David. *Concealed Carry Revolution: Expanding the Right to Bear Arms in America.* Berkeley, CA: Anewpress, 2021.

– "The Sociology of U.S. Gun Culture." *Sociology Compass* 11, no. 7 (2017): 1–10. https://doi.org/10.1111/soc4.12497

– "What's Next? Understanding and Misunderstanding America's Gun Culture." In *Understanding America's Gun Culture.*, edited by C. Hovey and L. Fisher. Lanham, MD: Lexington Books, 2018.

Yamane, David, Jesse DeDeyne, and Alonso O.A. Mendez. "Who Are the Liberal Gun Owners?" *Sociological Inquiry* 91, no. 2 (2020): 483–498. https://doi.org/10.1111/soin.12406

Yamane, David, Sebastian L. Ivory, and Paul Yamane. "The Rise of Self-Defense in Gun Advertising." *Gun Studies*, 2019, 9–27. https://doi.org/10.4324/9781315696485-2

Yang, Hyunmin Tim, Junhyoung Kim, and Jinmoo Heo. "Serious Leisure Profiles and Well-Being of Older Korean Adults." *Leisure Studies* 38, no. 1 (2019): 88–97. https://doi.org/10.1080/02614367.2018.1499797

Young, Lisa, and Joanna Everitt. *Advocacy Groups*. Vancounver: UBC Press, 2004.

Yousif, Nadine. "'A Pandemic of Grief': StatCan's First-Ever Data on Black Victims of Homicide Prompts Calls for Targeted Trauma Services." *Toronto Star*. November 17, 2020. www.thestar.com/news/gta/2020/11/16/a-pandemic-of-grief-statcans-first-ever-data-on-black-victims-of-homicide-prompts-calls-for-targeted-trauma-services.html.

Zivi, Karen. *Making Rights Claims: A Practice of Democratic Citizenship*. Oxford University Press, 2011.

Index